Numerous informative trade books exist on ADHD in childre
in its scientific understanding and management, but this is fa
der. The few popular books that do exist on adults with ADHD are sometimes filled with half-truths,
clinical yet unscientific "wisdom," distracting anecdotes, and outright falsehoods about the disorder,
including the possibility that it conveys some beneficial gifts to those so afflicted. For these reasons,
it is a real pleasure to read Tuckman's superbly rendered book on ADHD in adults, for it is so well-
reasoned, science-based, information-rich, to the point, and finally—useful! Apart from wishing I had
written it, I sincerely wish that you will read it.

—Russell A. Barkley, Ph.D., clinical professor of psychiatry at Medical University
of South Carolina Charleston and research professor of psychiatry at SUNY
Upstate Medical University at Syracuse

Tuckman has filled a huge gap in our understanding of adults who suffer from ADHD. He sheds light
where there was darkness, he clarifies the science behind adult ADHD, and, most importantly, he
brings theory into practice by providing a well-balanced model for helping those with ADHD using a
multi-modal approach to treatment: education, medication, coaching, and psychotherapy. Readers will
come away with practical tools to improve the lives of those suffering from this condition. This book is
a valuable contribution to the literature and will be a treasured resource.

—Harvey C. Parker, Ph.D., cofounder of Children and Adults with Attention
Deficit Hyperactivity Disorder (CHADD) and author of The ADHD Workbook
for Parents

Tuckman has authored a state of the art volume deftly blending science and clinical experience to
provide a reasoned, reasonable and eminently useful treatment guide for adult ADHD. He writes
from a strong scientific and clinical framework. It is clear in this volume that he has spent countless
hours helping adults with ADHD. Current in its scientific foundation and practical in its approach
to assessment and treatment, Integrative Treatment for Adult ADHD is an exceptional guide for
mental health professionals working with adults with ADHD. It is rare to find volumes directed at
mental health professionals that are scientifically accurate yet practical in approach. In his new book,
Tuckman has accomplished both.

—Sam Goldstein, Ph.D., research professor of psychology at George Mason
University.

Integrative Treatment for Adult ADHD is a wonderful gift for all mental health and health-care
professionals. Tuckman's vast wisdom and valuable interventions are delivered in a reader-friendly,
supportive tone. No stones are left unturned for readers seeking the best methods to diagnose and
effectively treat adults with attention deficit / hyperactivity disorder (ADHD.) This much needed,
well-researched, excellent book truly raises the bar for the standard of care for those adults afflicted
with ADHD.

—Jeffrey Bernstein, Ph.D., Author of: 10 Days to a Less Distracted Child, 10 Days to
a Less Defiant Child and Why Can't You Read My Mind?

Integrative Treatment for Adult ADHD *is full of practical strategies that you can use with your next client. Tuckman clearly understands the challenges that adults with ADHD face and what you can do to help them stay on top of life's demands.*

> —Nancy A. Ratey, Ed.M., MCC, author of *The Disorganized Mind: Coaching Your AD/HD Brain to Get Control of Your Tasks, Time, and Talents*

As a psychiatrist I am pleased to see Tuckman's Integrative Treatment for Adult ADHD *added to the armamentarium for all professionals who treat adults with AD/HD. As a psychiatrist I strongly support the concept "Pills do not make skills." Generally, along with psychiatric medication prescribed by the physician, psychoeducation, psychotherapy, and coaching are often needed to optimize the treatment of adults with AD/HD. The various disciplines need to better work together as a treatment team. The more each participant knows about the other team member's role and contribution to the treatment, the better off our patient will be. Tuckman's book goes a long way towards facilitating a better functioning and integrated multimodal treatment program for adults with AD/HD. Each discipline member of the treatment team should read this book and learn how to better their own role and more closely integrate it with the other professionals' contributions. For example, the more the therapists learn about medication, the better they can serve as liaisons to the medical/prescribing member of the treatment team. Now if only we physicians would learn more about cognitive behavioral therapy for AD/HD in adults.*

> —Philip Parker MD, psychiatrist in private practice in Southfield, MI, clinical assistant professor of psychiatry at Wayne State University School of Medicine in Detroit, MI, and Professional Advisory Board member of the Attention Deficit Disorder Association

Tuckman's book, Integrative Treatment for Adult ADHD, *is an excellent and much-needed resource for clinicians as well as clients. It is informative, well-organized, and written in a conversational style that is easy for all to understand, while still based on research findings. Tuckman's use of his own experiences in treating adults with ADHD adds a human touch to the complexities of this area of practice. The free online forms and other resources also are also a nice touch.*

> —James J. Crist, Ph.D., CSAC, clinical psychologist, clinical director of the Child and Family Counseling Center in Woodbridge, VA, adjunct faculty member at Argosy University, and author of *ADHD—A Teenager's Guide*

Tuckman has distilled the best of the best from research and clinical experience to provide a wealth of information as well as practical suggestions for managing adult ADHD. Jargon-free, well-organized, and user-friendly, Integrative Treatment for Adult ADHD *will be immensely helpful to both clinicians and lay readers struggling with ADHD.*

> —Barbara D. Ingersoll, Ph.D., author of *Your Hyperactive Child* and *Daredevils and Daydreamers*, member of the CHADD Professional Advisory Board, and 1997 inductee into the CHADD Hall of Fame for outstanding contributions to the welfare of individuals with ADHD.

INTEGRATIVE TREATMENT

for

ADULT ADHD

A Practical, Easy-to-Use Guide for Clinicians

ARI TUCKMAN, PSY.D., MBA

New Harbinger Publications, Inc.

Publisher's Note

Care has been taken to confirm the accuracy of the information presented and to describe generally accepted practices. However, the authors, editors, and publisher are not responsible for errors or omissions or for any consequences from application of the information in this book and make no warranty, express or implied, with respect to the contents of the publication.

The authors, editors, and publisher have exerted every effort to ensure that any drug selection and dosage set forth in this text are in accordance with current recommendations and practice at the time of publication. However, in view of ongoing research, changes in government regulations, and the constant flow of information relating to drug therapy and drug reactions, the reader is urged to check the package insert for each drug for any change in indications and dosage and for added warnings and precautions. This is particularly important when the recommended agent is a new or infrequently employed drug.

Some drugs and medical devices presented in this publication may have Food and Drug Administration (FDA) clearance for limited use in restricted research settings. It is the responsibility of the health care provider to ascertain the FDA status of each drug or device planned for use in their clinical practice.

Distributed in Canada by Raincoast Books

Copyright © 2007 by Ari Tuckman
New Harbinger Publications, Inc.
5674 Shattuck Avenue
Oakland, CA 94609
www.newharbinger.com

FSC
Mixed Sources
Product group from well-managed
forests and other controlled sources
Cert no. SW-COC-002283
www.fsc.org
© 1996 Forest Stewardship Council

RAINFOREST ALLIANCE CERTIFIED

Acquired by Tesilya Hanauer; Cover design by Amy Shoup;
Edited by Kayla Sussell; Text design by Tracy Carlson

Library of Congress Cataloging-in-Publication Data

Tuckman, Ari.
  Integrative treatment for adult ADHD : practical easy-to-use guide for clinicians / Ari Tuckman.
    p. ; cm.
  ISBN-13: 978-1-57224-521-1 (pbk.)
  ISBN-10: 1-57224-521-2 (pbk.)
  1. Attention-deficit disorder in adults--Treatment. 2. Attention-deficit disorder in adults--Alternative treatment. 3. Integrative medicine. I. Title.
  [DNLM: 1. Attention Deficit Disorder with Hyperactivity--therapy. 2. Adults. 3. Patient Care Management. WM 190 T898i 2007]
RC394.A85T83 2007
616.85'89--dc22

                         2007031839

12   11   10

10   9   8   7   6   5   4   3   2

I would like to dedicate this book to the literally millions of adults with undiagnosed and untreated ADHD who have struggled valiantly against their own hardwiring and others' misunderstanding. I hope that this book contributes in some small way to the too slowly growing awareness of adult ADHD in the clinical community.

Contents

■ The Consequences of ADHD ■ A Relevant Practice Niche
■ What This Book Covers

PART I: Understanding ADHD in Adults

CHAPTER 1

■ The History of the Diagnosis ■ What Is the True Prevalence?
■ Diagnostic Difficulties ■ Diagnostic Criteria ■ Gender Differences
■ Diagnostic Interview ■ Assessment Instruments ■ Brain Scans
■ Comorbid Conditions

CHAPTER 2

■ Etiology ■ Genetic Factors ■ Environmental Factors ■ Neurology
of ADHD ■ Unifying Theories

CHAPTER 3

■ The Evolving Personality ■ Situations That Obscure ADHD
■ Executive Functioning ■ Academic Functioning
■ Occupational Functioning ■ Daily Life Functioning ■ Psychological
Functioning ■ Social Skills and Relationships ■ Prognostic Indicators

PART II: The Integrative Treatment Model

Acknowledgments

I would like to thank several people for helping with this large endeavor. Wilma Fellman, M.Ed., LPC, provided valuable guidance on career counseling. Nancy Ratey, Ed.M., ABDA, MCC, and Jodi Sleeper-Triplett, MCC, provided eager and much appreciated feedback on the coaching chapter. Philip Parker, MD, reviewed the medication chapter and made many helpful suggestions. And Tesilya Hanauer and Kayla Sussell from New Harbinger Publications have been a joy to work with.

I'd like to thank Barry Gorman, MD, for his rather unassuming question of, "Do you have any interest in working with ADHD adults?" After ten years of consistently busy practice, the answer is still *Yes!*

I'd also like to thank my clients and the many people who came through the adult ADHD support group that I ran for Northern Virginia CHADD from 2000 to 2005. You taught me a lot, most especially why this is such important work.

On a more personal note, I'd like to thank my wife, Heather, for taking care of all those other things when I was busily tapping away on my laptop. Your continual support and understanding made it possible to squeeze this project into an otherwise already over-squeezed schedule. Thank you.

Foreword

From a developmental perspective, the field of adult ADHD is still in its infancy. Even though the first report of adults having problems with what is now called ADHD was published over a century ago in 1902, when George Still wrote about what he described as a "defect of moral character," recognition of ADHD as a legitimate adult disorder did not really take place until Dr. Paul Wender's pioneering work in the 1970s. In fact, it has only been in the last fifteen or twenty years that serious scientific study has begun to occur in the area of adult ADHD. This is indeed good news but we also need to remember that we still have a long way to go.

What we think we know about adult ADHD from anecdotal reports, testimonials, and clinical impressions may urn out not to be accurate when we subject it to rigorous scientific scrutiny. The way we truly advance knowledge in the field is through good science and this takes time and patience. The reality is that we still do not have much well controlled empirical research to guide us with respect to (a) understanding the impact and functional impairments the disorder has on a wide range of adult behavior and (b) understanding how to best assess and treat this complex disorder.

This state of affairs, however, has begun to change.. Now, we are beginning to understand that ADHD is associated with global impairment in functioning at all developmental levels: childhood, adolescence, and adulthood. Results from two recent major studies have demonstrated that both clinic-referred adults with ADHD and children with ADHD who are followed into their adult lives show impairment over a wide swath of human activity as adults (Barkley, Murphy, & Fischer, in press). These impairments extend well beyond mere inattention and impulsiveness and clearly demonstrate that ADHD is not a benign disorder.

The deficits that ADHD produces in executive functioning, planning, forethought, self-control, and working memory can have a serious impact on performance in major life activities. More specifically, when adults with ADHD were compared to both a community control group and a clinical control group, they were found to have more diverse and serious impairments in educational outcomes, occupational functioning, social relationships, sexual activities, dating and marital functioning, criminal activities and drug abuse, financial management, driving a motor vehicle, health and lifestyle habits, and in parent/offspring psychological morbidity. These studies strongly suggest that the ability to attend, exert self-control, and sustain attention, effort, and motivation is fundamental to healthy adjustment. Moreover, as children with ADHD get older, the stakes (and the associated impairments) get higher.

The scientific study of adult ADHD is important for another reason as well. As we all know, ADHD has always garnered its fair share of media skepticism and has often been a lightning rod for controversy. Critics claim we overdiagnose it, overmedicate our patients, and use it as an excuse for poor behavior. More often than not, the various media outlets routinely attack ADHD in a variety of ways ranging from criticizing assessment and treatment practices to questioning its very existence as a legitimate disorder. Those of us who take the time to understand the growing body of empirical research on adult ADHD know that these sorts of allegations not only have no merit, but can cause harm to those who truly struggle with this disorder.

Nevertheless, as professionals we should always keep in mind that good science, informed and skilled practitioners, and empirically based assessment and treatment practices will go a long way toward silencing these critics and protecting the credibility and integrity of this very legitimate and serious disorder. To the extent we as professionals can collectively employ practices that are based on sound scientific underpinnings, the more likely the disorder will gain the credibility and serious attention it deserves.

Given the new scientific findings about the potentially serious risks and outcomes for adults with ADHD, it is more important than ever to be able to identify the disorder accurately and to intervene effectively. Indeed, the consequences of undiagnosed and untreated adult ADHD can be devastating. To better serve this often hidden population of adults with ADHD, we need more clinicians who are well trained, who understand how the disorder presents clinically, who can reliably assess it, and who can accurately differentiate it from other psychiatric diagnoses and situational stressors.

Dr. Tuckman's book is an important step in this direction. Integrative Treatment of Adult ADHD skillfully addresses many of the common struggles that adults with ADHD encounter across multiple life domains. It is a valuable resource for any clinician who wants to learn more about how to identify, manage, and treat this commonly misunderstood disorder. Dr. Tuckman's clinical experience, wisdom, and understanding of adult ADHD shines through on every page.

Science will no doubt add to our understanding of this disorder as time goes on. In the meantime, Dr. Tuckman's book will serve a very useful purpose by increasing the awareness of adult ADHD among clinicians, primary care physicians, and other mental health professionals.

—Kevin Murphy, Ph.D.

Introduction

When I went into practice in 1998, the psychiatrist who ran the group practice I worked at asked me, "Do you have any interest in working with ADHD adults?" He told me, "They do better with medication, but they still need help with some basic life management skills." Even as a newly minted graduate, I certainly hadn't had any classes on ADHD in adults. Nonetheless, as a new graduate trying to scrape together a practice, I probably would have taken any referral. I began teaching myself about adults with ADHD and found a very good fit between what they needed and how I liked to work with clients.

What I discovered was not only a very rewarding specialty, but also a vast unmet need—ten years later, my work is still just as rewarding and the need almost as unmet. Although I now have more colleagues who share this special interest, the number of clinicians who work with adult ADHD has not kept pace with the need and desire for such clinical services.

Why a Book on Adult ADHD?

I had a little joke that I would use when I spoke about writing this book: "The good news is that there are no bad books on adult ADHD for clinicians; the bad news is that there are very few good ones." I can count on both hands the number of books for clinicians that exclusively address adult ADHD. This may explain why I can also count on both hands the number of colleagues I have in the therapist-saturated Philadelphia suburbs who specialize in working with ADHD adults. My hope is that my book will help to increase the number of informed clinicians who work with this underserved population.

It's ironic that ADHD is still more thought of as a childhood disorder, since there are actually more adults who have ADHD than there are children who do. Although the disorder may be somewhat more prevalent among children than adults, there are approximately three times as many adults as there are children in the United States (U.S. Census, 2000). Current estimates suggest that there are eight million ADHD adults in America (Ramsay & Rostain, in press), in contrast to the two to three million children.

Unfortunately, only a small minority of these adults has been diagnosed and is receiving appropriate treatment. The National Comorbidity Study found that only 10 percent of adults with ADHD had received treatment within the prior twelve months (Biederman, Spencer, Wilens, Prince, & Faraone, 2006). One of my goals for this book is to increase awareness of the disorder among clinicians who treat adults so that they can provide a more effective, targeted treatment that reduces premature termination or partial success.

The Consequences of ADHD

Myths abound about ADHD, ranging from it being excuse-making for poor parenting to being a creation of the pharmaceutical industry. Research, however, consistently shows significant differences in cognitive, behavioral, and social functioning between those with and without ADHD; and for children diagnosed with ADHD, there are significant risks for later maladjustment as adolescents in school and as adults in work and social performance (Barkley, 2006b).

Critics use the fact that most people have times when one or more of the criteria for ADHD fits an aspect of their behavior. However, neither ADHD nor any other psychiatric diagnosis is made based solely on one occasional symptom; the person must have a sufficient number of symptoms that persist over time and across different settings and that cause significant impairment. This quickly thins the crowd of people who merit the diagnosis. Losing your keys every now and then doesn't mean you have ADHD.

Some critics may say that those with ADHD just need to try harder, that the problem is one of motivation. However, a clever study proved what those with ADHD have known all along—that good intentions are not enough; that ADHD is bigger than motivation (Brown, 2005). The researchers measured the accuracy and persistence of ADHD children working on a long, boring computer task. They compared the effects of financial incentives and medication, their idea being that getting paid should have given the kids plenty of motivation to do well. Although both medication and money improved overall accuracy, the medication was significantly more potent; it also enabled greater persistence, which the promise of a financial reward did not. In other words, at its core, ADHD is more about neurology than motivation.

Here is a sampling of the sobering statistics on the impact of ADHD:

- Young adults with ADHD are more likely to have greater driving difficulties, including license suspensions and revocations, accidents where the car is totaled, hit-and-run accidents (Ellison, 2002), and accidents where bodily injury is involved, despite equivalent driving knowledge (Faraone et al., 2000).

- ADHD adults are two-thirds more likely to have been fired; three times more likely to have impulsively quit their jobs; one-third more likely to report chronic employment difficulties; and 50 percent more likely to have changed jobs in a given time period (Barkley & Gordon, 2002).

- ADHD adults with high school diplomas have annual household incomes that are lower by $10,791 and by $4,334 for college graduates (Editors, 2005).

- ADHD adults are twice as likely to separate or divorce and they report less marital satisfaction (Barkley & Gordon, 2002).

- ADHD adults begin to abuse substances at an earlier age and abuse substances more often. Their usage continues longer and they move from alcohol to drug abuse more rapidly (Wilens, 2004).

- ADHD teens are four to five times more likely to be arrested and 25 percent more likely to be institutionalized for delinquency (Young, 2000).

- More than half of ADHD children require academic tutoring; one-third may repeat a grade; one-third are placed in one or more special-education programs; half may be suspended from school; and up to one-third may drop out and not graduate high school, three times as many as non-ADHD students (Barkley, 2006c).

As disheartening as these statistics may be, they highlight the need for earlier as well as more effective treatment. They also highlight the struggles that the ADHD adults walking into our offices will have faced.

A Relevant Practice Niche

A large national survey found a 4.4 percent prevalence rate for ADHD in American adults, accounting for approximately eight million people (Ramsay & Rostain, in press). It's also worth keeping in mind that the prevalence of ADHD is much higher in the clinical population, even though many are diagnosed with anxiety, depression, or bipolar disorder. However, if the client's ADHD is neglected, there is a limit to the progress that can be made, particularly if the comorbid disorder is secondary to the ADHD. Even assuming that the prevalence of ADHD in the clinical population is identical to that of the general adult population—that is, one in twenty—we could then assume that most adult therapists have at least one ADHD adult in their caseloads, whether they know it or not and whether they address the ADHD specifically or not.

The incidence of the diagnosis of ADHD in adults doubled between 2000 and 2003 (Goldstein & Kennemer, in press), indicating that this is very much a growing area of clinical practice. Despite this, only 10 percent of adults with ADHD had received treatment within the prior twelve months (Biederman et al., 2006), indicating that there is still very much a need for qualified providers. As will be elaborated at length in this book, the treatment of ADHD adults involves far more than just medication, so there is a need for therapists who are familiar with all aspects of the disorder and its secondary effects. There is a shortage of therapists truly knowledgeable in this area, making it that much easier to build a practice and fill a caseload. As many ADHD clients have unfortunately discovered, general therapy skills are necessary but far from sufficient.

What This Book Covers

This book will provide a fully integrative treatment model for adult ADHD. I have taken the best of what previous authors, researchers, and clinicians have created and distilled it down to what you need to know to work effectively with this challenging but rewarding population. Much of this material is empirically based, but I won't bore you with too many of the details. The rest comes from my clinical practice—it has yet to be proven in scientific trials, but seems to work reliably with the clients that I and my colleagues see.

Part I, Understanding ADHD in Adults, begins with Diagnosing ADHD in Adults in chapter 1. This involves knowing both what is and what isn't ADHD by separating out the comorbid conditions that can muddy the diagnostic waters. In chapter 2, The Physiological Bases of ADHD, I provide just enough of the basics of neurology and etiologies to be useful in clinical practice. In chapter 3, The Impact of ADHD on an Adult's Life, I cover the many ways that a lifetime of undiagnosed and untreated ADHD can affect someone's pursuit of happiness and success in life. Although ADHD may be most obvious in the classroom, its effects go far beyond academics.

In Part II, The Integrative Treatment Model, I lay out the four facets of treatment that are necessary for the best outcomes with this population. This begins with chapter 4, Education as a Therapeutic Technique, to lay a foundation for the interventions that follow, by reducing stigma and building hope. In chapter 5, Medications and Other Biological Treatments, I review the commonly used medications, as well as proposed nontraditional treatments. Chapter 6, Coaching: More Than Obvious Advice, offers practical strategies that you can use to help clients better manage their daily obligations. Finally, in chapter 7, Adapting Psychotherapy for the ADHD Adult, I tailor traditional therapeutic techniques to address both the effects of previously untreated ADHD and to better enable the client to take an active approach to current treatment. An appendix of Resources for Clinicians and Clients appears at the end of the book.

In addition to the materials included in these book pages, there is also a large collection of materials available at no charge on my website, www.TuckmanPsych.com. You will find handouts to give to clients, as well as forms available for your use. Many of these forms appear within the pages of the book, but you may prefer to download and print them rather than copy from the book. Starting at this book's conception, the goal was to be user-friendly, and these online materials are very much in keeping with that goal.

PART I

Understanding ADHD in Adults

Before we move on to working with ADHD adults, we need to have a solid understanding of the disorder and its associated features. This first part of the book begins with making an accurate diagnosis since that is the prerequisite for effective treatment. Adult therapy clients who are earnest about making some changes in their lives but who are not making any progress toward that goal may have undiagnosed ADHD. The clinician's failure to address the ADHD may become a permanent roadblock, leading to frustration for both client and therapist.

I have to admit that even as an ADHD specialist, I have missed a diagnosis of ADHD in a client who came in for other reasons. I know it happens. Clients may have a complicated situation or more obvious reasons for their difficulties, such as an extremely dysfunctional upbringing, which can obscure another important cause for their struggles. As an example, an ADHD child with a verbally abusive parent may have attracted more abuse than a sibling would have because of her greater likelihood to be off-task. Granted, this doesn't undo or excuse the effect of the abusive parent's actions, but it may offer an explanation both for events that took place in childhood and any subsequent difficulties that cannot otherwise be sufficiently explained.

Although of course we try to adapt our interventions to the specific needs and processing style of each client, it's important to understand the countless ways that ADHD can have an impact on a client's life functioning as well as on his ability and willingness to make use of therapy. Sensible but overly detailed or complicated suggestions from otherwise intelligent and well-intentioned therapists often miss the mark with ADHD clients, which leads only to frustration and disappointment for everyone.

There are many reasons why a client may fail to have a sufficient response to treatment (Goldstein, 2006, October). The following list provides some of those reasons:

- Wrong diagnosis—this means both false positive and false negative

- Failure to appreciate intervening variables, such as the presence of ADHD, substance abuse, or abusive parents

- Insufficient treatment trials, perhaps based on unrealistic expectations

- Client's mind-set—pessimistic, doesn't fully apply herself, and so on

- Poorly informed clinicians

This part of the book will lay a foundation of knowledge about the diagnosis, etiology, and effects of ADHD, with the goal of enabling you to provide more effective treatment. This knowledge is crucial if you are to have any credibility with your clients, especially for adults with ADHD who have a tendency to feel misunderstood, based on legitimate experiences.

I have done many presentations on ADHD for members of the public and I often receive very appreciative comments along the lines of, "What you said really made a lot of sense. I feel like you really get it." I think these comments are less a reflection of my having said anything especially brilliant, as much as they are an indication that other professionals have not conveyed to their clients a basic understanding of what life with ADHD is like. This experience is even more valuable within a therapy context—the other place that I've received such appreciative comments.

CHAPTER 1

Diagnosing ADHD in Adults

The key to any effective treatment is an accurate diagnosis. This is as true for mental health and medical care as it is for automotive repair. An accurate diagnosis allows the professional and client to select and target interventions in the ways that are most likely to yield positive results. The alternatives are to shoot blindly or to pursue a path that is unlikely to prove beneficial. This is especially true of adult ADHD since it's a condition that's easy to misdiagnose—both by missing the diagnosis and by giving it when it is not truly present. The high level of comorbidity with ADHD means that it takes finesse to tease apart the origins of various symptoms, particularly when long-standing conditions such as anxiety and depression are secondary to a lifetime of ADHD-related struggles.

The History of the Diagnosis

What we call ADHD today has had a presence throughout the diagnostic classification systems of the last century. The evolution of the diagnosis shows an increasing understanding of the subtle and myriad effects of the disorder that go beyond the obvious problematic behavior. Unfortunately, until the last couple decades, ADHD was seen exclusively as a disorder of childhood that disappeared in late adolescence. This has had important implications for those who continue to struggle with the symptoms as adults. The symptoms of ADHD change less in late adolescence than do the environments in which these adults find themselves.

Unfortunately for ADHD youngsters, the classroom is an excellent screening tool for difficulties with inattention, hyperactivity, and impulsivity. When we enter the world of work and enjoy a greater latitude in choosing our environments, we tend to choose situations that favor our strengths and minimize the impact of our weaknesses. So, the child who could not sit still becomes a deliveryman who doesn't have to. This doesn't mean that all of his ADHD difficulties have disappeared, but rather that, at least in this aspect of his life, his ADHD difficulties may be less apparent.

One of the first official references to what we now call ADHD was made by G. F. Still in 1902 when he dubbed it "Moral Deficit Disorder" (Weiss, Hechtman, & Weiss, 1999). This plainly pejorative interpretation of ADHD behavior is well known to those who suffer from the disorder. This includes well-meaning family members and teachers who struggle to explain the ADHD person's seemingly self-destructive actions. In the 1930s, ADHD symptomatology was given the name "Minimal Brain Damage" and later "Minimal Brain Dysfunction" (Weiss et al., 1999). It wasn't until 1968 that the *Diagnostic and Statistical Manual-II* called it "Hyperkinetic Reaction of Childhood," finally approximating the disorder's current name (Jaffe, 1995).

The first studies demonstrating that ADHD persists into adulthood began to come out in the late 1960s (Barkley, 2006a). The first published empirical studies on the diagnosis and treatment of ADHD in adults came from Paul Wender's group in the late 1970s (Weiss et al., 1999).

SAY GOOD-BYE TO ADD

Despite the fact that it was retired in 1987 with the publication of the *DSM-III-R*, some people still use the old term of "ADD." This comes partly out of convenience, in that ADD rolls off the tongue more easily than ADHD. It also more easily lends itself to clever names, such as *ADDitude* magazine. In addition, some people will use ADD to indicate someone who has the predominantly inattentive type without hyperactivity, reserving the term ADHD for those with hyperactivity and impulsivity. However, given that it's been twenty years since ADD was replaced by ADHD, we owe it to the community to foster accuracy and minimize confusion.

In 1980, the *Diagnostic and Statistical Manual-III* called it "Attention Deficit Disorder." The *DSM-III* introduced two subtypes: "with hyperactivity" and "without hyperactivity." In response to the emerging studies that showed the continued presence of symptoms after adolescence, it also added "ADD, RT" (residual type) for adults who had outgrown the hyperactivity but retained significant difficulties with inattention and impulsivity (Jaffe, 1995).

The *Diagnostic and Statistical Manual-III-R* was published in 1987 and changed the name to "Attention-Deficit Hyperactivity Disorder," making the hyperactivity a key feature. "ADD, RT" became "ADHD, RS" (residual state). Three years later, the first newsletters targeted specifically at ADHD adults (*ADDendum* and *ADDult News*) began publishing, followed shortly thereafter by the first layperson's book, Lynn Weiss's 1992 *Attention Deficit Disorder in Adults: Practical Help for Sufferers and Their Spouses* (Jaffe, 1995).

As often happens, work by clinicians and publications for the general public precede empirical studies by researchers. Therefore, it should not be surprising that a search of psychotherapy journals shows that the first article focusing on psychotherapy for adults with ADHD was published as late as 1994 (Weiss et al., 1999). Given their unique needs, this goes a long way toward explaining why ADHD adults (perhaps undiagnosed) have had such difficulties finding therapists who can go beyond traditional psychotherapeutic techniques that are of such limited benefit to this population.

The *Diagnostic and Statistical Manual-IV* was published in 1994 and made an easily missed grammatical change with significant implications. The *DSM-IV* renamed the condition "Attention-Deficit/Hyperactivity Disorder." It added the slash between Attention-Deficit and Hyperactivity to signify that the disorder may include one or both symptom types. This was formalized by the inclusion of three subtypes: the predominantly inattentive type (ADHD-PI); the predominantly hyperactive-impulsive type (ADHD-PHI); and the combined type (ADHD-C) to indicate those individuals who display symptoms of both inattention and hyperactive impulsivity (Brown, 1995). The seemingly minor addition of the slash is important, signifying that people can have an attention-deficit or hyperactivity or both, but they don't need the hyperactivity in order to meet the criteria for the diagnosis.

It should be noted that the *DSM-IV* criteria are some of the most rigorous and empirically derived criteria ever created for the diagnosis. That said, there's still criticism that the *DSM-IV* criteria are more reflective of the symptom presentation in children than in adults. For those practicing in Europe and/or in some hospital settings, the *International Classification of Diseases-10* diagnostic coding system contains criteria that are very similar but not identical to *DSM-IV*'s for ADHD (Barkley, 2006b).

The *DSM-IV Text Revision* (*DSM-IV-TR*) was published in 2000, but is largely identical to the previous version, with the exception that the prevalence of ADHD went from 3 to 5 percent of school-age children to 3 to 7 percent (American Psychiatric Association, 2000). Both versions state that the data on the prevalence in adulthood are more limited. The first medication approved by the Food and Drug Administration for adults with ADHD was Strattera in 2003. Of course, the pediatric ADHD medications were being used off-label for adults before that, but it is still significant that it has been only a handful of years since adult ADHD was officially recognized in this sense.

What Is the True Prevalence?

Despite claims that ADHD is overdiagnosed among children, it's still underdiagnosed among adults, perhaps because it was only recently recognized that most ADHD teens become adults with significant and persistent deficits. As a result, many clinicians may not be sufficiently familiar with what to look for in adults. When it comes to effective treatment, an ADHD adult suffers from a missed diagnosis just as non-ADHD people suffer when they are mistakenly told they have ADHD. When considering the possibility of ADHD, clinicians should keep in mind that ADHD is only one possible cause of attentional problems (Weiss et al., 1999). As I sometimes joke, even the common cold has inattention and poor concentration among its possible presenting complaints.

Attention-Deficit Versus Deficit in Attention Regulation

Before going into the diagnostic criteria, let's spend a moment on the term "attention-deficit" since it's somewhat misleading. ADHD does not involve a deficit in attention per se, as in some people do not have enough of it, but rather in attention regulation—that is, keeping their attention on what is most important at that moment. *Attention regulation* involves a fluid monitoring of the environment and a constant decision-making process of whether to continue attending to the current object of focus or to shift to a more relevant object. This is a process that takes place in milliseconds. Errors in attention regulation occur both when someone shifts her attention when she shouldn't have, as well as when she stays put when she should have shifted.

As a practical example, if someone is sitting in a busy restaurant with many attention-grabbing stimuli, she needs to be able to stay focused on her companion in order to not come off as rude, while also shifting attention to the waiter when he takes the food order or brings the meal. Shifting her attention to extraneous stimuli too often can have serious social consequences, but so can failing to notice the waiter's attempts to break into the conversation. Both are failures in attention regulation.

At its extreme, this "locking-in" of attention is called *hyperfocus*, wherein the person becomes completely absorbed in an activity to the exclusion of awareness of the rest of his environment. The classic example of hyperfocus is demonstrated by the child who becomes so intent on a video game that he doesn't even hear his name being called. Another example would be the adult surfing the internet who doesn't notice that several hours have gone by. In response to this lack of awareness, the wife of a member of my adult ADHD support group suggested that he install a timer on the light switch in the study, so that he couldn't help but notice when it was time to stop. Unfortunately, he joked, he got used to working in the dark.

Obviously, that solution was not completely successful, but then it did become a matter of conscious choice rather than unintentional error, which is a completely different situation. Although hyperfocus is often used as an example of someone having good attention skills and, therefore, this demonstrates that this person's attention is voluntarily controllable, it actually shows poor attention regulation in that he is oblivious to everything else.

It's also worth noting that distractions can be external, that is, stimuli from the outside world may pull the person's focus away, as well as internal if the person gets lost in her thoughts rather than attending elsewhere. Or the person may remember to do something else and changes gears prematurely. Both shifts are problematic.

Barkley (2006c) and others have pointed out that people with ADHD have the greatest difficulty keeping their attention on tasks like paperwork, cleaning, and organizing that have little intrinsic appeal or minimal immediate consequences for completion or failure to complete. In contrast, interesting, novel, or personally meaningful activities seem relatively easy for people with ADHD to focus on (as they are for everyone). A frustrated spouse will point out this discrepancy, angry that she has to handle most of these less interesting tasks. What separates those with ADHD from those without it is the degree of difference between their performance on boring versus enjoyable activities. Everyone does worse on less interesting activities—but folks with ADHD do much worse.

Inconsistent Performance

This brings up another aspect of the deficit in attention regulation, that of inconsistent performance. People with ADHD perform some tasks quite well but not others; or they can't maintain a consistent performance for the same task over time. This may mean that sometimes they do great on mundane activities, like paying bills, but at other times they seem to forget completely about it. Or they may do well on a new activity, but then lose momentum over time.

For example, I had a client who was the top producer for his company when he started out as an insurance salesman. Within a few months, when the job had lost its spark, he became one of the lowest producers, much to his supervisor's confusion and chagrin. Unfortunately, it's this occasional good performance that becomes the most damning evidence against ADHD folks because it's seen as proof of their abilities. Any subsequent poor performance must therefore be more indicative of declining desire or motivation.

When it comes to assessing an individual for ADHD, the client's history will contain these inconsistencies and contradictions, which can be confusing to the unsophisticated observer. In fact, a pervasive inability to perform is more indicative of some other deficit, such as in overall intelligence, and may rule out ADHD as an explanation. Variability does not discount the validity of the diagnosis any more than periods of normal mood invalidate a diagnosis of bipolar disorder. In fact, the pattern of both better and worse performance is necessary to the diagnosis.

The Many Facets of Attention

When most people think of attention, they think of a single entity—you're either paying attention or you're not. In reality, attention is a very complex neurological function made up of numerous subfunctions. The four commonly cited subfunctions of attention include (Young & Bramham, 2007):

1. *Selective attention*—freedom from distractibility

2. *Divided attention*—the ability to simultaneously attend to two or more stimuli

3. *Shifting attention*—the ability to intentionally shift attention between two or more sources of information

4. *Sustained attention*—the ability to maintain attention with only limited reinforcement

It's usually difficulties with sustained attention that are the most problematic for folks with ADHD, since we all must occasionally deal with long and boring tasks that are necessary to keep our lives running smoothly (Young & Bramham, 2007).

Why Are More People Being Diagnosed with ADHD Today?

Critics of ADHD as a diagnosis have pointed to the fact that "suddenly" many more people are being diagnosed than in previous generations. They try to use this as evidence against the validity of the diagnosis, claiming that it's merely the overexuberance of the professional community and/or a convenient excuse for people's shortcomings. Although this is certainly true in some cases, I would make the argument that there are other more legitimate reasons that better explain the increase in the numbers identified.

Perhaps the greatest contributor here is the increased awareness in the professional community of ADHD as a relevant diagnosis for adults. Remember, it has been barely three decades since Wender published the first studies on ADHD in adults (Weiss et al., 1999). As with any condition, greater awareness brings greater identification. This is the whole point behind public awareness campaigns and advocacy organizations. The people who are now being identified have always struggled with symptoms like distractibility, disorganization, and poor time management before educational campaigns put the term "ADHD" into the public awareness. But they lacked a name for their condition as an explanation for their difficulties. Labels don't change the facts, but they can change our understanding of those facts and, hopefully, suggest likely solutions.

A second factor in the increased awareness of ADHD is that the last several decades have seen a marked increase in the pace and complexity of life in the Western world, making ADHD struggles more obvious than they would have been in the slower times of the past. We are all dealing with a constant flood of information, tasks, and possessions, and adults who have ADHD have a harder time handling this deluge and thereby their difficulties become more noticeable. However, this should not be taken to imply that the increased pace of modern life causes ADHD—it just makes it easier to tell who has ADHD. ADHD has been found in all countries where it has been studied at approximately the same prevalence, making it difficult to claim that there is a causative element (Conners, 2002).

In today's culture of cell phones and e-mail, where we are expected to be always available and respond immediately, there is less wiggle room than there was when we could buy ourselves some extra time by claiming that something was "in the mail."

In addition, the workplace has become both leaner and meaner, in that the secretaries, clerks, and assistants who would have covered some of an ADHD employee's weaknesses no longer exist in many companies. Moreover, the average American workweek has increased, as have commuting times and house sizes, meaning that there is more to take care of and less time in which to do it. This creates a situation where those with compromised efficiencies, for whatever reason, are more obvious.

Finally, increased toxins in the environment over the last half century, as well as the reduced nutritional values of processed foods, could be having an effect on neurological functioning. As a brain-based disorder, anything that influences brain development or functioning obviously has the potential to influence the manifestation or severity of ADHD. Although this theory certainly seems plausible, there is no real way to prove it beyond the tentative conclusions that can be drawn from correlational studies, with the obvious confounding variable that people with ADHD, or parents with ADHD, may have less healthy diets due to their difficulties with consistent life management. So the ADHD may be more the cause of a poor diet than the result.

The first two factors, that is, greater public awareness of ADHD and a more complex society that makes ADHD symptoms more obvious, do not reflect a change in the actual prevalence rates, but rather in the rate of identification. So these days we are identifying more of those who have ADHD, which can appear to be an increase in prevalence. The third factor, the effect of toxins and reduced nutritional values, however, if true, would indeed reflect an increase in the true prevalence of the disorder. The first two are certainly true; only time will tell if the third factor is true, as well.

Diagnostic Difficulties

Perhaps more than some mental health conditions, diagnosing ADHD accurately presents certain challenges. For instance, we all experience one or more of the symptoms of ADHD at times, but it's not pathological to sometimes experience inattentiveness, impulsivity, forgetfulness, or disorganization (Murphy, 2002). The challenge for the clinician is to assess the extent to which the client truly has difficulties that go beyond the norm in intensity, frequency, and duration; difficulties that are at the thin ends of the bell curve. In addition, since everyone performs better on interesting tasks than on boring ones, people with ADHD differ in that they are significantly less able to activate, mobilize, and sustain their attention when the task doesn't turn them on (Brown, 1995). This may be compared to how diabetics can handle a meal with small amounts of sugar but run into trouble with meals that fall beyond their body's threshold. So, at what point is a task boring enough that the clinician can "justify" the person's wandering attention?

The trouble here is that the term "clinically significant impairment" as used in the *DSM-IV* means different things to different people, thus making it impossible to come up with an objective standard beyond which there is a clear consensus that a criterion has been met (Murphy, 2002). For example, how many times does someone need to lose her keys for it to count? Of course, the same can be said for many other diagnoses as well—exactly how much psychomotor retardation does someone have to display for it to count toward a diagnosis of major depression? What this means is that every clinician will develop his own threshold for how much impairment is required to meet a particular diagnostic criterion and the diagnosis as a whole. This subject is covered more fully in the section What Constitutes Impairment? below.

Complicating this issue even further is the fact that inattention is such a universal symptom of mental illness that in isolation it provides little diagnostic specificity. If anything, it's a general marker for distress, but says little of its origin (Murphy & Gordon, 2006). Fortunately, although inattention is rather common, the symptoms of early-appearing chronic and pervasive disinhibition associated with the hyperactive-impulsive type are associated almost uniquely with ADHD, making for an easier diagnosis for those with these symptoms.

Furthermore, the high level of comorbid conditions common to adults with ADHD creates a tangled web of symptoms that can be difficult to tease apart (Murphy, 2002)—for example, to what extent is the client's distractibility explained by anxiety versus ADHD? Ironically, although some comorbid conditions such as anxiety and depression represent fallout from years of ADHD difficulties, they can develop a life of their own and actually dominate the clinical picture (Murphy & Gordon, 2006).

In addition to these clinical elements, there are also practical matters that can interfere with diagnostic certainty. Because ADHD is a lifelong condition, a positive childhood history is required to qualify for the diagnosis, but objective records, such as report cards or early job evaluations, or corroboration from other people, such as parents and teachers, can be difficult to obtain. Self-reported memories are vulnerable to inaccuracy, intentional and unintentional distortion, and incompleteness (Murphy, 2002). At the other end of the life span, corroborative evidence from the client's current life may also be difficult to acquire—although it's relatively easy and acceptable to get teacher input for a child, it's much harder or otherwise inadvisable to get that input from an employer (Murphy & Gordon, 2006). As a result, we are required to use our best judgment when dealing with incomplete data, but this is always the case when it comes to clinical work in the real world. In any case, we can safely say that those with no signs of disruption until college or later may have valid symptoms and impairment, but it's highly unlikely that they are due to ADHD (Murphy & Gordon, 2006). Rather, the diagnosis lies elsewhere.

I recently evaluated a woman in her midforties for ADHD. She did endorse many of the symptoms in her current functioning, but not in her distant past. Her symptoms had begun over the last couple of years, a period of time when she began menopause, became depressed, and began drinking heavily. Although I certainly understood why her primary care physician had thought about ADHD as a possible explanation for these difficulties, her history disconfirmed it, even though she had no documented proof of her prior functioning.

As is common when a condition becomes as well known as ADHD has, misconceptions can arise quickly. The increased awareness of ADHD in adults has resulted in much folklore, myth, and misconception among the public and professionals alike, "knowledge" that has not yet been empirically validated. Using these informal markers as official diagnostic criteria can lead to misdiagnosis if different people are using different criteria. The whole point of having official diagnostic criteria is to ensure that everyone is speaking about the same phenomenon. Granted, those of us in the trenches, faced every day with clients who come to us to ease their suffering, cannot wait for researchers to confirm every nuance before we act. As much as research should inform clinical practice, so too should clinical practice inform research. As individual practitioners, each of us needs to decide how far beyond the data we are willing to go and at what point we are no longer providing a service for our clients. Fortunately, people with bona fide ADHD leave a clear trail of evidence in their wake, as they go through lives that are a testament to their problems with attention, self-control, and/or hyperactivity (Murphy, 2002). Moreover, as with most disorders, it's those with mild or moderate symptoms who are more difficult to diagnose accurately.

It's also worth keeping in mind that these *DSM-IV* criteria were developed on children and field-tested only on children. Therefore, they may not as accurately reflect the presentation of the disorder in adulthood. It has been estimated that the current criteria miss about one-third of adults with ADHD (Barkley, 2006, October). As a result, the *DSM-V* should contain some important refinements. Barkley and his colleagues are focusing on executive function deficits as promising in separating not only those with ADHD from those with no mental health diagnosis, which is relatively easy to do, but rather to distinguish those with ADHD from those with some other mental health condition (Barkley & Murphy, 2006). In addition to fine-tuning the specific criteria, it's likely that the age by which symptoms must first be present for the diagnosis to be made will be changed, perhaps to fourteen or sixteen, since the current cutoff at age seven was rather arbitrary and creates too many false negatives.

Overdiagnosis of ADHD

Unfortunately, ADHD can be easy to overdiagnose, especially in self-diagnosis. Everyone experiences these symptoms at least sometimes so it's an easy diagnosis to endorse. Perhaps the growing popularity of electronic organizers is a testament to the fact that all of our lives are growing more complicated and difficult to manage. As with any disorder, greater public awareness leads to more people being diagnosed—both correctly and not. The good news is that those who truly do have ADHD are more likely to receive an accurate diagnosis and to seek appropriate treatment. The bad news is that those with other conditions, such as bipolar disorder or personality disorders, may also seize upon the label because it seems to explain their difficulties.

Related to this greater awareness of ADHD is the issue of social acceptability. Advocates have worked long and hard to increase acceptance of people with ADHD. (See the appendix for more information about advocacy groups.) This destigmatizing of the disorder cuts both ways. There are many reasons why people do not achieve as much as they would like, but ADHD has become a one-size-fits-all diagnosis for some people seeking an acceptable explanation for their difficulties. The downside of destigmatizing is that it makes it easier for the non-ADHD person to assume the label too. The common comorbid conditions that co-occur with ADHD or are confused with ADHD are discussed below, but it should be noted here that there are many nonclinical reasons why discrepancies may exist between intelligence and real-world performance:

inadequate social skills, personality style, unrealistic goals, a mismatch between demands and abilities, socioeconomic status, accessibility to educational/vocational opportunities, cultural issues, motivation, or having a relative weakness in selected areas (Murphy & Gordon, 2006).

Also, some people may seek the diagnosis with the hope of gaining special accommodations in school or work settings. This may be because they genuinely believe that they or their child deserve the accommodations, but it may also be seen as a way to get an edge in a competitive world. Alternatively, high-achieving parents may have difficulty accepting that their child may tend more toward average ability and seek out ways of improving the child's grades, either for the child's benefit or as a way of protecting their own egos.

Finally, a positive response to stimulants is not diagnostic, since most people function better with a stimulant, so a medication trial should not be used diagnostically (Murphy, 2002), including, "I did much better on my kid's Ritalin, so I must have ADHD, too." It's because of this near-universal benefit of stimulants that caffeine in its various forms is so pervasive in our busy culture. Therefore, some people may dishonestly seek a diagnosis of ADHD to gain access to prescription stimulants, believing they will then have an edge in the classroom or workplace. The difference between people with ADHD and those without is that those with ADHD, hopefully, will show a marked and pervasive improvement on the stimulant, more so than non-ADHD people will. Of course, the converse here is not true—failure to show an improvement on a stimulant does not invalidate the diagnosis.

Underdiagnosis of ADHD

Despite the potential to overdiagnose ADHD, it is probably more true that ADHD is still underdiagnosed among adults. Probably the biggest reason why many ADHD adults are missed is that mental health professionals still think of it as a disorder of childhood or they are unfamiliar with the signs and symptoms in adults. As a result, other diagnoses or explanations are given instead, such as anxiety, depression, fear of success, passive-aggressive behavior, or self-destructive tendencies. Although some of these explanations may also be accurate, the person's difficulties are not fully explained simply by these comorbid conditions. In some cases, the comorbid conditions are very much secondary to a lifetime of ADHD, meaning that treatment of the secondary elements will be of limited benefit. An analogy is bailing out a boat with a hole in the bottom, without fixing the hole first—the water will keep pouring in, despite your best efforts to get it out. (Comorbid conditions and rule-outs are covered in detail below.) I've seen many clients who had been in sometimes lengthy therapy previously and very clearly had ADHD which had never been diagnosed or addressed effectively.

Another possibility is that inappropriate measures or criteria were used to make the diagnosis and therefore failed to sufficiently pick up the client's ADHD symptoms. For example, a member of my adult ADHD support group was told by her psychiatrist that she couldn't have ADHD because she had managed to get a Ph.D., therefore, she did not exhibit the requisite level of impairment. What he didn't take into account was the fact that she had had to work twice as hard as her classmates just to keep up, which led to secondary anxiety and depression. This issue of inappropriate measures is also covered in detail below.

As this woman illustrates, some people manage to create significant successes in their life despite their ADHD, so success should not necessarily rule out an ADHD diagnosis, if any of the following bulleted items apply. Some people manage to scrape by or even become quite successful until their circumstances change and the environment exposes their ADHD weaknesses more significantly, resulting in trouble adjusting to the new situation (Weiss et al., 1999); for example:

- Retirement from the structured life of the military

- Divorce from a well-organized spouse

- Promotion or transfer to a less structured job or

- Leaving the workforce to stay home with children

It may also be that the client's parents served as "external executive functioner," keeping her on track until she left for college and then she had great difficulty when she couldn't provide that structure for herself (Katz, 2004). In later life, this executive function may be provided by roommates, romantic partners, and secretaries/assistants. In other cases, the ADHD person may have to work much harder or longer for the same successes. For example, she may need to come in early or stay late to get the same amount of work done. And, finally, some people with ADHD are successful because they find the right environment for their particular strengths and weaknesses, or they are very skilled in other ways such that others will tolerate their ADHD behavior.

For a diagnosis of ADHD to be made, the symptoms must have been present from early childhood. However, not all ADHD adults will have shown obvious symptoms in early life. This is not to say that the symptoms were not present, but rather that they may not have been as obvious. Individuals with high intelligence and without hyperactivity may not display as much of a history of academic difficulty and behavioral problems (Lavenstein, 1995). Symptoms of inattention are "silent" relative to the "noisy" symptoms of hyperactivity (Brown, 1995). As Thomas Brown joked at the 1999 CHADD conference, even the school janitor can diagnose the hyperactive kids because they are so obviously different from classmates.

For the hyperactive/impulsive students, high intelligence isn't much of a protector in the areas of self-control, organization, time management, or good judgment (Murphy & Gordon, 2006). Exceptions may arise if the person attended an extremely structured school that kept him in line or, conversely, attended an unstructured, chaotic school where his impulsive misbehavior was not notable. For example, I recently evaluated a college freshman who went to a private high school with small, supportive classes and had a mother who supervised his homework very closely. As a result, despite the fact that he could be the poster child for ADHD combined type, his grades were generally quite good because others kept him from going off the rails, and if he did go off, he could charm his way out of it. However, predictably, he wound up on academic probation his first year in college when all that structure and support was left behind.

If a student's struggles were obvious, explanations other than ADHD may have been used—such as poor motivation, "he'll grow out of it," or inconsistent parenting. Given the high heritability of ADHD, which will be discussed further in chapter 2, it is fairly likely that a parent has ADHD as well, so the child's struggles may be normalized under the logic of, "I was the same way but I turned out fine. We don't need to do anything about this."

Of course, most adults were children during a time when ADHD was not frequently diagnosed, even in children. For people who were born before 1980, unless they were quite uncontrollable, it's unlikely that they would have been diagnosed and treated as children. Therefore, lack of a diagnosis in childhood should not be construed as evidence against the presence of the disorder. Instead, you will need to do a present-day assessment of past functioning.

Giving someone an accurate ADHD diagnosis, especially if undiagnosed in childhood, can be a therapeutic intervention in and of itself. Newly diagnosed individuals often report immediate relief once they have a framework to explain their lifelong difficulties in academic, social, and/or personal functioning. After a lifetime of believing they are unintelligent, unmotivated, lazy, or inexplicably different from others, the diagnosis may be welcomed. This relief may be mixed with overwhelming feelings of sadness or anger because so much time has gone by and they endured so much potentially preventable struggle. This adjustment to the diagnosis will be addressed further in chapter 7, Adapting Psychotherapy for the ADHD Adult.

Diagnostic Criteria

The *DSM-IV-TR* (American Psychiatric Association, 2000) is the current gold standard of criteria used to make the diagnosis of ADHD. The criteria are as follows:

A. Either (1) or (2):

(1) Six (or more) of the following symptoms of inattention have persisted for at least 6 months to a degree that is maladaptive and inconsistent with developmental level:

(a) Often fails to give close attention to details or makes careless mistakes in schoolwork, work, or other activities

(b) Often has difficulty sustaining attention in tasks or play activities

(c) Often does not seem to listen when spoken to directly

(d) Often does not follow through on instructions and fails to finish schoolwork, chores, or duties in the workplace (not due to oppositional behavior or failure to understand instructions)

(e) Often has difficulty organizing tasks and activities

(f) Often avoids, dislikes, or is reluctant to engage in tasks that require sustained mental effort (such as schoolwork or homework)

(g) Often loses things necessary for tasks or activities (e.g., toys, school assignments, pencils, books, or tools)

(h) Is often easily distracted by extraneous stimuli

(i) Is often forgetful in daily activities

(2) Six (or more) of the following symptoms of hyperactivity-impulsivity have persisted for at least 6 months to a degree that is maladaptive and inconsistent with developmental level:

Hyperactivity:

(a) Often fidgets with hands or feet or squirms in seat

(b) Often leaves seat in classroom or in other situations in which remaining seated is expected

(c) Often runs about or climbs excessively in situations in which it is inappropriate (in adolescents or adults, may be limited to subjective feelings of restlessness)

(d) Often has difficulty playing or engaging in leisure activities quietly

(e) Is often "on the go" or often acts as if "driven by a motor"

(f) Often talks excessively

Impulsivity:

(g) Often blurts out answers before questions have been completed

(h) Often has difficulty waiting turn

(i) Often interrupts or intrudes on others (e.g., butts into conversations or games)

B. Some hyperactive-impulsive or inattentive symptoms that caused impairment were present before age 7 years.

C. Some impairment from the symptoms is present in two or more settings (e.g., at school [or work] and at home).

D. There must be clear evidence of clinically significant impairment in social, academic, or occupational functioning.

E. The symptoms do not occur exclusively during the course of a Pervasive Developmental Disorder, Schizophrenia, or other Psychotic Disorder and are not better accounted for by another mental disorder (e.g., Mood Disorder, Anxiety Disorder, Dissociative Disorder, or a Personality Disorder).

Code based on type:

314.01 Attention-Deficit/Hyperactivity Disorder, Combined Type: if both Criteria A1 and A2 are met for the past 6 months [ADHD-C]

314.00 Attention-Deficit/Hyperactivity Disorder, Predominantly Inattentive Type: if Criterion A1 is met but Criterion A2 is not met for the past 6 months [ADHD-PI]

314.01 Attention-Deficit/Hyperactivity Disorder, Predominantly Hyperactive-Impulsive Type: if Criterion A2 is met but Criterion A1 is not met for the past 6 months [ADHD-PHI]

Coding note: For individuals (especially adolescents and adults) who currently have symptoms that no longer meet full criteria, "In Partial Remission" should be specified.

Reprinted with permission from the Diagnostic and Statistical Manual of Mental Disorders, Fourth Edition, Text Revision *(Copyright 2000). American Psychiatric Association.*

What Constitutes Impairment?

It's worth keeping in mind that the requirement that symptoms be present "to a degree that is maladaptive" is not mere verbiage. The presence of a symptom does not automatically imply that it's impairing. For it to count toward the diagnosis, the symptom must actually cause impairment. Barkley et al., (2006, p. 2) define the symptoms of ADHD as "the behavioral expressions associated with this disorder—they are the actions demonstrated by those having the disorder that are believed to reflect that disorder (i.e., inattention, distractibility, impulsive responding, hyperactivity, etc.)." By contrast, "impairments are the consequences that ensue for the individual as a result of these behaviors. In short, symptoms are actions (behavior) and impairments are consequences (outcomes or social costs)." Impairments are the end result of the interactions between symptoms and their severity, the person's overall life situation, and adaptive behaviors. They're the combination of both risk factors as well as protective factors within the individual and provided by others (Goldstein, 2006, October).

In evaluating the presence of symptoms, be sure to ask the follow-up questions about impairment. Symptoms may be clinically interesting, but it's the impairments that drive the diagnosis, as well as bring people into treatment. Unfortunately the *DSM-IV-TR* does not provide specific criteria to define what constitutes impairment (Johnson & Conners, 2002). For example, how often does an adult need to lose her keys for it to count toward a diagnosis? And how do we define lost—when she can't find them after two minutes of looking, or one hour? What if someone else finds them the next day? Or they are never found again? Also, are the keys lost because they were put in the wrong place or are they lost because the person isn't good at finding things? Finally, who defines impairment? Is it the person herself who needs to be bothered by it or do other people have a vote? Often, people who are hypomanic are not bothered by their symptoms, whereas their families very much are. These questions point out that there is as much art as there is science in diagnosing ADHD, as with most other disorders. Each of us must set our own cutoffs for the level of impairment beyond which the presence of a symptom counts. The following dialogue may clarify the importance of assessing impairment:

Therapist: How do you do with staying organized?

Client: Oh man, not good. My stuff is always in chaos.

Therapist: How does that work out for you?

Client: Pretty bad. My girlfriend gets really mad with me since I always keep her waiting when I can't find something. I'm also kind of infamous among my friends—they never want to come over to hang out at my place. In college, I would sometimes lose textbooks for like a week in my room and get even further behind in the reading.

Therapist: What about at work?

Client: My boss is always giving me a hard time that my desk looks like a filing cabinet exploded on it, but I can usually find what I need. Well, eventually. He's pretty uptight anyway, but I do think that he reads too much into my messy desk and doesn't give me the harder projects because he's worried I'll screw them up.

This client has paid a price socially, academically, and vocationally for his inability to get places on time. In my opinion this warrants the cutoff for sufficient impairment.

Evolution of Symptom Presentation over the Life Span

The presentation of ADHD symptoms may vary over the person's life and across environments so the symptom complaints may vary—for example, the ability to sit still is more important in a classroom than it is for a retail salesperson. As stated earlier, the good news for adults is that they have a greater ability to choose their environments.

For example, I had a client who worked as a deliveryman for a restaurant supply company. He very much enjoyed the constant activity and chatting up his clients, so he was successful at work. The bad news for adults is that they are expected to function at a higher level and with less assistance from others—this same client's wife often complained about his difficulties in following through on projects at home. The good news for kids is that there are parents, teachers, and other adults to help them stay on track. The bad news is that they have much less flexibility about the environments in which they must function. I like to say that the classroom is one of the best screening tools for ADHD because it requires children to sit still and pay attention to lengthy and uninteresting lectures, as well as to track multiple assignments that may be less interesting than the class. Given such different social and vocational environments, it should not be surprising that there are inconsistencies between the findings in the child and adult literature.

In addition to these changes in environment, the ADHD symptoms themselves also change over the life span. Most notably, hyperactivity tends to quiet down into fidgetiness, subjective feelings of restlessness, and difficulty or aversion to sitting still. Adults may also find adaptive ways of dealing with this, like working two jobs, working in very active jobs, working long hours, or directing those energies into other pursuits. Whereas kids tend to be aimless in their restlessness, adults with ADHD may be more purposeful and put that energy to better use (Weiss et al., 1999). The fact that the most visible symptoms of hyperactivity and impulsivity tend to diminish in late adolescence may explain why ADHD was thought of as something that children grew out of. Ironically, though, in adulthood the consequences tend to be more severe. For example, impulsivity can also be expressed as low frustration tolerance and lead to rash decisions (Weiss et al., 1999). Impulsivity that leads to groundings and detentions in childhood can lead to job terminations, divorces, and jail sentences as an adult because the expectations for adults are so much greater. Adults are expected to function at a higher level of independence, consistency, and accuracy.

Therefore, despite the fact that some of their symptoms become less pronounced, many people with ADHD experience greater difficulties in adulthood. Whereas the problems that result from hyperactivity and impulsivity tend to be more dramatic, it is the slow erosion of inattention-based difficulties with organization that can cause some of the biggest problems for adults. For example, mundane tasks like grocery shopping, paying bills, and keeping track of items prove to be a constant challenge for ADHD adults, particularly those who do not have an organized and supportive partner. As organizational demands on the person increase, it is not surprising that these difficulties with inattention become more disabling. Some ADHD adults may adapt by choosing jobs that do not require sustained attention and by avoiding difficult activities like reading (Weiss et al., 1999), but even so, there is a limit to how much responsibility we can avoid as adults.

The fact that the hyperactivity and impulsivity tend to decline with age means that those with ADHD combined type (ADHD-C) will come to look more like those with ADHD predominantly inattentive type (ADHD-PI), at least superficially. But are they really the same? Probably not. Those who had ADHD-C as children will likely have greater difficulties with disinhibition than those who have always had ADHD-PI (Barkley, 2006b). It's unclear at this time what the clinical utility is of this distinction, but it bears keeping in mind as you take a childhood history.

Finally, there is some mounting evidence that women with ADHD may experience an exacerbation of symptoms as they go through menopause, as well as some fluctuation during the course of their menstrual cycles, both due to changes in hormone levels. It's possible that some older women will seek evaluation and treatment as their hormone levels drop during perimenopause, leading to a decrease in their ability to manage their lives.

Adult Versions of DSM-IV-TR Criteria

In this discussion of ADHD across the life span, it should be noted that some people do show a decline in symptoms over time and thereby fall below the diagnostic threshold but still maintain significant difficulties. This is the difference between *syndromatic persistence* wherein the person maintains full diagnostic status versus *symptomatic persistence* wherein the person maintains partial diagnostic status but is still impaired by the symptoms that remain. So, just because someone no longer meets full diagnostic criteria does not necessarily mean that he had a "full recovery." This is especially important to remember when looking at studies of adult ADHD, because how the researchers define terms and set inclusion/exclusion criteria for the study will obviously have an impact on the results.

For example, studies looking for syndromatic persistence will likely underestimate symptomatic persistence. Persistence of ADHD into adulthood varies from 4 to 80 percent depending on how you define and measure it (Faraone et al., 2000), which is quite a large difference. Overall, the *DSM-IV-TR* criteria become less sensitive to ADHD as people get older, leading to declining prevalence if you strictly hold to those criteria (Barkley, 2006f).

Because the *DSM-IV* criteria are slanted toward child-oriented examples, some authors have provided adult versions of the criteria (adapted with permission from Weiss et al., 1999, pp. 55–57, and Johnson & Conners, 2002, p. 74), as follows:

Inattention

(a) Frequent costly work errors despite "knowing better." Detailed and tedious tasks, such as doing income taxes, become very stressful. Accuracy is sacrificed for speed; does not recheck work.

(b) Difficulty staying on one task until completion before switching to something else—great starter, bad finisher. Difficulty staying with boring jobs. Dislike of reading for extended periods. Long conversations may become difficult to follow. Even enjoyable activities like watching sports for extended periods can become difficult to track.

(c) Frequently receive complaints about not listening, that it's difficult to get their attention, and that they forget things that seem to have been heard. Frequently may be seen as tuned-out. Others may see the person as spacey or not there; they need to repeat the person's name several times to get her attention.

(d) Difficulty with accurately following others' verbal or written instructions. Failure to follow through on commitments at home or work (not based on a conscious choice to simply not do the task). Inability to consistently keep accounts, pay bills on time, etc. Needs external deadlines to get things done. Difficulty following through on multiple requests made simultaneously. Jumps from task to task.

(e) Recurrent lateness, missed appointments, and missed deadlines. This may be hidden by certain tasks being delegated to a spouse or coworker or avoided. Does not plan ahead. Relies on others for order. Poor sense of time. Inefficient. Items on to-do lists are not completed.

(f) Long delays in responding to mail/e-mail, filing taxes, organizing old papers, paying bills, etc., due to procrastination, despite knowledge of the consequences.

(g) Frequently loses keys, cell phones, purses/wallets, work assignments, parked cars, household items, and so forth. Absent-minded. Loses organizers/PDAs (personal digital assistants).

(h) Sometimes puts significant effort into lessening distractibility—using white noise, multitasking, brinksmanship, or absolute silence. May work during off hours when there is less distraction. Difficulty filtering out unnecessary noise. Difficulty refocusing after being interrupted. Daydreams.

(i) Memory problems—for example, goes to supermarket with a mental list of items to buy and forgets half of them. Difficulty remembering where he put things, such as keys. Planning is difficult when important details are forgotten along the way. Forgets to use schedule or organizer. Uses others to help remember things. Frequently returns to home/office to retrieve forgotten items, but not due to compulsive checking.

Hyperactivity

(a) Fidgety—picks at fingers, shakes knees, taps hands or feet, talks with her hands, or changes position frequently. This may be more observable in the waiting room than in the office once engaged in discussion.

(b) Feels restless at long dinners out or during long conversations. May also feel restless when forced to wait. Difficulty staying seated through long TV shows, movies, or lectures. Prefers active pursuits.

(c) Subjectively feels like he always needs to be on the go or feels more comfortable with more stimulating activities. Paces or fidgets. Internal restlessness.

(d) Discomfort with just staying home for a quiet evening. May be a workaholic. Talks during movies. Has difficulty moderating speech volume.

(e) Others may complain of the frenetic pace the person sets for himself and others. Little opportunity to just rest, even on vacation. Always moving and unable to relax.

(f) Excessive talking wherein the other does not feel heard due to frequent interruptions. Can be seen as nervous nagging or interfering with appropriate social behavior at gatherings. Clowning, repartee, or other means of dominating conversations may mask an inability to engage in a balanced conversation. Takes a long time to get a point across. Often diverges into tangents and even interrupts herself.

Impulsivity

(g) Blurts out answers before questions have been completed. The person may feel that others talk too slowly and feels impatient about waiting for others to finish. Says things without thinking. Frequently puts foot in mouth.

(h) Irritated waiting for children or other slow people to complete something or when forced to wait on line. May be aware of their own intense efforts to force themselves to wait. May compensate by always having something to do. Impatient in traffic.

(i) Most often seen as socially inept in casual conversations or even with close friends—for example, impatience with watching others struggle with something without jumping in to help. Steps on people's toes. Violates others' space/boundaries and is seen as intrusive.

Obviously, these cannot be used as official diagnostic criteria, but they can give you a fuller picture of a client's functioning. As with most conditions, there is as much art as there is science in making a diagnosis.

Soft Signs

In addition to the above adaptations of the *DSM-IV* criteria adapted with permission from Weiss et al., 1999, pp. 55–57, and Johnson & Conners, 2002, p. 74, you can further flesh out the diagnosis by using the following soft signs of ADHD in adults.

These unofficial but common symptoms of ADHD provide more information about the client's areas of weakness. Many of these are outgrowths of the primary symptoms.

Inattention Soft Signs

- Some ADHD adults work hard at being organized but have little to show in terms of results—it's not just that they lazily don't try. Rather, they move things around but the objects don't wind up in better places because the person doesn't have a good organizational system into which to put things. This leads to feelings of hopelessness and avoidance of organizing.

- Often seen by self and others as not living up to their potential and that they could do better if only they cared more or tried harder.

- Complain of poor short-term memory and blanking out on very obvious things, like spouse's name at a party.

- Display poor prospective memory, that is, the ability to remember to do things in the future. For example, "I need to take out the trash when I get home tonight."

- Related to the above criterion, people with ADHD frequently miss turns/exits when driving, especially when going down familiar roads.

- Poor time management and/or procrastination which causes big problems at work and at home (Weiss et al., 1999).

- Hyperfocus, manifested as becoming engrossed in an activity to the exclusion of everything else. It may require repeated attempts to get their attention or lengthy stretches of time may pass unnoticed.

- Tendency to miss pieces of conversation or be briefly tuned-out—this may be noticed by themselves or others at the time or may become obvious only later, when others remember the discussion differently.

Hyperactivity/Impulsivity Soft Signs

- They are good starters, but bad finishers—have many half-finished projects at home and work. Get bored once they have the project figured out or it becomes routine.

- Trouble sitting and reading. If they do read books, they may read several simultaneously and probably not finish most of them.

- Tendency to blurt things out—they feel pressured to say their thought immediately for fear that otherwise they will forget it.

- Higher than average number of tickets for speeding/reckless driving.

- Regretful spontaneous purchases, large or small. This is not to be confused with manic spending sprees which tend to cluster more and be more excessive. A general inability to stick to a budget or an inability to mentally track how individual purchases fit into the bigger picture.

- Thrill-seeking behavior. This may be most obvious in physical tasks, such as motorcycle riding, where it results in frequent accidents and greater than average number of emergency room visits (Weiss et al., 1999). However, it may also take place in relationships, such as by creating dramatic situations or breaking up when the relationship becomes familiar and routine.

Other Soft Signs

- High caffeine intake, perhaps because it's the only thing that helps them to focus.

- Generally decreased quality of life and demoralization about the future and their ability to improve things for themselves (Weiss et al., 1999). Feeling of learned helplessness based on legitimate failures.

- Family or coworkers may feel more of the pain of the ADHD symptoms as a result of overfunctioning to cover for the ADHD person's shortcomings (Weiss et al., 1999).

- Related to the above, they may show a tendency to wind up with caretaker types in relationships who are then seen as too controlling.

- Difficulty achieving their potential at work, despite great mental effort. They may compensate by putting in extra hours to get the expected amount of work done (Weiss, et al., 1999). In addition, they may find that it's helpful to come in early or stay late because they are less distracted when the workplace is quieter.

- Great difficulty with the overly loose structure of college, leading to dropping out or needing extra semesters to graduate. Have a hodgepodge transcript with a broad array of courses, wide range of grades (A to F), and many dropped classes.

- General academic struggles such as repeated grades, difficulty with classmates, and complaints from others about irresponsibility (Weiss et al., 1999).

- Family history—about 25 percent of first-degree relatives (parents, siblings, and children) have ADHD (Weiss et al., 1999).

- Mood lability over a period of minutes or moments (Weiss et al., 1999), rather than the mood lability of bipolar disorder that occurs over a period of hours, days, or weeks. Prone to strong emotional reactions that take others by surprise both in their intensity and how quickly they dissipate.

■ Low self-esteem due to experiencing more rejection and failure than most peers. They may minimize their strengths, always feeling that they could have done better. New failures and mistakes bring back to mind a laundry list of past blunders (Weiss et al., 1999).

Gender Differences

As with many other disorders, ADHD may present differently in males and females. There has been debate in the field as to whether there truly is a gender difference in prevalence rates. The *DSM-IV-TR* puts the gender ratio at 4:1 to 9:1 in favor of males. However, it may be that the discrepancy is more indicative of referral biases than it is of true prevalence rates. That is, males are more likely to be thought of as having ADHD whereas females are more likely to be thought of as having depression or anxiety, even if they present many of the same symptoms as ADHD.

A second reason for the discrepancy may be related to the fact that males and females do not tend to present the same symptoms—for example, males are more likely to engage in aggressive and antisocial behaviors, which are more likely to prompt treatment (Ellison, 2002). Females are more likely to have the inattentive subtype and are less likely than males to have conduct disorder or antisocial personality disorder (Biederman, Faraone, Monuteaux, Bober, & Cadogen, 2004). A girl with ADHD who is doing poorly in school is more likely to withdraw and appear disinterested or depressed, whereas a boy is more likely to act out and get into trouble, making him more likely to be referred and diagnosed. In contrast, girls tend to suffer in silence (Ratey, Miller, & Nadeau, 1995) and are therefore less likely to be assessed for ADHD—either because they are not assessed at all or because they are assessed for depression or anxiety instead, which they may indeed also have. Interestingly, however, as self-referred adults, this bias is less likely to be relevant, which explains why the gender ratio balances out more in adulthood (Faraone et al., 2000).

When it comes to adults who have experienced a lifetime of struggle due to undiagnosed ADHD, it is not surprising that many women with ADHD seek mental health services to improve their functioning, mood, and self-esteem. Unfortunately, these women are more likely to be diagnosed with anxiety and depression than ADHD. Although it may indeed be true that they also are anxious and depressed, these are not the primary disorder, so, as a result, they tend to be treatment-refractory. Further complicating the differential diagnosis, ADHD females commonly report emotional instability characterized by fluctuating anxiety, depression, and sudden mood swings leading to difficulty with self-regulation (Young, 2002). However, it is unclear whether this is a feature of the ADHD or the result of a difficult lifetime. In either case, it muddies the diagnostic waters.

Future research will cast additional light on the true gender split. Refinements within the *DSM-V* criteria may improve diagnostic accuracy and eliminate a potential gender bias. Meanwhile, Patricia Quinn, MD, and Kathleen Nadeau, Ph.D., have edited *Gender Issues and ADHD: Research, Diagnosis, and Treatment* (Advantage Books, 2002), which serves as an excellent resource for this sometimes neglected half of the population.

Diagnostic Interview

In my practice, I use a two-hour diagnostic interview to assess for the presence of ADHD. It may not be perfect, but it's definitely a good place to start. As Thomas Brown says, "the most sensitive instrument for making a diagnosis of ADHD is a well-conducted interview" (2005, p. 182). Testing instruments are discussed in greater detail below.

Even if I've already spoken about this on the phone when setting up the appointment, I will generally start by asking the client, and anyone else who is present, why he thinks that he has ADHD. Some will report that a family member was recently diagnosed and the similarities prompted this evaluation. Others will have read a newspaper article or heard a TV or radio segment about adult ADHD. Still others will be referred by another professional who suspects ADHD but wants a better qualified second opinion to confirm it. I even had one client who had been unofficially diagnosed by his employees.

I do not use a set format for the interview, preferring to see where the client goes. I keep a running mental tally as the conversation flows, and I direct the discussion as needed to be sure that I ask all the questions I need to make an assessment. It is my personal opinion that overly structured interview forms can miss important spontaneous comments or deny the clinician the opportunity to explore those comments further. Of course, it takes a solid familiarity with the diagnostic criteria and associated features for both ADHD and the likely comorbid conditions and rule-outs to use this less formal approach, but I feel that it's worth it. This is especially true when the client being evaluated is a potential therapy client and you are simultaneously doing the evaluation and building rapport. Although it can be difficult to quantify, over time you get a feel for ADHD based on what your gut tells you. You can use the Adult ADHD Interview Form to unobtrusively keep track of the presence of diagnostic criteria, tone of the interview, collateral information, and comorbid conditions. You can also use the Areas of Impairment Form to keep track of the various ways that ADHD has affected the person's life, since significant impairment is required in order to qualify for the diagnosis. This may also be helpful in choosing areas to work on in therapy. Both forms are also available on my website, www.TuckmanPsych.com, for download.

ADULT ADHD INTERVIEW FORM

DSM-IV-TR Criteria

The symptom must be frequent, impairing, and present across multiple settings. Mark S for self-report, C for collateral report or information. Mark separately whether it was present in childhood and as an adult.

Inattention symptoms (need 6)

Child   Adult

_____   _____   Poor attention to details

_____   _____   Difficulty sustaining attention

_____   _____   Does not seem to listen when spoken to directly

_____   _____   Does not follow through on instructions and fails to finish tasks

_____   _____   Disorganized

_____   _____   Avoids tasks that require sustained mental effort

_____   _____   Loses things

_____   _____   Easily distracted

_____   _____   Forgetful

Hyperactive/impulsive symptoms (need 6)

Child   Adult

_____   _____   Fidgety

_____   _____   Difficulty remaining seated

_____   _____   Feels restless

_____   _____   Difficulty engaging in leisure activities quietly

_____   _____   Is often "on the go"

_____   _____   Talks excessively

_____   _____   Blurts out answers

_____   _____   Difficulty waiting turn

_____   _____   Interrupts or intrudes on others

Adapted from the *Diagnostic and Statistical Manual of Mental Disorders, Fourth Edition, Text Revision* (copyright 2000). With permission from the American Psychiatric Association.

Tone of the Interview

_____ Long-standing pain and frustration

_____ Sense of lost opportunities or regret

_____ Underachievement or failure to work to potential

_____ Interrupts you and himself or herself

_____ Wanders off topic

_____ Forgets the question or answers a different question

_____ Physically restless

_____ Distracted by items in the office or extraneous noises

Collateral Information Sources

_____ Previously diagnosed with ADHD

_____ Family member or significant other, if present, mostly confirms self-report

_____ Report cards or teacher comments are consistent with ADHD

_____ Results of assessment instruments are consistent with ADHD

_____ Family history of ADHD, especially in parents, siblings, or children

Comorbid Conditions

_____ Depression

_____ Bipolar disorder

_____ Anxiety

_____ Post-traumatic stress disorder

_____ Learning disabilities

_____ Antisocial personality disorder

_____ Substance abuse or other addictions

_____ Borderline personality disorder

_____ Sleep deprivation

_____ Head injury or medical conditions

AREAS OF IMPAIRMENT FORM

To what extent has ADHD impacted these various areas of the client's life? Mark S for self-report, C for collateral report or information.

Academic Performance

_____ Elementary school

_____ Middle school

_____ High school

_____ College and beyond

Occupational Performance

_____ Excessive job changes

_____ Been fired

_____ Quit impulsively

_____ Failed to advance

_____ Difficulty meeting deadlines

_____ Difficulty getting along with supervisors or coworkers

Daily Life Functioning

_____ Managing daily demands

_____ Time management

_____ Balanced lifestyle

_____ Money management

_____ Excessive driving tickets and accidents

_____ Excessive substance use

Psychological Functioning

_____   Self-image

_____   Self-efficacy

_____   Problem-solving style

_____   Overuse of avoidance

_____   Overuse of externalization

_____   Procrastination/brinksmanship

Social Skills and Relationships

_____   Reduced relatedness with others

_____   Puts foot in mouth

_____   Appears uninterested in others

_____   Reduced awareness of others' feelings

_____   Emotional outbursts

_____   Overly conflictual or imbalanced romantic relationships

_____   Inconsistent parenting

It's also important to remember that a diagnostic interview involves more than merely engaging in a symptom count, something that could be done in about five minutes. You are not only asking to see if the client has a particular symptom, you are also asking:

- **How long has the symptom been present**—a month? A year? As long as she can remember?

- **How frequently does she display the symptom**—once in a blue moon or several times a day? Only in one setting or across the board?

- **How much impairment does the symptom cause him**—is it kind of annoying or has it cost him jobs and relationships?

- **What's causing the symptom**—ADHD, a comorbid condition, or life circumstances?

It's the details that make all the difference when it comes to making an accurate diagnosis. For example, you may get a client who reports having difficulty concentrating at work; feels scattered, forgetful, disorganized, that he isn't functioning up to his potential; and he has great difficulties completing tasks that he has started. Initially, it may sound like he endorses many of the inattentive symptoms. However, further explanation reveals that he was recently promoted to a position that he has not been adequately trained for, yet he still has high expectations for a good performance. His academic performance and prior functioning do not indicate more than the usual number of inattentive symptoms and associated impairments. Stress and unhappiness from work are spilling over into his personal life—extra hours at the office mean less time to clean and organize his apartment—but he is otherwise functioning well outside of work.

At a superficial level, this man may indeed meet the criteria for ADHD by a simple symptom count, but he does not exhibit a lifelong persistence, across multiple settings, and to an extent that demonstrates he has experienced significant impairment. Most importantly, the cause of his symptoms is a bad job situation, not a neurological condition. Therefore, ADHD would not be an accurate diagnosis, although it's possible that he may have some subthreshold anxiety and depression.

The possibility of comorbid conditions makes it all the more important to make a careful assessment, for two reasons. First, many other conditions can look like ADHD superficially, so it's important to be able to tell the difference—this issue is covered at length below. Second, many adults with ADHD will also have one or more comorbid conditions that make it more difficult to accurately diagnose each condition. Therefore, the question here is not simply, "Does this person have ADHD, yes or no?" but rather, "Does this person have ADHD and/or another condition?"

There has been a lot of debate about the accuracy of adults self-reporting ADHD symptoms, especially from their childhood. However, studies have found that a self-report can meet a reasonable threshold for initial evaluation; but it should not necessarily be used to confirm the diagnosis (Goldstein, 2002). Unfortunately, historical data may not be otherwise available, leaving us to make our best guess. Of course, this limitation can be found with any condition that requires childhood history—including physical medicine. The good news is that research shows that more specific questions tend to elicit more accurate responses than open-ended questions, so we can increase the likelihood of getting good answers by asking good questions (Murphy & Schachar, 2000). This also means trying to avoid leading questions. The following list provides good examples of the types of questions to ask:

Too Vague or Leading Questions	More Specific Questions
Do you tend to lose things?	How do you do with keeping track of things like your keys, cell phone, hats, gloves, and other things like that?
Do you have trouble sitting still?	How do you feel when sitting through a long movie or meeting?
Did you have trouble paying attention as a child?	How did you do with paying attention to your teachers in middle school compared to your classmates?
Do you forget to do things?	If you had to remember to make a phone call when you got home this evening, how likely is it that you would remember it without writing it down?

Depending on the answers you receive, or the way that the client answers, you can follow up with additional questions.

It should also be noted that there are probably differences between those who seek an evaluation for ADHD specifically versus those who come to therapy for other or more general reasons, such as depression, relationship difficulties, or stress, but turn out to have ADHD. Some of those who come with the explicit goal of being assessed for ADHD are painfully obvious in their deficits and it becomes clear very quickly what the ultimate outcome will be. By contrast, those who come seeking treatment for other reasons, which also may be completely justified, may hide their ADHD symptoms with their more immediate concerns. It's only over time that you will begin to see that interventions that should have been helpful have not produced the expected improvements. Even as someone who specializes in adult ADHD, I have had clients where it has been months or even years before I began to think of ADHD as a relevant diagnosis, due to the degree of comorbid conditions or complicating circumstances.

Tone of the Interview

You should keep in mind that a diagnostic interview in a new clinician's office is a novel and interesting experience, which may mask the presentation of ADHD symptoms in the office (Weiss et al., 1999). These symptoms will become more apparent as the client becomes more familiar with you. For that reason the therapy client who was earnest and well focused initially may become much less so as her true difficulties reveal themselves over multiple sessions.

In addition to the facts gathered in a diagnostic interview, you should also pay attention to the client's affective quality. Adults with ADHD almost always communicate a sense of long-standing pain, frustration, and underachievement. They display an emotional "heaviness" about the type and degree of impairment they have experienced throughout their lives. They may become tearful and express despair, intense frustration, anger, a sense of lost opportunities, regret, low self-esteem, defensiveness, and sometimes learned helplessness. Although these folks can be very funny, if the overall tone of the interview is lighthearted and full of laughter, if the degree of disruption/pain/impairment seems minimal, or if the client is seeking improvement in only one or two areas of life, then ADHD is not the likely diagnosis (Murphy & Gordon, 2006).

You should also pay attention to the way that the person answers questions. Does he interrupt you and himself; wander off topic; or need to have the question repeated after talking for a while? Is he physically restless or distracted by items in the office or by extraneous noises? People with ADHD often must be interrupted or redirected as they go on and on when describing their symptoms and associated impairment. This could be indicative of their ADHD symptoms, as well as their psychological need to tell their story to a responsive audience. In addition, those with ADHD will have no shortage of examples to illustrate where their ADHD symptoms caused them difficulty. For example, when asked about losing things, the expected answer is more along the lines of "All the time! I'm always losing things" with the corresponding affect, than "Yeah, I sometimes lose things." Anybody, myself included, could answer in the latter manner. Those with ADHD will have suffered.

When inquiring about various symptoms, it's important to ask how long the person has been experiencing that symptom. Those with ADHD will give a clear answer that this has been going on for as long as they can remember; that this has always been true for them (Murphy & Gordon, 2006). When asked about certain symptoms, those with ADHD or their significant others will often give an extremely clear indication that that is a struggle for them, such as by laughing out loud (in an ironic way), shaking their head vigorously, rolling their eyes, or groaning. It's often helpful to watch for the significant others' reactions when you ask a question, since their body language can be equally informative.

The ADHD adult may have had childhood nicknames like "Calamity Jane," "space cadet," "the absentminded professor," "Dennis the Menace," or "dream girl"—nicknames they earned from their consistent and ongoing difficulties. There also may be stories that are legendary in the family that derived from ADHD symptoms (Murphy & Gordon, 2006).

For example, I had a client who routinely would have to ask the shop owner from down the street to call his mother to find out what he was supposed to pick up at the store because he so frequently forgot. Of course, this also made me wonder why his mother never wised up and gave him a list; perhaps she too had ADHD. Another client told me about how his mother was afraid of being reported to Child Protective Services because he so frequently earned himself a trip to the doctor's office because of his impulsive risk-taking behavior.

Even the initial phone call to set up the meeting can be informative. I once returned a call to a man who had asked for an ADHD evaluation. We arranged the time and set up an appointment to meet, but he was on his cell phone and couldn't write down the directions to my office. We agreed that I would call back immediately and leave the directions on his voice mail to be retrieved later. We spoke for an additional half minute and then hung up. I redialed him as agreed. However, rather than letting my message go to his voice mail, he picked up the phone! We both laughed at this as an example of his forgetfulness, joking that we had just done the evaluation. When we met, he did indeed meet criteria for ADHD.

When calling another prospective client, I was greeted with this outgoing message on her cell phone: "Hi, this is _____ . I'm either not available or I've lost my phone." As it turned out, this young woman very clearly had ADHD.

Perhaps the single best indicator of ADHD symptoms in childhood is unreliable and incomplete homework performance. It's therefore very useful to ask clients about their homework performance and to consider both the content and the affect of the answer. Doing homework consistently is the Achilles' heel of most ADHD students. Those with ADHD will often answer along the following lines (Murphy & Gordon, 2006, p. 445):

- ■ "I never did homework."

- ■ "I always copied someone else's."

- ■ "I did it five minutes before class."

- ■ "I could never sit still to do it."

- ■ "I could never keep track of all the books and papers."

- ■ "Even if I did it, I would lose it or forget to hand it in."

Of course, a simple failure to do homework consistently may be indicative of oppositional features or of a chaotic home life or caregivers who didn't value academics.

However, careful follow-up questioning will reveal that the choice to not do homework was not completely deliberate, at least initially. Rather, for an ADHD diagnosis, you're looking for comments: that despite their best efforts they couldn't focus, concentrate, or sustain their effort/motivation long enough to get it done consistently. Or they couldn't reliably track down what had been assigned and ensure that the necessary materials made it home and then back to school on time. Homework is very often a frustrating and emotionally charged issue for both parents and children, to the extent that a report of "no homework trouble" throws the diagnosis into serious doubt (Murphy & Gordon, 2006). Of course, after some years of struggle and defeat with homework, many ADHD students will simply stop trying and then it does become intentional, but a careful interview may be able to tease out that it did not start that way.

Collateral Information Sources

As with any diagnostic assessment, it can be helpful to include information from additional sources, if that is possible. This can include information from the past, as well as from contemporary sources. This information can be collected in person or over the phone through an interview, or it can be collected by mail through rating scales or questionnaires of current and past functioning, depending on the logistical considerations. Given that there will always be discrepancies, it's up to you to decide the relative weight to assign to various contrary pieces of information.

Because a diagnosis of ADHD requires the presence of symptoms since childhood, you have to find a way to assess those symptoms. Obviously, the client can answer questions retrospectively and be asked to provide specific examples, but some clinicians may worry about the influence of bias—minimizing or overreporting—be it intentional or not. Therefore, if possible, and note that often it isn't, it can be helpful to look at old report cards.

Alternatively, you can ask the client to provide a subjective memory of the report card comments he received. However, it should be noted that report cards tend to be more sensitive to hyperactive and impulsive symptoms than to inattentive ones, particularly if the student is a nice kid who seems to be trying. In the absence of report cards, it can also be helpful to have the client ask her parents what they remember her teachers' comments to have been. You're looking for comments like these (Weiss et al., 1999):

- Doesn't apply herself.

- Could do better or doesn't live up to potential.

- Needs to pay attention better.

- Needs to put in more effort.

- Doesn't hand in assignments.

- Disruptive in class.

- Organization needs improvement.

- Neatness needs improvement.

- Talks too much.

- Doesn't follow directions.

Another option would be to include parents of ADHD adults in the interview process if the client's report is contradictory or unclear. This is often geographically difficult, so it may need to be done by phone instead. Of course, given the high heritability of ADHD, it may very well be that one or both parents have ADHD. If so, they may not see their grown child's symptoms as abnormal. Alternatively, they may defensively protect their own self-esteem by denying or minimizing problems or by steadfastly holding onto the notion that this is not a disability, merely a different way of being.

As for assessing current or recent past functioning, it can be helpful to include a romantic partner or significant other who can provide a second perspective on the client's functioning. People with ADHD do not always monitor their own behavior well, so you may get a different story from significant others, especially about the frequency of difficulties. This can increase the number of clients who provide sufficient information to meet criteria (Weiss et al., 1999). In addition, the partner may have different expectations about how the world works and thereby find more elements of the client's functioning to be notable.

By contrast, someone with ADHD, especially if he also has an ADHD parent, may feel that a scattered lifestyle is normal. For example, I had a client who didn't think that his running out of gas on a semiregular basis was noteworthy—but his wife sure did! The other side of the coin is that sometimes the person with ADHD will rate her symptoms as more severe than others would, perhaps because many of the *DSM-IV-TR* symptoms are quite subjective, such as feelings of restlessness, and therefore may not be as obvious to others (Murphy & Schachar, 2000). Additionally, adolescents and young adults tend to minimize their difficulties, whether intentionally or not is unclear, so collateral information sources in these cases should probably be given more weight if there is a discrepancy (Murphy & Gordon, 2006).

It should also be noted that the significant other or romantic partner may have an agenda to either inflate or minimize the client's ADHD symptoms. Some partners may want to see the client as the troubled one in the relationship in order to take the spotlight off of her own difficulties, or even to play the role of the long-suffering martyr. Other partners may minimize the ADHD symptoms, attributing them to a lack of effort or other shortcomings that the client simply needs to overcome by trying harder.

Assessment Instruments

Assessment instruments can be efficient ways to gather a standardized and presumably accurate sampling of a person's functioning, potentially yielding a great deal of information for the savvy clinician. That said, there has been little success in creating a single instrument or battery of instruments that will accurately diagnose ADHD in individuals. Although researchers find significant group differences, there are still problems with the predictive power of these instruments—that is, the ability to correctly identify which group a specific individual belongs in (Goldstein, 2002). This is one of those areas where the needs of researchers differ from those of clinicians.

Researchers are interested in differences between group means (for example, people with ADHD tend to score lower on tests of executive functioning), whereas clinicians are more interested in individuals (for example, "How does this one client's scores on a test of executive functioning inform my decision about his diagnosis?"). Thus, studies that reliably find group differences do not necessarily lend themselves to clinical work.

For example, men tend to be taller than women, so if you compare the average height of a group of men to that of a group of women, you would indeed find a robust statistical difference between the two. However, there will be some men who are shorter than some women, so you cannot predict gender with 100 percent accuracy simply by measuring height—and those who are mislabeled may be quite offended. This is where the issues of predictive power and classification accuracy come in.

The trouble with using standard assessment instruments to assess for ADHD is that they were not designed for this purpose. However, since there are no tests that were, apart from the rating scales and the continuous performance tests which will be discussed later, we have to use what's available. In spite of the fact that this is done with good intentions and the desire to be helpful to our clients, it has led to practices that are not supported by the research. Of course, clinicians cannot always wait for the researchers when they have suffering clients clamoring for help, but perhaps there is a balance to strike here, since well-intentioned but inaccurate diagnoses are not all that helpful.

Some have theorized that standard psychological and neuropsychological instruments are poor measures of ADHD symptoms because of the instruments' highly limited sampling of behavior (typically twenty minutes or less per task) and their sampling of limited aspects of attention, impulsivity, or activity (Barkley, 2006b). ADHD is so multifaceted and different people have such broad arrays of strengths and weaknesses that it's easy to miss a diagnosis with an overly rigid interpretation of the results of an overly narrow instrument.

Related to this, another problem with the results of assessment instruments is less related to the instruments than to the interpretations that people make of them, which are the perceived benefits of objective measures. That is, because the instrument generates scores, percentiles, and/or graphs, these results must therefore be more accurate than the fuzzy impressions of a clinician. Although this is sometimes true, it's not always true. A knowledgeable and cautious tester will weigh the results of all of the instruments and incorporate them with the client's history, current functioning, and test-taking observations, and then make a decision based on the totality of the information. This will factor in the perceived reliability of the sources of information, as well as the extent to which the client's testing performance is representative of her true abilities.

Because of their lack of specificity with this diagnosis, traditional psychological and neuropsychological testing instruments should not be considered *de facto* parts of an ADHD assessment (Gordon, Barkley, & Lovett, 2006). They're good tools, but not for this job, so they should not be used beyond their capabilities—for example, a hammer will indeed get the cap off a beer bottle but it is not the best way to accomplish that goal. Rather, these instruments are most helpful when there is a credible suspicion that there is a comorbid condition, such as another neurological disorder, a learning disability, or a cognitive or emotional factor, that is either confounding the diagnostic picture or better explains the symptoms; or if there is too much inconsistency across the other data to make a diagnosis confidently.

Having said all of this, there will be times when assessment instruments must be used, but more for legal or policy reasons than clinical ones. Those seeking college accommodations, for example, may be required to provide a recent testing report, perhaps because it's assumed that it will be more objective and thereby more fair than a report from a diagnostic interview. As much as these policies ideally should be based in solid clinical reasons, this is not always the case, but we are required to comply with them nonetheless. However, the goal of these evaluations is different—rather than being done to guide therapeutic efforts, it's being done to justify the need for accommodations. So, clearly, different goals require different methods. The fact that objective testing is required for legal or policy reasons should not be construed to be an endorsement of these techniques in purely clinical settings. After all, do we really want politicians and administrators making decisions about our discipline's best clinical practices?

Neuropsychological Instruments

There is strong face validity to using neuropsychological instruments for the assessment of ADHD—given that it is a neurologically based disorder, it should be measurable by neuropsychological testing (Gordon et al., 2006). Unfortunately, neuropsychological tests can be problematic with this population because they are structured and novel, two characteristics that make it easier for those with ADHD to perform up to their potential. As a result, their performance is not indicative of their general level of functioning when familiarity and boredom are the real challenge.

In addition, the majority of adults with ADHD who would get tested for ADHD tend to show deficits that are relatively mild compared to the disorders that are traditionally assessed neuropsychologically, so the tests may lack sufficient sensitivity to pick up those deficits. Related to this, ADHD adults' executive functioning deficits may be more visible in the more complex environment of real life than in a controlled and distraction-free testing situation (Rapport, VanVoorhis, Tzelepis, & Friedman, 2001). Because of all these caveats, the wholesale administration of a full battery of neuropsychological tests as a routine element of an ADHD evaluation cannot be justified based on the research, especially in terms of diagnostic utility or utilization of health care dollars (Gordon et al., 2006). This is not to say that a good neuropsychological work up cannot be useful in detecting other types of difficulties, but it should not be the first choice if only ADHD is suspected.

Several tests are used to assess attention, among other things, and therefore may be used as part of an ADHD evaluation. However, you need to be very careful to not read too much into the results, based on what the research tells us. The Wisconsin Card Sorting Test, the Stroop Word Color Test, the Kaufman Hand Movements Test, the Rey-Osterrieth Complex Figure Drawing Test, and the Trail Making Test (Parts A and B) all display overall classification accuracies of only 50 to 70 percent (Gordon et al., 2006).

Two things should be pointed out here. First, flipping a coin has a 50 percent classification accuracy—that is, the rate at which it correctly identifies people with ADHD as having ADHD and those without ADHD as not having it. Second, if you do use these instruments, keep in mind that they tend to have more false negatives than false positives when it comes to ADHD.

Intelligence and Achievement Tests

Intelligence and achievement tests have not been found to be sensitive enough to use to diagnose ADHD. Despite being "common knowledge," there is no evidence that verbal/performance IQ discrepancies or IQ/achievement discrepancies have any bearing on a diagnosis of ADHD. IQ and achievement tests can, however, be helpful in determining if there are other cognitive factors that are contributing to inattention difficulties, such as demands exceeding abilities or the presence of learning disabilities. It also can be unofficially informative to watch the client's test-taking behavior, provided that you don't make too much of that data (Gordon et al., 2006).

Tests of Memory

Although many ADHD people exhibit memory difficulties, they are not deficits in long-term memory *per se* as much as they are the result of attention deficits that influence working memory. For example, the information is dropped out of working memory because something else grabs the person's attention. As a result, information is never actually encoded into long-term memory so there is nothing there to remember. In addition, some ADHD people have difficulties with recall whereby they become distracted at the very moment they are trying to pull information out of memory, such as items to buy at the supermarket. Once again, this is more of an attention issue than a true memory issue.

The existing tests of memory, such as the Wechsler Memory Scales-III (WMS-III), may not be sensitive enough to reliably pick up these kinds of memory difficulties under controlled testing conditions where there are few external distractions. Incidentally, internal distractions will remain but they may not be powerful enough to significantly influence the results. Studies have found that ADHD children do not have deficits in recall, long-term storage, and long-term retrieval, but they do have deficits in working memory (Barkley, 2006c). One final weakness of the WMS-III for diagnosing ADHD concerns the fact that it does not test prospective memory, a key deficit for those with ADHD (Nadeau, 1995a).

Rating Scales

The various rating scales on the market can be helpful in gathering information, but they are not a replacement for a good clinical interview nor a shortcut to a thorough understanding of ADHD and related disorders. Similarly, the Beck Depression Inventory-II hopefully would not be used in isolation to assess depression. As long as the rating scales are used judiciously, they can add something to the diagnostic process. They can help by asking about areas that may be forgotten in an interview or for highlighting things that the client may take as normal and therefore not worth mentioning, such as my client mentioned above who did not think that frequently running out of gas was notable.

Another benefit is that rating scales can be a way to get information from people who may not be able to make it into your office, such as a romantic partner or significant other, family members, friends, and coworkers. Finally, a rating scale filled out by the client before the session can save some time in session by allowing a more efficient use of the face-to-face time. However, it should also be kept in mind that what rating scales do best is "provide an organized report of behavior. They describe what the observer sees but not why it is being seen" (Goldstein & Kennemer, in press).

Of course, this doesn't mean that any information on the rating scales should be taken as definitive since different people have different sensitivities for what they will report, as well as different agendas and levels of defensiveness. For example, a parent who has undiagnosed ADHD may see the client's ADHD-related behaviors as normal and therefore minimize their severity on the rating scale. All in all, rating scales can be of some benefit if they serve to raise some flags that you can pursue in greater detail during the interview.

Five of the most commonly used rating scales for the evaluation of ADHD include:

1. Barkley's ADHD Rating Scale (Observer forms also available.)

2. Brown Attention-Deficit Disorder Scales

3. Conners' Adult ADHD Rating Scales (Observer forms also available. Long, short, and screener versions available.)

4. Adult ADHD Self-Report Scale-version 1.1 (Screener version also available.)

5. Clinical Assessment of Attention Deficit-Adult

Rating scales can be helpful in cases where the results of the interview and other corroborative sources paint an unclear diagnostic picture or if the client seems to have a borderline level of impairment. Having some objective data, imperfect as it may be, may add some diagnostic clarity.

Continuous Performance Tests

Continuous performance tests (CPTs) have been around since the 1950s in one form or another. They are specifically designed to assess attention. However, this should not be construed to mean that they are designed to assess ADHD specifically, since ADHD involves more than the types of attention required on these tests. The basic idea of these tests is to give subjects a boring, repetitive task that requires sustained attention and response accuracy. It usually involves responding to some stimuli, either visual or auditory, but not to others—that is, inhibiting impulsive responses. They test performance over time and compare the results to the pattern of results from various groups—ADHD versus non-ADHD/psychiatric versus nonpsychiatric. Currently, the available versions include the following:

- Conners CPT and Conners CPT II

- Intermediate Visual and Auditory (IVA) CPT

- Gordon Diagnostic System (GDS)

- Test of Variables of Attention (TOVA)

The theory behind CPTs is that errors of commission (responding when one should not) are indicative of impulsivity, and errors of omission (not responding when one should) are indicative of inattention. Unfortunately, for all their face validity, there isn't a sufficient correlation between the types of errors that someone makes and the ADHD symptoms that he displays. However, there is a slightly significant finding that ADHD adults tend to respond more quickly, suggesting impulsivity (Epstein, Conners, Sitarenios, & Erhardt, 1998).

The good news about CPTs is that they are the most reliable psychological test for distinguishing groups of ADHD children from groups of non-ADHD children. That is, there are significant differences to be found when comparing groups of ADHD people to groups of non-ADHD people, but this does not mean that it will be equally beneficial when trying to figure out which group a specific individual fits into. This is the classification accuracy problem discussed above.

CPTs are also sensitive to medication effects, so there is some utility in using a CPT to aid in finding the correct dose of medication. This is done by using improvements in CPT scores as an indicator of different doses' relative benefit (Gordon et al., 2006).

There is also one area where the CPTs are unmatched—that is, in detecting malingering. Perhaps more than most diagnoses, some people have an incentive to be falsely diagnosed with ADHD in order to gain special school or work accommodations, access to medications, or a diagnosis seen as less pejorative than their real disorder. Unlike clinical interviews or rating scales that are easier to fake bad, CPTs are too hard to fake, making them useful when malingering is suspected. Between-item variance and reaction-time variance are impossible for subjects to know or manipulate given that they occur in milliseconds. A lack of internal consistency in CPT scores, as well as extremely low scores, such as three standard deviations below the mean, suggests malingering (Quinn, 2002). Put simply, someone attempting to malinger on a CPT is likely to produce results so impaired that ADHD would be the least of their problems.

Unfortunately, apart from the detection of malingering, significant care should be taken when interpreting the results of CPTs in an ADHD evaluation, for multiple reasons. First, there are concerns about their ecological validity in that computer tests do not necessarily reflect the broad spectrum of attention skills used in real life (Weiss et al., 1999), particularly by an adult living a normal, multifaceted, interruption-prone life. Given this limited range of skills that is assessed by the CPTs, it should therefore not be surprising that one study found that one CPT correctly identified only 55 percent of ADHD subjects and 76.4 percent of non-ADHD subjects, which should give clinicians pause when interpreting the results for individual clients (Epstein et al., 1998). Once again, remember that flipping a coin will correctly identify 50 percent of ADHD individuals in a group comparison study. Overall, though, it appears that CPTs tend to have more false negatives than false positives, so you will be on somewhat more solid ground when discounting the negative results of a CPT than the positive, if the bulk of the other data says otherwise.

Projective Tests

There have been no studies that demonstrated any predictive validity of drawing, ink blots, or storytelling projective techniques in diagnosing ADHD (Gordon et al., 2006). However, such techniques can offer a great amount of other useful clinical information, particularly regarding the secondary psychological effects of a lifetime of undiagnosed and untreated ADHD. This information regarding the capacity for insight and openness, defense mechanisms, relatedness, affect modulation, and strengths will certainly be helpful in the psychotherapeutic process.

Structured Clinical Interview for DSM-IV-TR

The Structured Clinical Interview for *DSM-IV-TR* (SCID) surveys all major axis I diagnoses that can be helpful in ruling out other reasons for ADHD-like symptoms and for establishing the presence of comorbid conditions (Murphy & Gordon, 2006). The advantage of using a scripted interview is that it ensures that all relevant areas are covered. The disadvantage is that it can make the interview feel too rigid and not allow sufficient exploration of interesting items that may come up—and if the client does indeed have ADHD, many interesting things will come up, regardless of their relevance to the specific topic at hand. Whether you use the SCID or not, you should always screen for comorbid conditions, given the high prevalence in this population. More information on comorbid conditions, and their differential diagnosis, is provided below.

Assessment Instruments Conclusion

As with any diagnosis, clinical judgment factors in heavily when considering the accuracy and utility of various sources of information. Generally speaking, assuming that the additional data sources are reasonably reliable, more tends to be better. Testing data, although imperfect as noted above, can be of the greatest value when other sources are unavailable or of questionable credibility (Gordon et al., 2006). Certainly, there will be contradictions among and within the various sources, so it helps to have a larger sample size when seeking out trends in the data. This is the art that complements the science of assessment—interpreting a large collection of data points in a way that most accurately and helpfully captures what is going on with the individual client.

Brain Scans

There has been some interesting work done relatively recently on the use of brain scans to better understand the role of various brain areas in different conditions, including ADHD. Perhaps the best known currently, at least among the general public, is the work of Daniel Amen, MD, and his colleagues. Given Dr. Amen's success in promoting his ideas, it bears mentioning his work here because some clients may bring it up. Amen has written a number of books on ADHD for lay audiences, although he is best known for his work in the use of SPECT scans of the brain as a diagnostic instrument. SPECT, which stands for Single Photon Emission Computerized Tomography, works by sensing where injected radioactive glucose is metabolized in the brain. Areas of the brain that are more active metabolize more glucose, and thereby show up brighter on the SPECT scan. Based on this information, the clinician can match the subject's profile to those of groups of people who have been diagnosed with various psychiatric conditions.

There have been studies performed by others in the field that show there are indeed differences in the group means based on the psychiatric diagnosis. However, the fact that researchers can find differences between group means does not guarantee that clinicians can accurately diagnose individuals within those groups, a point that has been repeated several times in this chapter.

This confusion of group means versus individual results is the fatal flaw in the reasoning that clinicians can use SPECT scan results to make diagnoses at the individual level—there are simply too many errors, where a subject's brain scan says one thing but her behavior and symptoms say another. Given the significant cost of the scans, they simply don't add enough value to justify their use. Perhaps further refinements will change that but, at this time, low-tech procedures are still the best way to go.

Comorbid Conditions

Given the high probability, it's best to assume that an adult with ADHD will have a comorbid disorder and to plan diagnosis and treatment accordingly (Barkley & Gordon, 2002). The comorbidity of ADHD with other diagnoses is as high as 77 percent and many of these disorders also affect attention, so it's important to determine the contribution of each condition (Weiss et al., 1999). The three most important differentiators between ADHD and every other psychiatric disorder are as follows:

1.   The symptoms of ADHD have been present from childhood, in one form or another.

2.   The symptoms do not show significant fluctuations over short or long time intervals.

3.   The symptoms are present in most settings.

This will distinguish ADHD most clearly from the various comorbid conditions that often tag along or are mistakenly diagnosed in its stead. Once the presence of ADHD symptoms has been determined, you need to at least screen for possible conditions that are causing, contributing to, or comorbid to them (Brown, 1995). This has important implications for treatment in terms of the types of interventions likely to be successful and how you need to approach clients with these interventions.

Depression

Between 16 to 31 percent of adults with ADHD experience major depression; dysthymia occurs in 19 to 37 percent of clinic-referred ADHD adults (Barkley & Gordon, 2002). This is a sizeable minority and not surprising given the additional struggles that people with ADHD experience. Complicating matters, there is significant overlap between *DSM-IV-TR* criteria for depression and ADHD. Of the nine criteria for depression, seven are also somewhat associated with ADHD—diminished interest, decreased appetite, insomnia, psychomotor agitation or retardation, fatigue, feelings of worthlessness, and poor concentration (Weiss et al., 1999). Therefore, a cursory examination may misattribute which symptoms are caused by which disorder. This may also explain why women and girls are more likely to be diagnosed with depression than ADHD—if that is the clinician's bias, there's enough overlap to at least somewhat justify the misdiagnosis.

Sleep Difficulties

As for the sleep difficulties that are common to both disorders, people with ADHD often have difficulty falling asleep and usually attribute it to an overactive mind; that is, to a feeling that they can't turn off their brain. Depressed people's sleep disturbances are more likely to take the form of early morning awakening or excessive sleeping (Tzelepis, Schubiner, & Warbasse, 1995). People with ADHD may also be hard to wake up and are slow to get up to full speed in the morning, although this may be an artifact of not getting enough sleep the night before. See the section below on sleep deprivation.

Whereas depressed people tend to exaggerate their perceived shortcomings, ADHD adults will often have a larger kernel of truth in their feelings of worthlessness following years of underachievement (Tzelepis et al., 1995). Unfortunately, their pessimism may be based on a realistic assessment of their abilities, derived from an accurate evaluation of their past performance. Of course, they know they have the potential to do better, but they have never been able to harness that potential, so their pessimism is not based solely in a low mood.

Bipolar Disorder

The symptoms of bipolar disorder can mimic those of ADHD. All seven criteria for mania may be found to varying degrees in adults with ADHD: grandiosity, decreased need for sleep, overtalkativeness, racing thoughts, distractibility, psychomotor agitation, and excessive involvement in pleasurable activities that have a high potential for painful consequences (Weiss et al., 1999). The differential diagnosis is based on the degree to which these symptoms are displayed and their frequency—in ADHD they will be less extreme but will be more common; in bipolar disorder they will be more pronounced when they occur but will also wax and wane more significantly. Those with true bipolar I are easy to separate out because of the extent of emotional lability, the perception of possessing special abilities, a severely reduced need for sleep, and potentially psychotic symptoms. It can be more difficult with those with bipolar II where the hypomanic symptoms are not as pronounced (Murphy & Gordon, 2006).

In this case, we use other markers. One marker is the age of onset—often in childhood with ADHD, later for bipolar, at least for the most obvious symptoms. Duration of symptoms and deviation from baseline is also relevant here—mood lability is common among some people with ADHD in that they can display quick and sometimes intense changes in mood, but these mood shifts may last moments or hours, not days or weeks as they do in bipolar disorder. In addition, ADHD adults do not generally feel euphoric in the way that those with bipolar do and they are also less irritable (Weiss et al., 1999). As one would expect, there is no cyclical pattern to the moodiness of an ADHD adult, so a client's emotional lability and irritability are instead the result of impulsivity and low frustration tolerance (Tzelepis et al., 1995), not the brain rhythms of bipolar disorder. ADHD folks have a chronic and pervasive pattern of impairment over time and across situations, whereas the patterns of those with bipolar disorder tend to be more episodic and are seen as uncharacteristic of the person, especially behaviors such as reckless spending sprees and a significantly stronger libido. Although it can be difficult to be certain of the precise family history if the relative did not receive professional treatment, a family history of bipolar disorder is more suggestive of bipolar disorder in the individual than it is of ADHD. Finally, past response to medications can be suggestive (Murphy & Gordon, 2006), but medications should not be prescribed to help clarify the diagnosis, especially because ADHD medications can spark a manic episode in those with that tendency.

Anxiety

The inattentiveness and forgetfulness of ADHD make for many unpleasant surprises. ADHD adults have learned over the years that they are not good predictors of what will happen next. Also, they are often caught unprepared for events they may remember only when prompted (at which point it may be too late), as well as events they may have missed completely when they were supposed to have been informed about them. Therefore, it makes sense that one study found that half of the adults referred for an evaluation of ADHD met criteria for at least two major anxiety disorders. Other adults may not reach the full criteria for the diagnosis, but that doesn't mean it is not present, and disabling to some degree. When anxiety is comorbid with ADHD, it will exacerbate problems with self-esteem, adaptive functioning, and stress tolerance, as well as some cognitive areas like working memory (Weiss et al., 1999), not to mention a client's willingness to take a chance on new strategies.

Many ADHD adults describe chronic tension and anxiety resulting from frequent procrastination and the anticipation of disappointment and failure. It's expected that adults will be able to complete most tasks of daily life relatively easily, so when the ADHD adult struggles so much with such tasks, they can become a source of worry. Additionally, ADHD adults are at greater risk for developing social phobia due to a lifetime of embarrassment, humiliation, and rejection by peers and adults in response to their ADHD behaviors, such as not waiting their turn, saying inappropriate things, forgetting, and interrupting/intruding. They come to learn that they do inappropriate things but do not know how to stop it, so they may simply avoid some social situations (Tzelepis et al., 1995).

In the diagnostic process, it's important to keep in mind that inattention can be caused by both anxiety and ADHD, so it's important to figure out if the inattentiveness is coming from two separate entities or one. This can be accomplished by exploring when and why the person gets anxious and seeing how that correlates with her inattentiveness. Someone with anxiety will not be uniformly anxious across all settings and situations, so there will be more variability in her level of anxiety-based inattentiveness. Interestingly, some ADHD adults compensate for disorganization by becoming obsessively rigid and controlling, even beyond the point of benefit (Weiss et al., 1999).

There was one member of my adult ADHD support group who kept everything in plastic organizing containers with labels because it was the only way to prevent total chaos. Ironically, his non-ADHD wife was the messy one in comparison. The presence of anxiety is important to assess because it can complicate treatment with stimulants, which is discussed further in chapter 5.

It's possible that some people will seek an ADHD evaluation based on a decline in their performance that is due more to stress than to anything inherently neurological. In fact, ADHD guru Ned Hallowell wrote a book called *CrazyBusy: Overstretched, Overbooked, and About to Snap! Strategies for Coping in a World Gone ADD* (2006). Obviously, a fast-paced lifestyle will not give someone ADHD, but the resulting overload can appear similar to ADHD in superficial ways. However, this is nothing that dropping some obligations can't cure. You can differentiate what is stress-based by assessing to what extent the deficits are correlated with higher stress levels. However, those with ADHD tend to lead more stressful lives because of their inefficiencies in managing everyday demands. Therefore, the best distinction will be that those with stress-based ADHD-like symptoms will not have the lifelong history of difficulties. In addition, they will not display the full range of primary and secondary ADHD symptoms.

Post-Traumatic Stress Disorder

The presence of post-traumatic stress disorder (PTSD) can have such a severe impact on an individual's functioning that it will have to be addressed first before you can even assess for the presence of ADHD, much less treat it. Unfortunately, hyperactive and/or impulsive adults with ADHD who tend to be stimulus-seeking or thrill-seeking are more likely to encounter traumatic events and are potentially more reactive to the events they do encounter (Weiss et al., 1999). Those with predominantly inattentive symptoms are more likely to miss the warning signs that could have predicted or prevented problems and thereby find themselves in difficult situations. The disturbing literature on ADHD and driving is illustrative of ADHD people's elevated risk for traumatic situations. Diagnostically, there should be little confusion between PTSD and ADHD, except in the most cursory of evaluations.

Learning Disabilities

People with ADHD may be more likely to have learning disabilities. This added wrinkle can have a significant impact on their functioning and ability to be successful. The degree of the impact depends on the nature and severity of the learning disability, how it interacts with the ADHD symptoms, and what skills the environment demands from the individual. A psychoeducational evaluation may be necessary to better understand the precise learning disability that is present. Although it's overkill to put every adult through a full battery of tests, it may be warranted for those whose difficulties seem to go beyond the norm of ADHD or those who do not make good progress in treatment.

Antisocial Personality Disorder

Children with ADHD are more likely to evoke negative and/or unsupportive reactions from their caregivers, especially if they are undiagnosed and untreated. This leads to predictable increases in defiant behavior which can evolve into oppositional defiant disorder (ODD) and conduct disorder (CD), the precursors to antisocial personality disorder in adulthood. This negative outcome is generally more true of those with hyperactive and impulsive symptoms than it is of those with predominantly inattentive symptoms (Barkley & Gordon, 2002). A self-reinforcing process can be set up wherein the child is seen as a bad kid because of his ADHD-based unruly behavior, he evokes negative reactions from adults, and then fails to improve his self-regulation skills, which only exacerbates the situation. This is especially true if the child has an impatient and reactive (untreated) ADHD parent.

There's often a question raised as to the intentionality of the person's ADHD-based behavior. Whereas ADHD people can make some of the same social transgressions as those with ODD/CD/antisocial personality disorder, it's less intentional with ADHD—they may be just as surprised and disappointed as everyone else about their mistake. With a defiant person, there is what I call "the screw you factor"—she knows she did it but either doesn't care about the consequences or is purposely aggravating people. The ADHD adult's mistakes come more from a neurologically based lack of awareness or the secondary effects of poor planning that make negative outcomes more likely. If someone has progressed to the point of meriting the diagnosis of antisocial personality disorder, then the ADHD is merely the tip of the iceberg, and there are severe limits as to how much progress that person can make in treatment—or even will want to make.

Substance Abuse and Other Addictions

Active substance abuse can mimic ADHD symptoms in terms of disinhibition, poor attention, poor short-term memory, and restlessness. More so than with the general population, there is a significant overlap between ADHD and substance abuse. One study found that half of the adults with ADHD had a lifetime history of substance abuse versus one quarter of the control group. Looking at it from the other direction, it has been estimated that 15 to 25 percent of adult addicts and alcoholics have ADHD (Wilens, 2004). ADHD could predispose someone to substance abuse or other self-medicating behaviors in two ways: first by making poor choices about when and how much to abuse which is caused by acting impulsively and not thinking about the consequences, and second by self-medicating the painful feelings and low self-esteem that result from a lifetime of undiagnosed and untreated ADHD. However, it also should be noted that, contrary to what we might expect, those with ADHD are not more likely to abuse cocaine or stimulants. Rather, as with the general drug-abusing population, marijuana is the most popular (Spencer, 2006a).

If someone has a strong history of substance abuse, it can be difficult to know which symptoms come from what. In these cases, it may be best to initiate treatment for the substance abuse and then reevaluate for ADHD after three to six months of abstinence (Tzelepis et al., 1995) to eliminate the confounding variable of substance-induced effects. This may be easier said than done, though, in that it may be necessary to address the ADHD in order to improve the likelihood of the person staying clean. This is the unfortunate irony of those with the double whammy of ADHD and substance abuse—it can become a real dilemma as to which to address first. This issue is addressed further in chapter 5 on medications. The irony is that the stimulants, which are the most commonly prescribed medication class for treating ADHD, also have a potential for abuse, making most clinicians leery of giving them to those with a history of substance abuse.

Of course, even if you're able to get an accurate picture of the person's current functioning after some period of sobriety, someone with a strong history of substance abuse is not likely to give a reliable report about her history and may lack good insight into her behavior, making the results of the interview flawed. In these cases, additional weight may be given to collateral sources, if they are available (Tzelepis et al., 1995). This is when clinical judgment and a small dose of luck become more important.

Borderline Personality Disorder

People with borderline personality disorder (BPD) can appear to have ADHD due to the chaos in their lives, inconsistent performance, and mood lability. However, people with BPD feel much more rage and emptiness, have a stronger fear of abandonment, suffer from more identity issues, and exhibit more manipulative behavior (Weiss et al., 1999). For those with BPD, their difficulties are more mood-based and therefore are more correlated with what is happening in their daily life. They will be more dysfunctional during times of greater emotional distress. In addition, the persistent self-defeating patterns of those with BPD are qualitatively different from the inattention-based difficulties of those with ADHD.

Sleep Deprivation

There has been some talk (mostly superficial reports in the popular media) that ADHD is caused by sleep deprivation and thereby can be "miraculously" cured when the person is taught better sleep habits or some other similar intervention is made. Although poor sleep can indeed cause cognitive deficits that may appear somewhat similar to some ADHD symptoms, this certainly doesn't mean there is a causal link. Diagnostically, we would expect sleep-based deficits to remediate as soon as a normal sleep pattern is restored. However, many ADHD people do indeed have sleep difficulties, for multiple reasons.

The first reason is more of a time-management issue, in that procrastination may force those with ADHD to stay up later to finish the night's activities. Alternatively, they may hyperfocus on an enjoyable activity and not notice that it is long past the time to get into bed. Finally, they may knowingly stay up too late doing an enjoyable activity, despite full knowledge of the price to be paid the next day.

Beyond these lifestyle matters, it does seem that people with ADHD have some true difficulties with sleep. For some, it can be that it is difficult to quiet their mind when they lie in bed, making it difficult to drift off to sleep. In fact, I've had more than one client who, counterintuitively, would take a small dose of stimulant if she could not slow her thoughts enough to fall asleep. We can only assume that less than a full night's sleep, regardless of the cause, just exacerbates ADHD folks' functional difficulties. If significant sleep difficulties remain after the lifestyle contributors are successfully addressed, often not an easy matter, a sleep study may be warranted to rule out sleep apnea and other sleep disorders separate from the ADHD that may be contributing to the person's difficulties (Lavenstein, 1995).

Head Injury and Medical Conditions

Injury to the brain in the frontal lobes can cause acquired executive dysfunction, marked by deficiencies in planning, organization, motivation, initiation, mental flexibility, attention, and impulse inhibition. This can look like ADHD, which is not surprising given that ADHD is thought to result from a dysfunction in the frontal lobes. As with many of the differential diagnoses, the most distinguishing feature will be the lack of a lifelong history of difficulties. Rather, there will be a specific onset following the brain injury (Lavenstein, 1995).

It's generally not necessary to refer for further medical evaluation, such as a physical or neurological work up, as a routine part of the diagnostic process. However, if the client has a medical condition that seems complicated, or he is experiencing many other symptoms unrelated to ADHD that are not being medically monitored or treated, then a referral may be in order simply to rule out other potential etiologies. However, there is currently no medical test for ADHD.

Conclusion

It will be interesting to see what the *DSM-V* will hold for this diagnosis, especially in relation to adults. There is talk of further refining the three subtypes and perhaps splitting them apart, making the inattentive subtype a different diagnosis altogether, or adding more subtypes, such as the proposed Slow Cognitive Tempo to describe those who tend to be more passive, low energy, and given to daydreaming. The predominantly hyperactive-impulsive subtype may be eliminated because it is mostly diagnosed in young children at an age when attention is not really relevant or measurable. Over time, the vast majority of these children tend to grow into the combined subtype when their inattention becomes more apparent; thus the hyperactive-impulsive subtype may not really be all that clinically useful (Barkley, 2006b). It's also possible that the combination of ADHD and conduct disorder represents a distinct disorder rather than a common comorbidity (Barkley, 2006, October). It will also be interesting to see if separate criteria are given for adults, since the current criteria tend to be more descriptive of children, resulting in potential underdiagnosis. It would also be good if they included more information about how ADHD presents in girls and women, rather than just in boys and men.

ADHD is somewhat of a paradox—in some cases it can be diagnosed quickly and easily, yet it can just as easily be misdiagnosed if you aren't careful. In some cases, the diagnosis is given when it shouldn't be, yet in others it isn't given when it really should be. The client pays a price for both of these types of errors. Therefore, as clinicians we owe it to our clients to get it right, even if our conclusions aren't what they want to hear. Fortunately, a careful assessment can be quite accurate and sets the stage for treatment that is targeted most effectively.

It's also worth keeping in mind that the mere act of making the diagnosis and reframing the reasons behind the client's lifelong struggles can be therapeutic all by itself. Finally your clients may have an explanation that is less pejorative, and perhaps unchangeable, than pinning their troubles on laziness or selfishness. This moment of revelation or confirmation is more likely to be beneficial if the client and whoever else is present are provided with information about the diagnosis and common treatments, to provide a sense of hope for the future. This is covered more fully in chapter 4, Education as a Therapeutic Technique, but ideally treatment begins with the moment of diagnosis.

CHAPTER 2

The Physiological Bases of ADHD

This chapter will be short and sweet—just long enough to provide you with some foundation of knowledge for clinical practice, without going into more detail than most clinicians require—or, frankly, are interested in.

Etiology

As with much of physical or mental illness, it's not completely clear what causes ADHD. Nevertheless, we can say with certainty that the expression of ADHD is a combination of both genetic and environmental factors, with genetic factors having the greater impact. Each subject is covered separately in this chapter, following a brief discussion of some of the less plausible theories of causation that have been proposed.

Doubtful Theories of Causation

I will begin with the theories that lack any real empirical support, before moving on to those that seem more plausible. Some of the more commonly cited of these unsupported theories propose that ADHD is caused by refined sugar, food and other allergies, food additives, folic acid deficiency, and even fluorescent lights (Weiss, Hechtman, & Weiss, 1999). Refined sugar and artificial food colorings in particular gained notoriety from supporters of the Feingold diet, which is covered in greater detail in chapter 5, Medications and Other Biological Treatments.

Parenting behavior is sometimes cited as a causative agent in the development of ADHD. Put simply, some people believe that bad parenting causes ADHD. There is a small amount of simple logic to this, in that parents of ADHD children do tend to use fewer positive parenting techniques. However, the proponents of these theories ignore the fact that children affect parenting behavior at least as much as parents affect children's behavior. That is, untreated ADHD children are better at pushing their parents past their limits, such that these parents employ fewer positive behavior management techniques and use more negative ones. Therefore, the studies that show some support for the poor parenting theory may be measuring the result rather than the cause. As further proof, studies have demonstrated that the introduction of medication that controls the disruptive ADHD behavior leads to improvements in the parents' behavior as well as the children's (Barkley, 2006d). Thus, the more accurate statement is that ADHD children cause bad parenting.

A third theory that has some simplistic face validity holds that current society has more hyperactivity as a result of the increased tempo of our lives. However, there is no evidence that supposedly "slower" societies have less hyperactivity (Barkley, 2006e). As discussed in chapter 1, the more likely scenario is that ADHD symptoms are simply more obvious and debilitating in our fast-paced world. This is similar to saying that a white shirt is more obvious against a black background than it is against a white one, but we would never say that the black background caused the white shirt.

Finally, some have proposed that ADHD is the natural, genetic outgrowth of those who, earlier in our evolutionary history, were society's hunters, in contrast to the majority, who were farmers. This theory holds that the quick reaction times and distractibility characteristic of ADHD actually were evolutionarily adaptive during our species' prehistory, but modern society does not value those traits any longer. Even if this unsophisticated understanding of evolution were true, it doesn't change the reality that people with ADHD need to function now in our current society, not in some vision of life many thousands of years ago. This theory is clearly an effort to make ADHD people feel better about their struggles—it's not that they are defective, they were simply born in the wrong era.

It's certainly worthwhile to help people with ADHD feel better about themselves, but this sort of "feel-good" relabeling carries some significant risks. First, its rosy homage to the skills of ADHD people runs the risk of minimizing the impact of the true suffering that those with ADHD experience on a daily basis. Second, if ADHD is seen as some sort of adaptive condition that no longer fits the needs of society, critics of the diagnosis may use that as justification to undermine or repeal the hard-won legal protections that people with ADHD now enjoy. This would be a real step backwards. I appreciate these authors' sentiments, but as will be discussed throughout the remainder of this book, true self-esteem comes from both the joy of success and the acceptance of our weaknesses.

Genetic Factors

In contrast to some of the dubious theories mentioned above, studies have found a strong genetic component to the expression of ADHD. Twin studies show that genetics play the major role in the expression of ADHD traits (Barkley, 2006e). For example, there is an 81 percent concordance rate in identical twins as opposed to 29 percent in fraternal twins. In addition, about one in four first-degree relatives (parents, siblings, and children) of someone with ADHD also have ADHD (Weiss et al., 1999). In practical terms, we can therefore assume that if someone has ADHD, there is a very good chance that at least one other person in the same family has it as well. Although these concordance figures suggest that there is still some room for environmental factors, they also show that ADHD is one of the most heritable of the mental health disorders. The precise genes involved are still being identified, but it's already clear that there are probably multiple genes involved, all contributing to some small and additive degree (Faraone & Khan, 2006).

Environmental Factors

The nongenetically based variation in the manifestation of ADHD seems to be limited to events that occur to the individual, such as prenatal exposure to nicotine or alcohol, early exposure to lead, stroke, brain trauma, and low birth weight, rather than to shared events, such as a parent's child management style or socioeconomic status. Maternal smoking has been found to have the strongest association with expression of ADHD symptoms (Barkley, 2006e). Given that it is a neurologically based disorder, obviously anything that affects brain development has the potential to influence the likelihood of developing ADHD symptoms. Therefore, prenatal, neonatal, perinatal, and early childhood events may play some role in determining who displays ADHD symptoms and with what severity.

Neurology of ADHD

ADHD is thought to involve structural and/or functional differences in the frontal lobes, basal ganglia, and cerebellum, and possibly the anterior cingulate gyrus (Barkley, 2006e). Additionally, differences in the volume of brain matter in the prefrontal cortex, cerebellum, and possibly striatum have been found (Arnstein, 2006), making for less neural machinery to do the work of these areas, potentially creating predictable functional differences. There are some who cite these studies and interpret them to mean that ADHD medications lead to a degeneration of brain matter, but the causality goes the other way—those with less brain matter probably tend to have more severe ADHD and, therefore, are more likely to be taking medication. The medications themselves do not affect brain volume (Biederman, 2006, October).

The neurochemical dysfunction appears to be mediated by dopaminergic and adrenergic systems, with little direct influence by the serotonergic systems. This conclusion is based on the fact that people with ADHD experience a temporary remission in symptoms when taking stimulants that are dopamine and norepinephrine reuptake inhibitors, but do not benefit from serotonergic antidepressants. There is also some indirect evidence from animal research and research on non-ADHD humans to support this idea (Barkley, 2006e).

As discussed in chapter 1, paying attention is a complex and multifaceted process. Like most cognitive functions, it involves an interplay between many brain areas. However, as with any complex process, good functioning requires that all of the components are working properly, whereas only a single flaw is required to limit functioning. In addition, given that someone can have relative strengths and weaknesses across these varying areas, it should not be surprising to see a diversity of presenting symptoms across clients.

Unifying Theories

The *DSM* tends to be atheoretical in its approach, favoring an objective description of symptoms. Yet why is it that we see the particular clustering of symptoms that we do? And why don't we see other symptoms as well or instead? Creating an explanatory model is obviously a more difficult undertaking than merely documenting co-occurring symptoms, yet such a model can provide a deeper understanding of the disorder to guide both research and intervention. I review two of the primary theories below.

Barkley's Response Inhibition Theory

Russell Barkley (1997) has developed an extremely detailed, well-reasoned, and empirically supported theory of why and how ADHD presents. This highly ambitious undertaking is only superficially elucidated here. Barkley sees the primary deficit in ADHD as that of behavioral inhibition. It is this most basic ability that allows us to ignore stimuli in the moment in order to employ our executive functions to achieve our goals more effectively. Behavioral inhibition refers to three interrelated processes (Barkley, 2006g):

1. Inhibiting the initial response to an event, thereby permitting a choice of whether or how to respond.

2. Stopping an ongoing response, thereby permitting a delay in the decision to respond or continue responding.

3. Protecting this period of delay and the self-directed responses that occur within it from disruption by competing events and responses. This is known as "interference control" or "freedom from distractibility."

There must be a delay in responding for the other executive functions to have time to act. Therefore, the other executive functions are dependent on this ability. It sets the stage for their performance and protects that performance from interference. Success as an adult requires the ability to delay gratification so that greater future goals can be achieved over smaller immediate goals. This is especially true for those situations where the pursuit of future goals involves sacrifice in the moment (Barkley, 2006g). For example, "I would like to lose weight but I want to eat one of those donuts." Unfortunately, many with ADHD exhibit what has been called *delay aversion* wherein they become impatient and go for the smaller immediate reward rather than holding out for the larger reward down the road.

Barkley specifies four executive functions that interact fluidly, as follows:

1. *Nonverbal working memory*, which allows someone to hold events in mind and mentally manipulate them. This leads to hindsight, forethought, a sense of time, time management, self-awareness, and nonverbal rule-governed behavior.

2. *Verbal working memory*, which allows self-reflection, problem-solving, rule-governed behavior, generation of rules and meta-rules, reading comprehension, and moral reasoning.

3. *Self-regulation of affect/motivation/arousal*, which allows self-regulation of affect, social perspective-taking, and self-regulation of motivation and arousal in the service of goal-directed action.

4. *Reconstitution (planning and generativity)*, which allows the analysis and creation of rules and goal-directed behavior.

The executive functions feed into *motor control/fluency/syntax*, which allows the inhibition of task-irrelevant responses, execution of goal-directed responses, execution of novel/complex motor sequences, persistence, sensitivity to response feedback, flexibility, task reengagement following disruption, and internal control of behavior.

Because of this complex interplay, ADHD is primarily a deficit in behavioral inhibition, but with secondary deficits in executive functioning and self-regulation. Those with ADHD do worst in the situations that require self-regulated persistence of effort, rather than persistence that is externally derived from a situation that is inherently rewarding, such as playing a video game. Although those with ADHD possess the ability to think through their actions before jumping into them, they too often don't do so because they tend to leap without looking. When a delay is forced or they are able to muster one, they are able to engage their executive functions and perform well.

This behavioral inhibition theory has several implications for clinical practice (Barkley, 2006g):

■ Because those with ADHD tend to lose sight of the future consequences of their actions, it's important to make those future consequences more salient in the moment that a decision is made. Also, natural consequences are often too distant to figure prominently enough in their decision-making process; they get drowned out by more immediate rewards.

- Given that internal behavioral controls are often insufficient, it's important to provide stronger external controls by reducing external distracters and increasing cues that support the desired behavior.

- Provide more external time markers, be it clocks or count-down/count-up timers.

- Increase the saliency and strength of shorter-term rewards to enhance the weak longer-term internal rewards, by building in rewards for completing steps along the way to a larger goal, for example.

- Encourage and prompt the process of thinking out plans, for example by writing down ideas and moving those thoughts around "physically" rather than only mentally.

Brown's Six Clusters of Executive Functioning

Brown (2005) also sees ADHD as a disorder based in executive function deficits, but he clusters those functions differently than Barkley does. Brown does not agree with Barkley's assertion that behavioral inhibition is the primary deficit of ADHD which then creates other secondary difficulties. His six clusters are as follows:

1. *Activation*—organizing, prioritizing, and activating to work

2. *Focus*—focusing, sustaining, and shifting attention to tasks

3. *Effort*—regulating alertness, sustaining effort, and processing speed

4. *Emotion*—managing frustration and modulating emotions

5. *Memory*—utilizing working memory and accessing recall

6. *Action*—monitoring and self-regulating action

Any individual may have relative strengths and weaknesses in her abilities within these six clusters. Brown's framework can be useful for understanding a client's performance and thereby targeting interventions more precisely.

Conclusion

Although the specific details are still being worked out, there is little doubt that ADHD is very much a brain-based disorder. However, at this time, that knowledge does not directly translate into clinical practice, except to the extent that there is now some vindication for those who have struggled with these difficulties to know that their problem is not caused by a bad attitude or laziness.

CHAPTER 3

The Impact of ADHD
on an Adult's Life

Hi Dr. Tuckman,

I was diagnosed with ADD last year. I have suffered from various symptoms since childhood. I often find myself not being able to handle the pressure of life. Just getting simple things done, and I am single with no kids. ADD has long affected my relationships, my work habits, my finances, etc. I am now at the point where I really can't deal with it any longer. Last year after my diagnosis, I refused to take my meds. And this just perpetuates the problems. My anxiety level is extremely high. And I get to the point where I want to shut myself off from society ... which is where I am now. My doctor retired last winter, and I am looking for someone new. Please let me know if you are accepting new patients.

This e-mail from a prospective client neatly captures all of the struggles of the adult with ADHD. In one short paragraph, this woman summarizes what a life with untreated ADHD is like. She is overwhelmed in all parts of her life, yet is ambivalent about treatment. She is experiencing significant comorbid conditions. She is in need of help, but is having trouble finding a qualified professional. In short, this woman is going under. What's most remarkable about this e-mail is that it's not at all remarkable—the only unique aspect it has is that it arrived at a time that I was gathering materials for a presentation on adult ADHD. I have received countless similar e-mails and phone calls from adults with ADHD as well as from others on their behalf. As this e-mail so concisely illustrates, ADHD affects all aspects of life functioning. This goes far beyond the well-publicized difficulties in the classroom.

This chapter discusses the various ways that ADHD impacts people's lives, including both the direct effects and the secondary outcomes of a lifetime of undiagnosed and untreated ADHD. Of course, sweeping generalizations are always risky; nonetheless, there are certain characteristics common enough that they bear mentioning. It's important for therapists to have a solid understanding of this material if they are to be most helpful to their clients. Much of this knowledge will serve as a foundation as you do therapy with these clients—these are things to look out for or even ask about directly, if they are not mentioned by the client. In addition, some of this knowledge will be useful when you educate your clients about ADHD and normalize their difficulties, and thereby replace the unproductive explanations they may have used previously.

Put simply, ADHD creates demonstrable limitations in every major realm of functioning (Barkley & Gordon, 2002). Thomas Phelan used the term "ADHD octopus" to describe the pervasive effect of ADHD on someone's life and family (2002, p. 242). ADHD reaches its tentacles into all aspects of the person's life—and even into other people's lives. These effects can then cross spans of time, as the experiences of the ADHD child set the stage for what's to come in adulthood.

This brings up an important point. In this chapter, I often refer to the effects that ADHD has on children's lives, rather than refer directly to the effect on adults' lives. There are two reasons for this. First of all, there is much more data available on children with ADHD than on adults, so we are left to extrapolate. Granted, there are mitigating factors that may minimize or alter the effects of childhood events as the person grows up and creates a life as an adult, but we can safely assume that there will be carryover effects nonetheless for at least some proportion of ADHD adults. Second and related to the first point, what happens in childhood does indeed carry forward into adulthood, so even if the direct effect occurs earlier in life, it can still influence what comes later. For example, the child who does poorly in school will have reduced academic and vocational options when grown. The child who experienced more teasing as a result of his ADHD-based social difficulties may be less likely to trust people as an adult. Our present is a product of our past, so don't make too much of the gaps in the literature on adult ADHD.

In the most general sense, we can say that the greater the number and severity of ADHD symptoms, the greater the number of areas in which someone will exhibit impairment in young adulthood. This is somewhat more true of the symptoms of inattention than it is of hyperactivity. More specifically, more severe ADHD symptoms almost universally lead to a high risk of impairment. Interestingly, children and adults with ADHD exhibit a positive illusory bias in their self-ratings, often rating their competence and performance as better than they actually are (Barkley et al., 2006). Therefore, you may get an overly confident or optimistic self-report when you ask about these difficulties, so perhaps these reports should be taken with a grain of salt.

The Evolving Personality

Ramsay & Rostain (2005c) describe ADHD as an "Axis 1.5 Disorder" (p. 336), describing the way that ADHD folks' executive functioning style affects their interactions in their social and physical environments from an early age. By influencing the events the person with ADHD encounters, as well as the meanings she makes of those events, followed by the influence of those meanings on future events, the ADHD places a strong evolutionary pressure on the person's developing personality. This will influence her core beliefs about herself and her ability to be effective in the world, as well as her beliefs about relationships, and her interactions with others. Just as other aspects of temperament have a tendency to push someone's personality in certain directions as the person interacts with and is rewarded and punished by the world around him, so, too, do the typical ADHD weaknesses and difficulties affect the person with ADHD.

This is why, although everyone is an individual and must be treated as such, we can use broad brushstrokes as a reasonable starting point when describing or working with a new client. After all, this is the whole point of diagnosis—it suggests that certain strategies are more likely to be helpful than others.

We should also keep in mind that the adult who seeks an evaluation for ADHD may be quite different from the adult who was diagnosed with ADHD in childhood. Granted, the younger someone is, the more likely she is to have been diagnosed in childhood, given the increase in awareness of ADHD. But putting this historical factor aside, generally, we can assume that those who are not diagnosed until adulthood are likely to have had and continue to have less severe symptoms or better compensatory skills, or both, such that they did not warrant earlier intervention. We then also need to consider the effects of those interventions—both the positive, intended ones, as well as the negative ones related to the perceived stigma of being different or defective. Those diagnosed as children or adolescents will have had a different life than those who struggled undiagnosed and untreated. As time goes by, we will see the ratio between these two groups shift, as more of the ADHD adults seeking our services will have been diagnosed as children before entering our offices.

Situations That Obscure ADHD

It should be noted that ADHD may be less apparent in certain situations, such as when children are engaged in free play or when adults are engaged in less complicated tasks. ADHD symptoms are most obvious in situations where the demands of the task or environment exceed the person's ability to sustain attention, regulate activity, and restrain impulses (Barkley, 2006b). In much the same way, a diabetic's blood sugar regulation difficulties become most obvious after an overly sugary meal and seasonal affective disorder (SAD) is most apparent in the winter months.

The presentation of symptoms depends not only on the symptoms inherent in the person, but also on the surrounding environment. ADHD children display fewer behavioral problems in new or unfamiliar surroundings or when tasks are unusually novel, but they increase their level of deviant behavior as familiarity with the setting increases. As a result, the problematic behaviors may be observed more by family members than by acquaintances, if those interactions are interesting enough to keep the ADHD person focused. Thus, the family members may feel as though they are not believed when they discuss the struggles at home, adding insult to injury. I've had spouses complain that their partner seems to do quite well at work where he has a secretary or assistants, but performs much worse at home where the spouse needs to play that supportive role.

Perhaps the most obvious example of the effect that environment can have on the expression of ADHD symptoms is that of children playing video games, although similar examples can be found for adults engaged in very enjoyable activities, as well. I call this the "Nintendo Effect" because it's such a stark difference. The rapt attention displayed when playing video games is often touted as proving that an ADHD child can focus really well when he wants to; therefore, the difficulties he exhibits elsewhere are assumed to be more a matter of desire or choice.

There are two problems with this assumption. First, as discussed in chapter 1, the overly rapt attention displayed when playing video games is actually a sign of dysfunctional attention regulation. This hyperfocus is problematic because it's too much of a good thing. The second problem with the motivation assumption is that studies have found that even with highly stimulating video games, ADHD children look away more and have more problems with their performance compared to non-ADHD children (Barkley, 2006b). Thus, even video games are not immune from ADHD's sometimes subtle effects.

Executive Functioning

There is growing consensus in the field that ADHD is primarily a deficit in *executive functions*, a broad range of generally higher level cognitive functions (Barkley & Gordon, 2002) that usually operate without conscious awareness (Brown, 2005). Given the importance of executive functions in meeting the complex and ever-present demands of adulthood, deficits in this area can cascade into a multitude of troubles. Executive functions are often thought of as the general class of self-directed actions that people employ to modify their own behavior and thereby maximize future, over immediate, consequences. This can include such functions as response inhibition, working memory, resistance to distraction, strategy development, planning and future-directed behavior, flexibility, problem solving, organization, self-regulation of emotion/motivation, and social intelligence.

A significant price is paid by those lacking these various skills. Life as an adult in this society is complicated enough to serve as an excellent screening tool for those with executive function deficits. Unless an ADHD adult has someone else in her life, or several people who take over the tasks that she is weak on, or serve as the safety rails to keep her from going too far off the tracks, the ADHD will create noticeable problems in most areas of her life. These various secondary effects are elaborated upon throughout the rest of this chapter.

Three areas of executive functioning bear specific discussion: working memory, sense of time, and persistence of effort. Each is addressed in turn.

Working Memory

Working memory is crucial to the performance of any task that involves integrating two or more pieces of information, whether it's two things happening in close proximity, such as tracking a conversation, or connecting a current piece of information with something from long-term memory, such as considering how a new task will fit into an existing schedule. It enables people to hold and process some pieces of information while simultaneously attending to others. It is used in almost every aspect of daily life, from participating in conversations and reading, to setting priorities and adapting flexibly to new developments (Brown, 2005). If a person's working memory tends to blink and drop pieces of information, all sorts of errors are likely to occur, in that the rest of the brain's processing machinery will be severely limited in its inputs and outputs by this bottle-neck. An analogy is that of a computer with too little RAM that runs slowly, has operating errors, and crashes. So, for example, someone with ADHD may know that he must live within some budget constraints. But when faced with a tempting purchase, he may not be able to integrate fully how this purchase fits into the bigger picture of his current finances, future income, and pending expenses, only to realize later that he is running out of money prematurely. Many of these types of errors look like bad judgment or foolhardiness, but it's really that the person has lost some of the relevant information from his mental calculations and therefore makes a flawed decision.

Sense of Time and Prospective Memory

Sense of time is the inherent ability to know, at least in a general sense, how much time has passed while doing a particular activity. Unfortunately, the sense of time is much more fluid for people with ADHD than it is for other people, in that for those with ADHD, five minutes of a boring activity can feel like an hour, and an hour of a pleasur-able activity can feel like five minutes. I can recall countless examples from my clinical practice of situations where ADHD clients have gotten themselves into trouble because of their inability to monitor the passage of time. They might be the clients who missed important meetings because they didn't realize that hours had gone by while they were surfing the internet. Or the clients who made commitments to themselves (or others) to spend a significant amount of time on uninteresting tasks, only to find that they had spent much less time and accomplished much less than they were supposed to do.

Sense of time is extremely important in today's society given that time deadlines are ubiquitous. Virtually all domains of major life activities require planning, forethought, and otherwise remembering what needs doing and, just as importantly, when it needs to be done. It's not usually the case that ADHD adults don't know what to do, but rather they don't do it when they know it would be best to do it (Barkley & Gordon, 2002). For example, they know it's important to pay the electric bill on time, but that doesn't always translate into actually getting the envelope into the mail before it's too late. What this comes down to is called *prospective memory*, which is the ability to remember to remember.

For example, "I need to go through the bills when I get home tonight," or "I have a report due at work at the end of the week." Life involves countless examples where prospective memory is more important than a memory for specific facts (e.g., Columbus discovered America in 1492) in terms of daily functioning (Nadeau, 1995a). It has been said that ADHD creates "time blindness or future myopia" (Barkley & Gordon, 2002, p. 62).

These difficulties with prospective memory are fundamentally different from the situations in which the person consciously decides that she doesn't want to do something. For example, filing papers is seen as horribly boring and thereby avoided, despite knowledge of the sometimes significant negative consequences. When the situation is due to a failure to remember, the task doesn't even enter consciousness for a decision to be made. On these occasions, the ADHD person may be as surprised and disappointed as anyone else that the task wasn't completed.

Of course, most people eventually run out of patience and stop believing that the ADHD person simply forgot to do the probably uninteresting task; instead, they peg the person as irresponsible or selfish—and a liar to boot. For the ADHD person, this can add insult to injury, as he is forced to deal with both the pragmatic consequences of the failure, such as a late fee on the electric bill, as well as the social fallout, such as his romantic partner, once again, becoming upset with him. Unfortunately, as the story about the boy who cried wolf teaches us, even the most trusting people eventually stop believing the promises.

Persistence of Effort

For adults with ADHD there is strong and consistent evidence of difficulties in the self-regulation of motivation, particularly *persistence of effort* (Barkley, 2006c). This is why those with ADHD can engage in personally interesting or meaningful activities for hours on end, and yet be able to put in only a fraction of that time on boring tasks like filing, cleaning, and studying. In contrast to those without ADHD, those who have the disorder display a much larger difference in their performance between enjoyable and boring activities. It takes a much greater force of will to stay with these boring activities than it does for non-ADHD people. Unfortunately, success in life often requires the ability to complete many uninteresting tasks on an almost daily basis. Those weak in this ability pay a price in every domain of life: educationally, financially, socially, and occupationally.

Academic Functioning

ADHD is best known for the negative effect it has on students' academic performance. Partly this is due to the demands of the classroom and homework assignments that pull strongly for ADHD deficits. The tasks required for being a student tap into many typical ADHD difficulties with distractibility, poor memory, disorganization, and others. The statistics on ADHD students' academic success are predictably sobering. As an example, one large longitudinal study found that one-third of the hyperactive students failed to graduate from high school, compared to none in the control group. In addition, only 21 percent of the hyperactive group had ever enrolled in college, compared to four times as many of the control group (Barkley, 2006f).

In general, ADHD can affect a person's ability to apply her intelligence effectively in the world and adapt to challenges (Ellison, 2002). ADHD students are often penalized for their inconsistent, or abysmal, homework performance, even if they manage to do quite well on tests that show a mastery of the material. Even those students who are motivated to do their best may still miss too many assignments or turn them in too late or incomplete. The unofficial grade profile of the bright ADHD student is A's and B's on tests but C's and D's, or worse, on homework.

Having a high IQ can be a protective factor in the classroom because it gives the student a greater cushion to make up for the lost efficiencies that come with ADHD. When parts of the lesson are missed due to distractibility, for example, brighter students are often able to fill in the blanks based on what they did catch. These gains aside, they will still have difficulties in the areas of self-control, organization, time management, or the exercise of good judgment (Murphy & Gordon, 2006). Unfortunately, for almost all ADHD students, the difficulties they have in performing up to their potential are well-known to themselves and others, resulting in frequent comments from parents, teachers, and classmates about those difficulties. Predictably, these negative school experiences often lead to negative feelings toward academic achievement. This in turn leads to declines in motivation in order to protect self-esteem—"I don't care. School is stupid anyway." It's easier to stop trying than to continue to suffer the criticism.

For example, a colleague of mine obtained the following responses from an ADHD high school student on an assessment questionnaire (J. R. Ramsay, personal communication, May 2006):

Feelings about middle school: "sucked"

Feelings about high school: "sucks"

Feelings about college: "is going to suck"

Although this disengagement can be protective in the short-term, it obviously compounds the problem over time, in that learning in school is a progression that builds on earlier learning. Therefore, problems can develop later due to unintentionally missing things, as well as intentionally tuning out, which serves as a self-esteem saver (Ellison, 2002). I call this phenomenon "Swiss cheese knowledge," wherein the student has a general sense of the subject, but is lacking bits and pieces that she may not be aware of. This can create problems later when that missing information is needed. Sometimes ADHD students are behind academically, not because of skill deficits but because they can't muster the great force of will necessary to make themselves practice in subjects requiring repetitive and sustained effort for mastery, such as math (Goldstein, 2002) and foreign languages.

Beyond these secondary psychological struggles, high school is often a real challenge for ADHD students, even under the best of circumstances. Native intelligence is no longer sufficient to get them through as the reading and writing assignments get longer—unless their abilities still far exceed demands, they may no longer be able to get by on catching most of a lecture and scribbling out homework at the last minute (Nadeau, 2002). Today, high school students are increasingly expected to manage the planning and execution of assignments that span longer and longer time intervals and cannot be completed at the last minute without experiencing enormous stress.

These escalating demands weigh heavily on ADHD students' weaknesses, creating a tinderbox of family tension as the teen pushes for independence from parental oversight. Predictably, many parents find it easy to justify their overinvolvement, despite vehement protestations to the contrary. Parents often find it easier to gain grudging acceptance from younger students and may be unaccustomed to dealing with this level of resistance.

Unfortunately, the characteristics of high school that are most troublesome for ADHD students only get worse in college. Whereas, in earlier years, parents and teachers would oversee and review the student's work, perhaps intensively, in college it's almost completely up to the student to be responsible, leading to a painful lesson in being careful about what one wishes for (Weiss et al., 1999). In contrast to the relatively easily accessed student support staff available in secondary school settings, few colleges provide that level of support. Even if there is a disabilities counselor available, it's very much incumbent on the student to initiate and maintain contact, which few do—and even fewer do before the situation reaches a crisis. Many college freshmen with ADHD sink quickly under the combination of virtually complete freedom and the seemingly limitless distractions that pull them away from schoolwork. As a result, college can be a difficult transition for many ADHD students. They must learn how to manage the increased academic demands while simultaneously managing living on their own, and setting a schedule conducive to meeting those demands.

Given this mismatch between the ADHD college student's skills and the demands placed on the student by the college, it's not surprising that an unfortunate number do not graduate in their first attempt. This then puts them in a double bind—accept jobs that are in line with their educational level but below their abilities, or risk further failure and frustration by returning to school to get the degree that would give them access to the higher level jobs in which they could be successful (Weiss et al., 1999). Although the same academic demands will still be present the second and third time around, a returning adult has a better sense of the purpose of education and knows how earning a diploma can lead to better things after graduation if she can survive the challenge.

In addition, hopefully, the ADHD student will have learned ways to cope and be able to take a more active approach in dealing with the limitations of her ADHD and other weaknesses, such that she can be more successful. This vanquishing of a past failure can have important implications for her self-esteem.

Unfortunately for those whose academic performance doesn't match their abilities, for whatever reason, access to certain jobs or careers is tied to applicants' grades and test scores. This doesn't mean that the person couldn't be successful in the position or educational program, but that he is likely not to get the chance to prove himself. As a result, ADHD-based academic difficulties in early life can carry forward far beyond the school years. This is not to say that every person needs to go to college or work at a white-collar job. Rather, it's a matter of having the opportunity to pursue the paths that would be a better fit for the person's interests and overall abilities. Those with poor academic records close off some of those options prematurely and have fewer opportunities later in life, perhaps forcing them to settle for careers that are less rewarding, both financially and psychologically.

Occupational Functioning

Work is a major part of adult life, so it isn't surprising that ADHD adults seek help to become more successful in this part of life, especially if they have chosen or found themselves in a situation that pulls on too many of their weaknesses. The demands of the workplace can differ significantly from those of the classroom, which is both bad news and good news for those with ADHD.

I'll start with the negatives first. ADHD adults are two-thirds more likely to have been fired; three times more likely to have quit impulsively; one-third more likely to report chronic employment difficulties; and 50 percent more likely to have changed jobs in any given time period (Barkley & Gordon, 2002). Employers rate ADHD employees in more negative terms on measures of meeting job expectations, getting along with supervisors, working independently, and completing work assignments (Ellison, 2002). ADHD employees often get into trouble by not understanding their supervisors' or coworkers' expectations, by choosing an inappropriate career, or by not having the self-confidence to deal with these sorts of dilemmas (Crawford & Crawford, 2002).

ADHD behavior can be difficult for coworkers to tolerate, especially when it affects them too, as in a group project or where their work is dependent on someone else's. I have many, many examples from my clinical practice, but one particular client comes to mind. He lost several jobs due to his tendency both to procrastinate and miss deadlines, despite his ability to do what was required of him. Although he was somewhat bothered by his brinksmanship, his coworkers were far more disturbed by it, leading his bosses to fire him when repeated requests to improve weren't heeded.

On the plus side, compared to school, it can be easier for an adult with ADHD to be effective at work. Although many of the same skill deficits remain, adults have a greater choice of work settings than students do, so they can find jobs that are a better fit. Furthermore, work performance may be measured in ways they can better meet, tasks may be more interesting, or the job itself may provide more structure (Weiss et al., 1999). For those who succeed at work or managed to get themselves through college or graduate school, it may be possible to have an assistant manage the details that often elude them. This brings to mind an extremely hyperactive client who worked as a day trader to meet his need for constant stimulation, and who had enough self-knowledge to hire an assistant to handle the paperwork so that the trades actually went through.

Some ADHD adults may succeed in their first jobs, when the demands placed on them are generally lower or when there is more oversight to keep them on track. However, they may begin to struggle following a promotion to a position that requires them to do the planning and oversight. The skills that made them successful in their previous position are not sufficient to make them successful in the new position. Alternatively, as demands at home increase, they may no longer be able to make up for inefficiencies at work by staying late, so their job performance begins to suffer.

Adults with ADHD may display some common dysfunctional work habits. One of these is called *pseudoefficiency*, which is the tendency to complete low priority but easy tasks while avoiding harder but more important tasks, such as returning phone calls rather than finalizing a report. Because they look and feel busy, they create an illusory sense of getting a lot done, while time ticks down on items that should be a higher priority. Granted, we all can admit to doing at least a little bit of this. The ADHD folks just do much more of it.

A second dysfunctional habit is that of *juggling*, which is jumping to new, and thereby more exciting, projects before finishing projects that are partially completed and no longer interesting (Rostain & Ramsay, 2006a). In order to assess this tendency, I will often ask as part of my diagnostic interview whether someone is a much better starter than finisher. Those with ADHD routinely answer yes—and their spouses will vigorously and exasperatedly confirm it. Ultimately, it may come down to the eleventh hour before the person finally gets into gear with a task and completes it, even though he had plenty of opportunities to do so earlier. As with pseudoefficiency, the person gives the appearance of being busy, and perhaps he is, but most projects at work and in life don't give partial credit—it's either done or it isn't. A report is either finished or it isn't. A room is either completely painted or it isn't.

Daily Life Functioning

This section deals with the myriad tasks adults are required to engage in to keep their lives running smoothly, from paying bills to buying groceries. Few of these necessary activities are exciting or satisfying, but there are significant problems or penalties that arise from not completing them on time. These are the sorts of tasks where there is no reward for doing them, since it is expected that they will be done without undue struggle or complaint. Most people see them as a necessary evil, but not as inherently difficult. Perhaps more so than most people, those with ADHD too often live their lives by following a negative reinforcement model in which they engage in an activity at the very last minute to stop or avoid an aversive stimulus (Goldstein, 2006, October). For example, they will finally get around to cleaning up the living room only to stop their romantic partner from griping. Or they will scramble to get the electric bill in the mail only to avoid a late fee. Although this sometimes serves to get the job done, it's not as inspiring as living to pursue more positive rewards.

Although ADHD can lead to dramatic disasters, most of the time it's the smaller and more frequent problems that cause the most damage to the person's and family's peace of mind and quality of life. For many with ADHD, after a lifetime of turmoil, unpredictability, and last-minute scrambling, they develop the belief that instability and chaos have always been and always will be a part of their life (Rostain & Ramsay, 2006a). Their prior efforts at consistency and stability failed, so they are disinclined to try again, even if a therapist makes seemingly unsubstantiated promises that this time can be different.

The Daily Grind

Many ADHD adults have underdeveloped life management skills (Nadeau, 2002), which lead to frequent crises, as well as to a slow and steady decline punctuated by periods of frantic catch-up activity. Because ADHD has been present since early childhood, it contributes to difficulties in acquiring appropriate coping skills which further exacerbates problems over time (Safren, 2006). Organizing a household requires coordinating many unrelated parts and activities and entropy is a constant threat (Dixon, 1995); it requires a consistent input of energy simply to maintain the status quo. For this reason, ADHD has been called "a disorder of routine task management" (Barkley & Gordon, 2002, p. 61). What separates ADHD folks from others is their difficulty with handling the daily requirements of life that are not necessarily difficult in isolation, but can become overwhelming in total. The analogy is that of snowflakes—pretty one by one, but scary in an avalanche. For too many ADHD adults, much of life feels as though they are running half a step ahead of that avalanche.

One reason the mundane tasks of life management can seem so hard to stay on top of is that ADHD adults frequently feel driven to move on to the next experience, that being stuck in the same moment for too long begins to wear on them (Ratey, Hallowell, & Miller, 1995). This can be a real problem for tasks that demand persistence, despite boredom and sameness. Of course, these elements describe many tasks. This often means that many tasks are started but many fewer are ever finished.

On the other side of the coin, the ADHD adult may unintentionally find her attention pulled from activity to activity before she completes the first one. As one of my clients described to her husband, it isn't that she decided to skip wiping up the spilled syrup, merely that she was constantly being pulled to another task, like making the kids' lunches, getting dressed, and feeding the dog; so the syrup spill simply disappeared from her radar screen, even though she knew it would take only a moment to wipe it up, and that her husband would be upset to find it on the floor that night. This type of problem repeats constantly in her life, in a million variations. It isn't that she doesn't know what she should do, but rather that she has trouble making it all happen within the fleeting twenty-four hours of the day.

Adults with ADHD experience breakdowns with many facets of time management. Good time management requires planning; prioritization; remembering the plan; thoughtful midcourse corrections when unexpected variables come into play; sticking to the plan despite appealing distractions; accurately predicting how long something will take; keeping track of the passage of time during an activity; and shifting flexibly from one activity to another as the plan requires (Nadeau, 1995a). As with every chained activity, this one is only as strong as its weakest link. Predictably, time management becomes increasingly important as the demands on the person increase and there is less slack time to absorb the inefficiencies.

Related to this issue, one near universal complaint of those with ADHD is their difficulty in maintaining a balanced lifestyle that involves appropriate self-care. Given ADHD folks' poor self-regulatory abilities and their difficulties with establishing new habits, it isn't hard to imagine that these deficiencies could adversely impact their diet, exercise, hygiene, sleep, and other habits that affect their health (Barkley & Gordon, 2002). Therefore, in addition to the primary ADHD symptoms, these secondary effects may further erode their efficiency, well-being, and mood.

Many ADHD adults also have awful money management habits, and possibly poorly developed skills, too. This is partly due to impulsive spending, but also to not being organized about balancing their checkbook, creating a budget, paying bills on time (even when they have the money), and keeping the necessary records for taxes (Nadeau, 2002). This can have major consequences, in terms of finances as well as self-esteem, relationship dynamics, stress, and mood. Many ADHD people "leak" money in small ways that add up to large sums, like paying cab fares when running late, buying lunch because they didn't have time to make it at home, and so on. If credit cards are used, this is especially hard to notice at the time.

Additionally, many adults with ADHD lack the ability to see how individual purchases fit into their whole financial picture, just as they have difficulty budgeting their time. Whatever is directly in front of them has more pull on their decision-making process than the amorphous concept of budgetary planning, thus causing unpleasant surprises as the end of the month draws near.

I had one client who was so overwhelmed by tracking her finances that she simply didn't bother. If she wanted something, she bought it. This despite the fact that her parents had bailed her out of credit-card debt twice already, which she felt awful about, and which justified her critical mother's overinvolvement in her life. Granted, we can understand her mother being critical, but she also used her daughter's bad money management skills as an opportunity to take unfair shots at her.

At the time of each purchase, my client turned a blind eye to the consequences; this was partly based in her neurology and partly in her psychological defenses. Of course, she later felt guilty and ashamed about spending the money. So, as often happens with ADHD, what starts as a simple neurological deficit winds up playing out in complex intra- and interpersonal dynamics that must be addressed in psychotherapy while coaching strengthens the client's basic skills.

Driving and Drama

One area of modern life that is being increasingly studied in relation to ADHD is driving performance; this is because of the great risks associated with even fleeting lapses of attention or impulsive actions. It has been proven across a growing body of literature that drivers with ADHD exhibit pervasive and multilevel impairments. Both self-ratings and ratings by others indicate that people with ADHD employ significantly fewer safe driving habits (Goldstein, 2002). Young adults with ADHD are more likely to have greater driving difficulties, including license suspensions and revocations, accidents where the car is totaled, hit-and-run accidents (Ellison, 2002), and accidents where bodily injury is involved—all despite equivalent driving knowledge (Faraone et al., 2000). Once again, the problem is often not one of not knowing what to do, but rather of doing it reliably and consistently.

Obviously, some of these difficulties stem from neurologically based cognitive dysfunction. Despite most people's automatic behaviors when behind the wheel of an automobile, driving requires many simultaneous skills of attending to what is happening inside and outside the car; predicting what other drivers are likely to do and responding accordingly; sustaining attention; ignoring distractions; and so forth. Given the potential cognitive complexity of this task, it isn't surprising that ADHD deficits show up here and lead to a much higher likelihood of driving problems. All it takes is one moment of lapsed attention at precisely the wrong moment for something awful to happen.

Additionally, there are also the poor choices related to lifestyle matters, such as speeding when running late, driving when sleep-deprived, or driving recklessly due to thrill-seeking. I had one ADHD client who, at the mere age of twenty, had racked up twenty-two tickets for moving violations and even wound up spending time in jail as a result. Even for a sixty-year-old, that would be an impressive collection of driving violations, but for someone who'd been driving for only five years, it's staggering.

Finally, those with ADHD are twice as likely to become addicted to cigarettes, which can have drastic health and financial effects over time. ADHD folks also tend to prefer drugs to alcohol, with marijuana being the most popular drug of choice. Once addicted, they're also more likely to maintain their addiction longer (Spencer, 2006a). This clearly has significant secondary effects on their quality of life, occupational and social functioning, and overall happiness. Also, active substance abuse or dependence can have significant effects on the diagnostic process and subsequent treatment.

Psychological Functioning

Although ADHD is a neurological condition, its effects on functioning create significant secondary psychological effects. Through experience after experience, the ADHD influences and shapes the evolution of the personality in some of its most fundamental ways, such as self-image, self-efficacy, problem-solving style, and relating to others.

These features may become at least as important to address in treatment as the primary symptoms. In fact, the unhappiness deriving from these outgrowths of the primary symptoms, these impairments in functioning, provide the motivation that drives ADHD adults into treatment.

Adults with previously undiagnosed ADHD tend to share certain personality traits, such as acceptance of chaos, avoidance of boredom and certain types of tasks, and thrill-seeking behaviors, all of which have an effect on their lives. Undiagnosed ADHD will have caused a lifetime of difficulties and deeply embedded certain patterns of living, thinking, feeling, and acting that will take time to change, even when the core symptoms of ADHD are addressed with medication. For example, people with ADHD are ten times as likely as the larger population to develop a personality style characterized by pessimism, helplessness, and disorganization, and are half as likely to develop a personality style characterized by empathy, extroversion, and motivation (Goldstein, 2002).

Self-Image and Self-Efficacy

The psychological effects listed above shouldn't be surprising given that the ADHD adult, and many of the people around her, know that there is something wrong that stops her from being more successful. Even when they do achieve some success, many ADHD adults feel like imposters and struggle to hide their inadequacies from family and coworkers (Nadeau, 2002). The lifetime of difficulties they've experienced, despite their potential for success, creates a mixture of confusion and shame which leads to an uncertain self-image (Weiss et al., 1999). They often feel like failures, defective, incompetent, and socially undesirable (Ramsay & Rostain, 2005b). This is not uncommon. People with hidden disabilities frequently have difficulty developing a healthy self-esteem because of the failures and frustrations they face. They lack sufficient experiences of personal mastery, of undertaking and accomplishing personally chosen tasks. Instead, they often suffer from excessive guilt and self-blame (Crawford & Crawford, 2002) because they know that they could do better than they do.

Since our feelings about ourselves are shaped by the reactions we experience from the people around us, it's important to understand how people tend to react to ADHD behavior. In general, most people have a set of assumptions and inferences they use to make sense of others' behavior—this is necessary to understand the social world. As a rule, people assume that behavior is motivated and intentional, with some exceptions where they can see an act is unintentional or influenced by specific circumstances. Thus, ADHD mistakes are not attributed to neurological factors that are difficult to control and cannot be seen, especially if the ADHD person can sometimes perform well.

Rather, the ADHD behavior is attributed to conscious choice or personality characteristics. Most people tend to assume that anything mental is completely controlled by choice and not influenced by genetics or biochemistry, whereas physical ailments are much less frequently seen as under the person's control. Therefore, people who have a mental illness, especially ADHD, are judged negatively for making bad choices. This can cause self-doubt and self-hatred in the ADHD individual as others, and thereby himself, assume that he could do better if only he tried harder, cared more, and was less selfish (Harman, 2004).

To make matters even worse, ADHD children tend to be more closely monitored and managed than their peers, which has important implications for their development. Of course, the parents can justify this degree of oversight, given that the child has more difficulty staying on track without it, but some parents' overprotectiveness may derive more out of managing their own anxiety than it does from the child's true need for structure. In these situations, the child is given even fewer opportunities to manage her own destiny and is thereby even less prepared to do so as an adult.

Certainly, the dilemma for every parent is to find the optimal balance between the competing demands for independence and guidance, a line that's often seen more clearly in retrospect. Parents of ADHD children struggle even more with striking the appropriate balance, but it's probably safe to say that they tend more toward the guidance end of the spectrum. Unfortunately, this often well-intentioned position can deprive the child of opportunities to practice independence, thereby undercutting her ability to self-manage, as well as her confidence in her own abilities. This can create a situation where she experiences much more conflict about her desire for independence—she hates being controlled by others, yet knows in her heart that she may need it. With age, this dynamic shifts from parents to bosses and romantic partners, causing tension in these important relationships.

Ramsay and Rostain (2005a) write about the self-mistrust that many ADHD adults feel. That is, after countless mistakes, failures, and misrememberings, they've learned that they can't trust their memories or their commitment to get things done, even important things. Every task to be completed can evoke a feeling of dread, as they wonder whether they will be able to get it done on time and of sufficient quality. Every task becomes a ticking time bomb of potential trouble.

Defense Mechanisms

One way ADHD people try to escape their painful feelings is to adopt an attitude of apathy toward the chaos in their lives. They may procrastinate and get to an important task eventually or they may avoid it completely. After all, they rationalize, it doesn't count as failure if you don't really try or if you can blame it on circumstances, like, "I did it at the last minute, so how good could it have been?" Although hardly the ideal solution, it's somewhat understandable if they are pessimistic about the likelihood of good effort yielding positive results.

This indifference can be mind-boggling and anxiety-arousing to the people around them, including therapists, who see the price they pay—or may soon pay—and feel compelled to push the ADHD person to do something to avert disaster. The client with the poor money management discussed above is an excellent example of this. She confesses she hates the emotional price she pays when she has to borrow money from her mother, as she too often does; yet she has had great difficulty changing her ways so that she won't have to rely on maternal help. Note that this client eventually did make some progress in this area—but it wasn't easy.

So, despite clear evidence of the cost of these ADHD behaviors, some clients may be hesitant to work on changing them, for fear of losing part of who they are in the process—of not being themselves anymore. The problematic patterns are thereby retained. Some clients may compensate with magical thinking, whereby problems are avoided with the unreasonable belief that everything will somehow work out just fine or that an easy solution will present itself and be effective. These various avoidance techniques are reinforced by the relief experienced when the clients escape the uncomfortable feelings of impending failure, guilt, self-reproach, and negative self-evaluation, even though they haven't actually addressed the problem itself (Ramsay & Rostain, 2005a).

When things, predictably perhaps, don't work out well, they may externalize responsibility for the difficulties, playing the victim of circumstances or unreasonable others. Although well-meaning others may initially bend to accommodate the ADHD adult, over time they will likely burn out and either disappear or cease to be so forgiving, giving even less than they otherwise would. In this way, ADHD adults cut themselves off from potential resources and allies without fully realizing why people get angry with them or go missing from their lives (Ramsay & Rostain, 2005a). Taken a step further, they may begin to assume that everyone will eventually get frustrated with them or single them out negatively, and preemptively keep their distance or assume the worst. This obviously then becomes a self-fulfilling prophecy.

Taking these deficits together, the ADHD adult may become hypersensitive to failure or the possibility of failure. Rather than seeing setbacks as temporary and learning experiences, they view them as yet another indictment of their bad character. Unfortunately, they have plenty of experiences with failure, certainly more than most people. There's a popular book whose title succinctly captures this misattribution and overgeneralization that many ADHD adults suffer from: *You Mean I'm Not Lazy, Stupid, or Crazy?!* (Kelly & Ramundo, 2006). These are the assumptions that the ADHD folks and others quite logically make to account for their self-defeating and otherwise inexplicable behaviors. As a result, they lack persistence in solving problems, because the first failure, or even hint of failure, is overwhelming. It can be difficult to convince them otherwise, because they have quite a database of well-intentioned and reasonable advice that has proven largely unhelpful, such as "take the first ten minutes of each day to plan your activities." Such advice didn't take into account their ADHD—the first ten minutes of the day are long gone before they even remember they were supposed to plan things out ahead of time.

As a consequence, they may hesitate to believe that new strategies may be at all helpful, including those coming from a therapist well-versed in ADHD. If they do try something new and it doesn't work out, they may lack the resilience to ride out the disappointment and frustration and maintain motivation. Flooded with anxiety, self-doubt, and self-deprecation, they will retreat from the challenge.

One way of dealing with this cascade of painful feelings is to wait until the very last minute to do things. Although they go through a long stretch of semiconscious awareness of an impending deadline, they are mostly able to push those negative feelings aside. The mad dash at the last minute then absorbs their full attention and quiets the chatter of critical inner voices. In addition, given the near ubiquity with which ADHD folks report this tendency, there seems to be some physiological aspect to it; it may be that the adrenaline rush (so to speak) helps them to focus in a way that a far-off deadline does not. So, if they did start working on a project far in advance, whatever work they did would be done halfheartedly and not be very productive. Although people with ADHD are certainly aware of the additional stress they face by engaging in this brinksmanship, it's exceedingly difficult for them to motivate themselves to start things earlier.

Finally, some ADHD folks experience insatiability in their pursuits, quickly growing bored with whatever was once interesting (Brooks, 2002), be it relationships/friendships, jobs, hobbies, or living situations. Predictably, constantly chasing the next thing leads to upheaval and lost momentum each time they start over. For example, someone who changes jobs or careers too frequently never earns any seniority and the perks that come with it, including promotions, recognition, and pay raises. Alternatively, someone who gets bored in relationships as soon as the honeymoon glow fades will quickly pursue a new romance rather than build something more meaningful.

These tendencies can become socially "expensive" as friends begin to view the ADHD person as flighty and exhausting to be close to. Consequently, the person may not have a network of longtime friends to provide support during difficult times. The psychological defense of *escape into action* may be related to this. With this defense, the person avoids dealing with difficult emotions or the problems that elicited them by jumping into activity instead (Ramsay & Rostain, 2005a). Although their impulsivity will neurologically predispose them to act this way, there is also the added layer of a psychological defense mechanism.

Taken together, all of the difficulties that emerge with ADHD make people prone to additional psychiatric disorders. Some studies have found lifetime rates of alcohol abuse or dependence in one-quarter to one-half of all ADHD adults; up to one-third of this population may have another substance abuse or dependence; one-quarter to almost one-half suffer from generalized anxiety disorder; and up to one-third of all ADHD adults suffer from major depressive disorder (Barkley, 2006f). These figures are obviously much higher than those found in the general population and are a testament to the psychological toll that adults with the disorder pay for undiagnosed and untreated ADHD.

Social Skills and Relationships

ADHD can have a significant effect on social functioning, in both obvious and subtle ways. For the sake of presentation, these effects are categorized into different sections, but the dynamics from one can certainly take place in another.

Social interaction involves a complex interplay vulnerable to disruption in many ways:

- Hyperactive and impulsive actions and comments can be off-putting if they diverge too far from others' expectations.

- Inattention can cause the ADHD person to miss important aspects of the communication, causing the other person to feel that she isn't being listened to.

- Besides the obvious practical problems that can result from these ADHD-based lapses, such as missing an important piece of information, the social ramifications can be even greater if others extrapolate from these experiences.

We all seek to understand why others do what they do and, in that process, we tend to assign our own motives to others' behavior. For example, if we don't pay attention to something it's usually because we view it as unimportant. Therefore, when the ADHD person seems to not be attending, we assume that the conversation or our opinions generally aren't important to him. As a result, ADHD people are often seen as irresponsible, self-centered, or rude.

Studies have found that ADHD children are not chosen as frequently to be best friends or partners in activities as other children are (Goldstein & Kennemer, in press). Unfortunately, ADHD children are aware of these difficulties with predictable impacts on their self-esteem. In addition, they tend to experience more high incidence/low impact problems, which cause them to become less socially accepted, as well as experiencing more low incidence/high impact problems, which lead to social rejection. Even though the children are aware of the consequences for their difficulties, they continue to have difficulty adapting their behavior accordingly.

General Social Skills

Follow-up studies of hyperactive children show that as adults they have problematic interpersonal relationships and significantly fewer social skills (Barkley & Gordon, 2002). ADHD adults often rate themselves as less skilled at regulating their social behavior. They may be vigilant about violations of social norms and have good intentions, but still have difficulty controlling their behavior. They report difficulties in engaging others in conversation and in their self-presentation skills, including tactfulness and their ability to adjust their behavior to be appropriate to the situation; moderating expressions of strong emotions; and controlling nonverbal displays. Taken together, they too frequently put their foot in their mouth, and have trouble with social engagements because they are seen as insensitive and inconsiderate (Friedman et al., 2003).

As with many other areas, they often know what the right thing to do is, but they have difficulty doing it consistently. One member of my adult ADHD support group described a job interview where he wondered to himself halfway through, "Have I sounded like an asshole yet?" This elicited an understanding reaction from the group who knew well what he was saying. What's notable is not only his pessimistic expectation, but also the fact that he wouldn't necessarily have realized that he was crossing a line at the time.

ADHD adults also have trouble recognizing others' emotions because they miss important cues that show how an interaction is going or that it's going down a new path. It's not really that they lack the ability to read social cues, but rather that their attention may be elsewhere in the moment. Although these empathic failures are unintentional, ADHD adults may be seen as self-centered or uncaring about others' feelings. However, these receptive deficits may be less obvious than their expressive deficits, which are more likely to result in more immediate feedback. By contrast, the difficulties arising from their receptive difficulties may surface later only if a misunderstanding is revealed (Friedman et al., 2003). As a result, the ADHD adult may remember an interaction differently than others do and be completely unaware of what she's missing.

Taken together, it should therefore not be surprising that ADHD adults tend to have significantly fewer social acquaintances and close friends. This isn't necessarily by choice, since they report more difficulties keeping friends (Barkley, 2006f). I have had many clients lament their lack of connection to others, sometimes for reasons they understand, sometimes not. Given the multiple protective effects of close relationships, this is concerning for more than immediate reasons.

Romantic Relationships

Given the social difficulties discussed above, it shouldn't be surprising that ADHD adults are twice as likely to separate/divorce and report less marital satisfaction (Barkley & Gordon, 2002). Too often a dynamic arises wherein the partner is pushed by the ADHD person's difficulties to take on more and more responsibility to ensure that tasks and chores are done completely and on time. The stereotype is that of an overfunctioning caretaker and an underfunctioning ADHD partner. Initially, this is a good balance, in that the caretaker enjoys being needed and able to do things her way, and the ADHD partner is more than happy to jettison some of his responsibilities.

Unfortunately, as the non-ADHD partner begins to realize the full extent of her partner's difficulties and thus the enormity of the demands that fall to her, she becomes increasingly demanding, which brings up too many bad memories of being controlled for the ADHD partner. At this point, the two begin to polarize each other, with the non-ADHD partner becoming increasingly angry and resentful and nagging more. Meanwhile, the ADHD partner becomes increasingly avoidant and/or passive-aggressive about helping out. The stability of the non-ADHD partner comes to be seen as boring or controlling and the spontaneity of the ADHD partner comes to be seen as irresponsible. Eventually the non-ADHD partner gets burned-out, feels depleted, and distances herself emotionally as a last ditch effort to feel less overwhelmed. This is often the time when treatment is sought out, as both partners are frustrated, to varying degrees, with the stalemate and negative interactions.

Weiss et al. (1999, p. 248) have listed the top ten complaints of the non-ADHD partner:

1. He doesn't care about me—e.g., forgot my birthday.

2. She's annoying—e.g., doesn't put the milk back in the fridge.

3. He's impossible to live with because I can never plan anything.

4. She doesn't listen well so we have unsatisfying conversations.

5. It's like being married to a child I have to look after.

6. She never follows through.

7. He makes love too quickly and expects me to turn it on and off just as quickly.

8. She always has some project that's more important than anything else.

9. Things have to be so structured for him to function at all that it's dominating both of our lives.

10. He explodes and says hurtful things. When he apologizes, it's done for him but I still carry it around with me.

Given these complaints, and the couple's likely ways of dealing with their frustrations, it shouldn't be surprising that intimacy suffers. The non-ADHD partner can burn out over time as a result of the peaks and valleys of the relationship, temper outbursts, lack of empathy, poor resolution of conflicts, and lack of communication (Ratey, Hallowell et al., 1995). It can be difficult to continue to reach out and make the relationship work when she feels as though she isn't getting enough back for her efforts. Interestingly, ADHD adults don't necessarily have problems with the emotional aspects of intimacy but rather in demonstrating it, such as remembering to bring up topics of importance to his partner, listening intently without interrupting, and staying attuned to his partner's mood states through the day (Weiss et al., 1999). As with so many other issues, they generally know what the right thing to do is, but that knowledge doesn't translate reliably into the necessary action.

Given that ADHD affects every other aspect of relationship functioning, of course it also affects sexual functioning. In fact, ADHD adults are ten times as likely to have some sort of sexual adjustment problem (Barkley & Gordon, 2002). Commonly cited are issues related to the timing and frequency of sex; amount of foreplay; and balancing both partners' sexual needs from moment to moment. Perhaps not surprisingly, an effective medication regimen can improve things in the bedroom, too, by helping the ADHD partner to maintain attention, be more aware of her partner's needs, and display an improved capacity to delay gratification (Weiss et al., 1999). Of course, because the most commonly used medication class, the stimulants, will have mostly worn off by the end of the day, changing the time to engage in sex may be necessary to take advantage of this improvement.

Parenting

The effect of ADHD on the ability to parent is discussed here in its own section because of the significant impact that it can have on this major life activity. First let's cover the positives. It has been said that ADHD parents benefit from having more energy to better keep up with active children and that they're also good at showing enthusiasm for their children's activities and having fun (Weiss et al., 1999). For example, I had a client who took great pleasure from playing video games loudly with his children. It can also feel really good to a child (or anyone, for that matter) to be hyperfocused on.

However, as with most other parts of life, ADHD brings some significant negatives to parenting. Compared to work and school, parenting activities can be quite unstructured, which often results in difficulties completing agreed-upon tasks, thus causing the other parent to become irritated. Many women who are successful in the professional world have a greater struggle as stay-at-home mothers, especially of young children—there are far too many interruptions where they can't just close their office door, too many crises of the moment, and too many divergent tasks to juggle (Dixon, 1995). They may also have difficulty setting limits consistently and effectively—partly because they have difficulty self-regulating, but also because they may be tired of always being told no; so they don't want to take on that role themselves.

Predictably, the price paid for not setting consistent limits is that the children may act out more, thus making the ADHD parent more prone to emotional outbursts. Contributing to this short fuse, the parent may feel overwhelmed trying to manage children's complicated schedules of after-school activities and ensuring that everyone gets everywhere on time and with all the necessary belongings, a task that sometimes requires the skills of an executive secretary (Weiss et al., 1999).

Less tangibly, inattention and distractibility may be interpreted by children as boredom with them. Alternatively, parents may miss the subtle and fleeting opportunities to really connect with their children. Hyperactive parents may have greater difficulty enjoying the quiet times that children need or the repetitive play that young children engage in (Weiss et al., 1999). I had a client with four children who described the agony of playing simple little games with her youngest because she felt she had done it a million times already. Another client spoke of the guilt she felt when she repeatedly brought her son to school late, since he was paying the price for her time-management difficulties. More traumatic are the late pickups after school or the times when the parent completely forgets to pick up the child. Finally, growing up in a messy, disorganized household doesn't provide any of the children with a good role model or teach any organizational skills, even if the children themselves don't have ADHD.

The effect of ADHD on a family depends on who in the family has it, how many people have it, how severely, and whether the non-ADHD members have other difficulties

(Weiss et al., 1999). Parents with ADHD are often told, in a guilt-inducing way, to take parenting classes or read books on how to be better parents, but that rarely helps—usually, they already know what they're supposed to do but they can't maintain the consistency to keep the new habits going. It's similar to giving someone with crutches advice on how to improve his basketball game—it merely adds insult to injury. Given the continued struggles of the ADHD parent, it isn't surprising that the non-ADHD parent often becomes the overfunctioner. Attempts to shift some of the load to others can result in disaster or it takes more time to teach and monitor than to do it oneself, so the pattern continues. This dynamic will persist until the non-ADHD parent becomes overloaded, burned-out, and resentful.

Perhaps this is why households with ADHD, especially if more than one family member has it, tend to be characterized by conflict, anxiety, noise, and disorganization. When anger and chaos are more the norm than the exception, the parents are likely to blame themselves and each other, making the situation even worse (Phelan, 2002). ADHD people, especially the hyperactive/impulsive ones, tend to be louder than other people—not only yelling in anger, but also in sudden outbursts of enthusiasm or excitement. They do more general banging and knock down more things. This constant barrage of noise can be overwhelming for those who need quiet time.

The problematic relationship dynamics don't end if the marriage does. If the non-custodial parent has ADHD, he is likely to be labeled as the bad guy, irresponsible, and unreliable, despite his best efforts. He may compensate by playing the role of the fun parent who doesn't enforce limits in the same way the custodial parent does. This may come easily to him but it also further angers the custodial parent who bears most of the parenting burden when it comes to setting limits and keeping the children on track, leaving her feeling undermined and powerless (Weiss et al., 1999). As a result, the parents may become even less able to communicate in a civilized manner.

I had a client who complained vehemently about his ADHD ex-wife's unwillingness or inability to ensure that their son completed his homework when he stayed with her. This father was understandably concerned about his son's welfare but felt powerless to change his ex-wife's behavior—and moralistic about the need to do so. She admitted that she needs to do better, but she also believed, much to the father's frustration, that a few missed homework assignments aren't the end of the world, an understandable position given her own academic history. This typifies the difference in priorities between divorced parents where one has ADHD.

Prognostic Indicators

This chapter has discussed the many and varied ways that ADHD can have an impact on someone's life. Much of this has focused on undiagnosed and untreated ADHD, although much of the same, to a lesser degree, can probably still be said for those who have had some treatment. This section summarizes the factors that tend to lead to more negative or positive outcomes. Obviously, no single factor is as predictive as a combination would be. For many adults with ADHD, this list will serve more as a basis for understanding or explaining the past, whereas for younger adults or children with ADHD, this list may serve as a reminder of the importance of early intervention.

The following items have been correlated with more negative outcomes for those with ADHD (Ellison, 2002):

- More severe ADHD symptoms and/or comorbid conditions

- The presence of aggressiveness or conduct disorder

- Social or adaptive impairment beyond that which stems from the ADHD itself

- Traumatic events

- Lower socioeconomic status to the extent that it creates additional psychological and emotional strain on the family

- Family instability, such as divorce/separation

- Parental psychopathy and/or alcoholism

By contrast, the following items have been correlated with more positive outcomes for those with ADHD:

- Treatment has a mitigating effect (Ellison, 2002). Earlier and more intense treatment probably leads to better outcomes.

- Lack of impulsivity (Goldstein, 2002), which makes the child far less likely to have comorbid oppositional defiant or conduct disorder, compared to children with the combined subtype who are more aggressive and intrusive, and hence rejected (Barkley & Gordon, 2002). The presence of either of these comorbid conditions will exert a powerful negative influence on the person's development.

- Greater intelligence (Ellison, 2002), in that more raw intellectual power partially compensates for some of the lost efficiencies resulting from the ADHD.

- Special talents, interests, and experiences that build self-esteem (Ellison, 2002).

- An environment that promotes structure and predictability (Nadeau, 2002).

- A school or work environment that accommodates ADHD traits (Nadeau, 2002).

- Social support from family and friends who accept the negative and appreciate the positive in the person (Nadeau, 2002).

Few of these negative and positive prognostic indicators should be surprising. Moreover, research has shown there are certain predictions we can make based on the subtype that characterizes the person. In general, children with ADHD-C are more likely to be male, oppositional, and aggressive; they are more rejected by peers; have lower self-esteem; and are more depressed, all of which certainly fits together. By contrast, those with ADHD-PI are more likely to have math-related learning disorders; suffer more from internalizing disorders, such as anxiety or depression; have relatives with more internalizing problems; are shyer, more passive, and more withdrawn with peers; have less well-developed social knowledge; and possibly are less responsive to stimulant medication (Barkley, 2006d). Taken together, these prognostic indicators carry forward from childhood into adulthood, setting people up for certain outcomes that are more likely than others.

Conclusion

This chapter is intended to provide an overview of the many ways that ADHD can impact someone's life, as well as the lives of family, friends, and coworkers. Some of the ways are obvious and well-known, others are more subtle. It's important for a therapist working with an ADHD adult to have a solid understanding of these myriad consequences of undiagnosed and untreated ADHD, if the therapy is to be as effective as it could be. These adults have suffered a great deal over the course of their lives, not only from the direct consequences of their ADHD-based behavior, but also from the secondary effects of explaining to themselves why they continued to do things that clearly did not work. In the integrative treatment model that follows in the next section, psychotherapy will be targeted to address these specific sequelae.

I began this chapter with an illustrative e-mail from a potential client. I will end it with another e-mail, as well. This particular client was referred for an evaluation by his current therapist who suspected the client had ADHD but wanted a second opinion to be sure. I met with him for a two-hour diagnostic interview and concluded that indeed he did have ADHD. I explained the integrative treatment model and sent him back to his psychiatrist to start him on something for the ADHD to supplement the antidepressants he was already taking. Although this sounds like a relatively straightforward undertaking, this client's difficulty with completing this process provides a window into his difficulty with getting most things done. After all, he brings his ADHD to his treatment, just as he brings it to everything else in his life. As I said about the opening e-mail, this client's struggles are rather typical. Really, the only thing that's noteworthy here is that I got it as an e-mail at a relevant time. I performed my evaluation in mid-June and this e-mail arrived in early October, more than three months later.

I had been wanting to contact you for a while now but seems like there has been a constant stream of little interruptions. This is how things like this often go for me. Since I last contacted you there have been a few events but very little has actually changed. I saw my primary doctor in late August. He thought my blood pressure was low enough (140/80) to give some ADD medication a try ... as long as I monitored the pressure myself. Then I saw my psychiatrist a few weeks later and after a long discussion and what seemed like a difficult decision, she gave me some samples of Strattera. Then things got a bit tricky. Before I started I needed to get a blood test that my primary doctor wanted done. Originally just a routine check (liver, cholesterol, etc.). I had some slightly elevated liver numbers in the past but he did not think it was anything serious. My psychiatrist and I decided the best route was to get this test before I started the Strattera and then get another test after I was taking the Strattera.

When I left my psychiatrist's office I felt a little confused and concerned if all this was going to really be the best way to proceed. But then ... also ... about that time I was running low on my blood pressure medication and had submitted for a 90-day mail refill. The refill was running late in arriving and I did not want to start the Strattera while there was a risk that I might run out of the BP med for a few days before I received it. So I waited ... and then the blood test slipped a little too. Then I had a minor accident with my car (long story) the week before Labor Day and I had to deal with getting the car repaired. That really threw things off for a good 2 weeks. I had a hard time dealing with starting new medication, etc., while still concerned about getting my car fixed ... and I was pretty busy with work ... and a few other minor things were going on.

Finally around the middle of September things seemed to settle down a little bit ... and then I get into these modes where I hate to start stirring things up again. Meanwhile the blood test has slipped. I think about doing it and then forget. I have to fast before it. My psychologist has also been away for the past few weeks. I last saw her on Sept 5th ... and I see her tonight. So ... I am at a point right now where I need to get in for the blood test and then start the Strattera ... but for whatever reason it is not as easy as it sounds to do. I am supposed to see my primary doctor in 3 weeks so I definitely need to get the blood test before then.

Does all of this sound confusing? Actually, I have felt reasonably good for the past 2-3 weeks but just not getting a whole lot done. I guess we'll see where we go from here after I see my psychologist tonight.

The Strattera didn't do much for him, kicking off another round of delays and appointments with his psychiatrist. It was eight months after our evaluation that he was finally started on Adderall, which is what he is taking now.

PART II

The Integrative Treatment Model

The goal of treatment is to help ADHD adults be "more consistent, predictable and independent" (Goldstein, 2006, October). As with many diagnoses, but perhaps even more so, the greatest improvement comes from an integrative treatment approach. Not everyone needs or receives all of this, but it is an ideal to strive for. The four parts of the integrative treatment model espoused in this text include the following:

1. **Education** to increase the client and family's understanding in order to reduce unproductive blame and increase the likelihood of success with preselected strategies more likely to be successful.

2. **Medication** to reduce the negative effect of symptoms on functioning.

3. **Coaching** to help the client develop better habits at work and home to create a variety of successes and build feelings of competence by suggesting specific strategies based on a thorough understanding of typical ADHD strengths and weaknesses.

4. **Psychotherapy** to address the effect of undiagnosed ADHD on the client's self-image and self-efficacy, as well as comorbid conditions and willingness to try new strategies.

Although medication treatment for ADHD is perhaps the best-known treatment and can be quite helpful in reducing the core symptoms of inattention, hyperactivity, and impulsivity, this doesn't usually translate directly into full improvements in daily functioning, such as in the areas of time management, organization, planning, and self-esteem (Ramsay & Rostain, in press). Of course, it's these functional deficits that directly cause suffering and therefore they are what drives clients to seek treatment. This is where the other three pieces of the integrative treatment model come in—or, as the saying goes, "pills don't teach skills." Medications treat the core symptoms of ADHD, whereas education, coaching, and therapy address the side effects, emotional sequelae, and/or comorbid conditions that come from a lifetime of undiagnosed and untreated

ADHD (Murphy, 2006). By treating the core neurological symptoms, medications can be thought of as improving functioning from the bottom up, whereas psychosocial techniques are a helpful top-down adjunct, by addressing functional problems, modifying negative thought patterns, and building coping strategies (Rostain & Ramsay, 2006b).

In practice, there may not be any clear lines between education, coaching, and psychotherapy, but it helps to break them apart for discussion. You may find yourself alternating between looking at the past and the present in a fluid way—as I like to say, "We can't leave the past in the past if it's still happening in the present." By helping your clients achieve greater success today, you help them move beyond yesterday's failures. Both coaching and therapy are necessary, but neither is sufficient. You can't make ADHD adults feel better about themselves through therapy if they are still experiencing the same problems that made them feel so bad in the first place. Merely offering strategies, however, will not be sufficient if your clients don't fully apply themselves and use those strategies because of pessimism about the outcome or interfering comorbid conditions. Each treatment method is more effective when accompanied by the others.

Basically, treatment involves three goals, of which the four parts of the integrative treatment model are the means to those ends:

1. Identify through education and coaching those strategies that are most likely to be helpful.

2. Help clients, through coaching and therapy, to work on functional improvement by pushing themselves to use those strategies, even if it means cutting across the grain of where their natural tendencies lead them to. This is often much easier to accomplish with the right medication regimen.

3. Help clients, through therapy, to accept that certain skills will never become strengths and that they have many other good qualities. This is easier if they make some progress in other ways and can avoid or remove themselves from situations that are too likely to be problematic. For example, I could take a million music lessons and would never gain the ability to play by ear—that is simply not a skill I am destined to master.

As elaborated at length in chapter 3, The Impact of ADHD on an Adult's Life, ADHD deficits will have a direct or secondary effect on virtually all aspects of the client's life. Fortunately, the gains made from treatment will have similar direct and secondary effects.

Part of your work may involve helping clients to seek out environments that better match their strengths and weaknesses. What you can't achieve by internal changes, you may accomplish through external changes. This may bring up the possibility of going against societal or familial expectations, particularly in areas or families with high academic expectations that the ADHD adult simply cannot achieve. For example, it may be wiser to advise these clients to go to college part-time or take time off first—or maybe not even go at all.

There are no quick fixes for ADHD. Rather, treatment is an ongoing process that requires a consistent input of energy if gains are to be maintained. Treating ADHD is much like managing diabetes—it's less of a destination than a lifestyle. It may, however, be similar to working with clients with a history of chronic depression or bipolar disorder. Clients may take long breaks from treatment, but then reengage as their life circumstances and demands change.

Perhaps more so than treating children, adults may respond better to psychosocial treatments because they are more aware of their difficulties and therefore more motivated to work on them (Safren, 2006). Unlike past treatments that addressed only part of the puzzle, by employing an integrative treatment approach, you can put that motivation to better use.

CHAPTER 4

Education as a Therapeutic Technique

Because most people tend to view ADHD symptoms as something they should be able to control, and therefore feel bad about when they don't, education about the effects of undiagnosed and untreated ADHD on an adult's life is crucial for the newly diagnosed. As with most mental health conditions, but even more so, you need to help your clients to understand it, frame it as something treatable, and instill hope and optimism for the future for them to become sufficiently motivated to work at and follow through with their treatment program (Murphy, 2006). In fact, such education is almost universally agreed on as the necessary first step in treatment (Ramsay & Rostain, in press). This education can be provided directly in session or through recommended books, articles, or websites.

Whereas therapy with ADHD kids may focus primarily on behavior modification instituted by parents and teachers, a large part of the therapeutic work with ADHD adults involves helping them to reconceptualize their identities in light of their having ADHD. With greater understanding, it becomes easier for adults to deal with the cognitive, emotional, and self-esteem problems. Therefore, therapy with ADHD adults must include an educational element to remove the unproductive self-blame the client may feel (Hallowell, 1995). To assist in this process, the following client handouts are available for download on my website, www.TuckmanPsych.com.

- ADHD: Not Just for Kids Anymore

- Is the Problem ADHD or Motivation?

- ADHD & Couples

- Integrative Treatment for Adult ADHD

- ADHD Resources

ADHD's history as a diagnosis perfectly captures the difficulty that many people have in understanding it. In 1902, George Still called it Moral Deficit Disorder to explain the seeming inability of these children to do the right thing. Based on the name he chose, his assumption was clearly that the children's behavioral deficits were caused by a lack of morals, motivation, or desire, rather than lack of ability. This highlights the interesting ethical question of our responsibility for our actions and two errors in logic that people often make.

First, there is the moral fallacy in which people are blamed for their biologically based symptoms, under the assumption they have some control or choice over them. Second, there is the biological fallacy in which people are absolved of all responsibility for their actions if there is a biological basis for their disorder (Weiss, Hechtman, & Weiss, 1999). Of course, some sort of middle ground is probably more appropriate for situations in which there are elements of both biology and free will. Education helps ADHD adults to understand the nature of the biological challenges they face while maintaining their responsibility to address those challenges. Therefore, despite their additional struggles, it is still incumbent on these adults to find success and happiness.

How Education Helps

The process of educating an adult with ADHD works at two levels, the emotional and the pragmatic, both of which are equally important. The emotional level involves reframing the *attributions* your client has made of his lifetime of ADHD difficulties. That is, how does the client explain his difficulties to himself? The pragmatic level involves teaching your client about ADHD in general so that he can create and implement better strategies for dealing with life's challenges. These two are obviously interrelated in that the client is more likely to feel better about himself if he can achieve some successes in the present, but he is also more likely to attempt those new strategies if he can reframe past difficulties in a less pejorative way; a way that provides him with some hope for something better.

The Emotional Aspects of Education

The emotional aspects of education address the misattributions based in the moral fallacy, thereby neutralizing the resulting unproductive blame, guilt, shame, and frustration. The popular book on adult ADHD is appropriately titled, *You Mean I'm Not Lazy, Stupid, or Crazy?!* (Kelly & Ramundo, 2006) because without ADHD as an explanation for these problematic behaviors, those labels are, unfortunately, what you're left with. Related to this, education also challenges the pointless "shoulds," such as, "I should be able to remember to do these things." That may or may not be true, but since it doesn't happen, it's better to work on accepting these limitations without continued self-flagellation, which doesn't lead to any real improvements.

The saying "Would you rather be right or happy?" captures this mind-set nicely. In other words, the client may be right that she should be able to remember better, or at least it's not a point worth arguing, but being right won't make her happy if she continues holding herself to an unachievable standard. Therefore, ultimately, it may be wiser to let go of this notion and try to come to some acceptance of her limitations.

This brings us to the secondary psychological features of undiagnosed and untreated ADHD. A lifetime of feeling different from others, of experiencing far more struggle compared to peers, and more failures and disasters has predictable effects on the client's self-esteem, self-efficacy, motivation, and outlook on life, which often leads to comorbid depression and anxiety. For that reason, part of educating the client involves discussing how a neurological condition can lead to predictable psychological sequelae. The often negative meaning that's made of the problems stemming from ADHD deficits, and the resulting negative feelings, is the insult added to the injury. By finally understanding why her past worked out the way it did—and could not have worked out differently—the client is better able to accept what needs to be done to improve her life in the present. The secondary psychological characteristics are then separated from their neurological underpinnings in a way that offers some possibility of a different interpretation of those primary symptoms, as illustrated in the following dialogue with a client in her late thirties who had just been diagnosed.

Client: I never did as well in college as I thought I should have. I mean, I did okay, but I had to drop a bunch of classes like halfway through the semester when it became obvious that I couldn't rescue my grade. I made up most of the classes in the summer when there weren't as many people around.

Therapist: Actually, that's really typical of undiagnosed ADHD college students. You should feel really proud of yourself that you got out in four years. I have a lot of clients who took five years or more, or had to come back later to finish, if they ever did.

Client: I always felt really self-conscious that my friends seemed to have a much easier time of it than I did. Even now, I still feel embarrassed about it.

Therapist: The thing is, college is a really hard place for untreated ADHD folks. Being smart and meaning well isn't always enough. There are a million distractions and no one there to keep you on track. It takes really good skills and habits to keep track of everything, plan out your time, juggle short-term assignments with the big papers due later, and all that other stuff.

Client: Yeah, I always felt like I was scrambling just to keep up. It's not that I didn't want to do the work, it was just that every noise in the dorm was distracting and everything else seemed more interesting. And then the end of the semester hit and I went into panic mode to get everything done. It was awful, and I would always promise myself to not do it this way again, but I always did.

Therapist: That kind of procrastination is classic for ADHD college students. Of course you know that you're going to pay the price later, but the distraction of the moment is still more powerful than the fuzzy long-term goal. That's the way your brain is wired. The immediate thing will grab your attention much more than the far away thing.

The Pragmatic Aspects of Education

Education also works at a second level, the pragmatic one. That is, knowing that someone has ADHD suggests certain strategies are more likely to be effective, making them more likely to improve problematic behaviors. This is the whole point of diagnosis, whether for mental health treatment, medical care, or even auto repair—it helps to provide a short list of appropriate interventions rather than having to shoot blindly. Therefore, there's a cost to both missed and mis-diagnoses in that the interventions tried are less likely to be helpful. Many ADHD adults have sought treatment previously that did not explicitly address their ADHD, making the treatment less beneficial; so, predictably, they may not be optimistic about trying another intervention. Therefore, knowing that they are dealing with ADHD now, and that they are working with a therapist who is knowledgeable about it, means that this go-round is likely to prove more helpful. If more of the same tends to lead to more of the same, then perhaps something different will lead to something different.

How and When to Educate

In practice, education takes a nonjudgmental and problem-solving approach that doesn't get bogged down in addressing past wrongs. Rather, it's focused on helping the ADHD person, the romantic partner, and family members to understand some of the negative/angry responses he received in the past and how to avoid such responses in the future (Weiss et al., 1999). It's important for the client to participate in the brainstorming process that will combine your knowledge of ADHD with his knowledge of his strengths, weaknesses, and life circumstances. This results in a greater emotional investment from the client because the solutions come partly from his own input, which builds his self-esteem and also models a process that he can apply elsewhere.

Some of the education will take place in session as a quick aside based on what the client is reporting. For example, when a client describes a situation where she logged onto a conference call late because she didn't notice the passage of time, you might say something like, "Lots of people with ADHD have trouble remembering ahead to do something without a reminder." Alternatively, you might use a mini-lecture explaining that ADHD is often associated with a poor sense of time, particularly when the person is absorbed in whatever she is doing in the moment. Note that given ADHD folks' short attention spans it's best to limit your explanations to less than two minutes unless you can see that the client is right there with you.

You can also recommend books, magazines, or websites that the client or family can read outside of session—see the appendix for a list of resources. You can also provide copies of articles or information sheets of your own or someone else's making. Many of these are provided on my website, www.TuckmanPsych.com, and are available for free download. Because one of the soft signs of ADHD is a tendency to start many books but to finish few, it may be better to recommend more circumscribed readings to not set up the client for yet another failure. Alternatively, you can give her permission ahead of time to skip around, skim as needed, or to read several books at one time in order to keep her motivated and at least reading something about ADHD. In fact, we once joked during an adult ADHD support group that it would be easy to write a book for adults with ADHD since all the writer needs to do is write the first half and then repeat it, because few readers with the disorder would ever make it to the second half!

Although most of the educating is done at the beginning of treatment, occasionally it will come up again as clients' lives evolve and they face new situations (Murphy, 2006). These can either be externally driven events, such as the birth of a child or a job change, or internally generated, as the client makes progress in the treatment and begins to address new issues.

Involving Family Members

Many romantic partners and family members will complain that the ADHD affects them at least as much as it affects the ADHD adult because they often feel they must play rescuer and provide a safety net. Too many tasks fall to them—especially the boring ones. Unfortunately, there's usually a fair bit of truth to their complaints, even if their self-righteous anger can make them seem unsympathetic.

The client may call on you to set his family straight, hoping that your professional authority will cut through their skepticism and tendency to write off any explanations as yet more excuse-making. Although I wouldn't necessarily call this true family or couples therapy, I very much find it helpful and appropriate. Some basic education about ADHD can drastically reduce the amount of tension in the household.

For most ADHD adults, it will be their romantic partner who is included in the treatment. However, because of their greater need of being bailed out than their peers, some ADHD adults may still be overly dependent on their parents for financial or logistical support, so you may want to see their parents or other family members. However, for the remainder of this section, I use the term "romantic partner," but the same lessons apply to any family members. Educating romantic partners eliminates their attribution errors and all the mistaken assumptions that arise from it, such as:

- "If he cared more about his family/job, then he would do better."

- "She's just selfish and self-absorbed and doesn't want to do better."

- "I'm powerless to do anything different and it will never get better."

- "It's my job to be the responsible one and hold it all together."

Given their degree of suffering, it's important to involve romantic partners in the treatment. However, because they are likely to be at least partially burned-out by this point, engaging them in anything that involves extra work on their part will be a tough sell. Therefore, the sales pitch should point out that their attendance in sessions would be a relatively small investment that will lead to greater returns in saved effort and increased happiness later.

The more the romantic partners know about ADHD, the easier time they will have in restoring balance in the relationship and reversing the overfunctioning that they are likely to be doing. Just as the ADHD adult will gain more from treatment if she is actively involved in the process, so too will the others in her life. As tempting as it might be to expect the ADHD adult to overcome all her challenges by herself, unless her partner does at least some of the work, a mutually satisfying relationship will be difficult to achieve.

Working with the romantic partner will follow two separate but interwoven themes. The first is helping the ADHD adult to become more effective. For example, telling the ADHD adult in the morning to bring home a gallon of milk after work is unlikely to achieve the desired result. However, a quick call on the cell phone during the ADHD adult's drive home is far likelier to get the job done. The partner may complain that she shouldn't have to be responsible for that reminder call, and perhaps she shouldn't have to be, but the reality is that such a small additional effort will probably result in milk in the fridge. This is that "Would you rather be right or happy" mind-set again. By framing it as a choice that the romantic partner makes in the pursuit of her own happiness, rather than being at the mercy of her partner's ADHD, the non-ADHD partner is more likely to accept the small additional effort. Here's another example:

Client: It really bugs me to have all his stuff cluttering up the table in the entryway to our house.

Therapist: I know it doesn't look great to have that stuff there, but his ADHD makes it hard for him to remember it all if he puts it somewhere else.

Client: But why should I have to look at his stuff? Why can't he just work on remembering it?

Therapist: You guys could try having him just remember it, but that hasn't really worked so far. So, you can either find a way to live with having his keys, wallet, cell phone, and work folders out on the table or you can go back to the mad scramble every morning when he tries to find it all or forgets some of it. The choice is yours, but the third option of having it all put away and him still remembering to take it all isn't really an option here.

Of course, both partners need to have a say in these negotiations, but it works better if they are both informed about the ADHD partner's particular deficits. This allows them both to take an active problem-solving style to address these difficulties collaboratively rather than one partner trying fruitlessly to convince the adult with ADHD to do better.

The second theme in working with romantic partners is that of picking their battles and letting natural consequences do their thing. This topic is covered more fully in chapter 7, Adapting Psychotherapy for the ADHD Adult, but there is an educational element to this theme as well, in terms of letting some things go without worry or resentment. This is easier to do with the issues that don't directly impact the non-ADHD partner as well. For example, leaving it to the ADHD partner to get out the door on time to meet a friend or make it to a club meeting. This shouldn't be the non-ADHD partner's problem and therefore doesn't deserve comment. Of course, if the ADHD partner does ask for help with the task, then that invites the other partner's reactions.

Creating an ADHD-Friendly Lifestyle

It's almost too obvious to say that everyone benefits from a stable, rejuvenating lifestyle. Of course, actually living it is another thing. More so than for many other people, this is especially true for those with ADHD who often seek out or find themselves in a lifestyle that worsens their ADHD—chaotic, unstructured, or too extreme. For example, I had a client who routinely stayed up too late, either working on the computer or watching TV, and then, predictably, he felt awful and was less productive the next day. He knew this was causing problems, but he couldn't manage to break the habit on his own, partly because of poor time management through the workday and partly because of a "consequences-be-damned" attitude at the time.

A fair bit of time across many sessions was spent with this client on the habits and cognitions that maintained this unhealthy pattern. As with many ADHD adults, his unbalanced lifestyle was both a symptom of ADHD difficulties and an exacerbation, making it important to address both, as well as making it more difficult. Unfortunately, maintaining a balanced and structured lifestyle requires certain skills that many ADHD adults don't have or are weak on; so, it may always be an uphill struggle to achieve such a lifestyle, but that doesn't mean they shouldn't try. I wish I could claim that this client made significant and lasting improvements in this arena, but at least he did make some progress.

Part of the process of creating an ADHD-friendly lifestyle involves working with the client to become less reactive and more proactive, to learn to look ahead to stressful times and plan accordingly to avoid crunch times (Nadeau, 1995a), and to manage the small daily stuff that snowballs into big problems. This requires them to use their time well and have their possessions generally organized. Unfortunately, disorganization of time and disorganization of possessions usually go hand in hand, in that if people are too busy, they don't have the time to organize, yet being disorganized wastes a lot of time, making them even busier.

Some ADHD adults may simply give up, claiming that there's no point to it anyway, since it's impossible for them. Others may embrace the chaos and claim that they prefer it that way. If this is the position they are taking, at least outwardly, it's worth spending some time discussing the price they pay, both tangibly, such as late fees on bills and frayed social relationships, as well as psychologically, such as feeling constantly overwhelmed, dreading and avoiding certain items/tasks, and so on, to increase their motivation to begin to address their problems with organization. Given the likelihood that their many attempts in the past were failures, they will be much more willing to make another attempt if you can convince them that, with proper treatment, perhaps they can be more successful now than they were in the past.

Client:	My office is a total mess. It takes me ten minutes to find anything and some things I just don't find. At least not when I'm looking for them.
Therapist:	It's frustrating wasting time like that, especially since you have so much work to do.
Client:	I know. My boss is getting on me about it too. I told her that I would try to get it organized, but I don't think she believes me anymore. So maybe that's good judgment on her part!
Therapist:	Sounds like it! But I don't know, maybe it's not so hopeless. The trouble before was that you kept doing the same things that didn't really work the first time, but since it was all you had, you just kept on doing it. But now that you know about your ADHD and you are taking meds that seem to help, maybe this time can be different.
Client:	I don't know. I've gotten a lot of advice in the past. Everything works for about a day—and then nothing. I'm not really sure why I bother.
Therapist:	Well, if more of the same just leads to more of the same, it makes sense that you're skeptical. You should be. But the difference now is that you know about your ADHD and can use strategies that are more likely to be effective.
Client:	I guess.
Therapist:	If more of the same leads to more of the same, then you gotta do something different to get something different. Well, coming in and talking about your ADHD is different. Checking out those websites I told you about is different. Taking the meds is different. Maybe there are enough new inputs that the outcome can be different.

An ADHD-friendly lifestyle emphasizes (Nadeau, 2002):

- Good sleep patterns

- Proper diet

- Frequent exercise

- Controlled substance use

- Tolerable stress levels

- Appropriate stimulation

- Supportive social relationships

- Career choices that cater to strengths without playing on too many weaknesses

I like to call this the New Year's resolution stuff—the changes that we all aspire to. As hard as it can be for anyone, it's especially difficult for those with ADHD in that the planning and consistency required are very much an uphill climb for them. Despite the additional work required, ADHD adults are better off getting on track sooner rather than later, before they have made life choices that are difficult to undo or recover from (Nadeau, 2002)—like early marriage and divorce, incomplete education, having children before being ready to handle the responsibilities, and substance abuse.

In order to avoid reinventing the wheel, the pursuit of an ADHD-friendly lifestyle needs to take into account what is known about ADHD in general combined with the specific preferences of the individual. For example, certain habits will be much more difficult to ingrain—like taking half a minute every hour to do some deep breathing and focusing, as a way of fighting stress. Although it's a fine idea, it's not likely to be used enough to really be all that helpful. Instead, it will become yet another failure, yet another task they didn't do, yet another indictment of their character.

Of course, in seeking an ADHD-friendly lifestyle, clients shouldn't interpret this to mean a sterile, routine-driven monotony. Even assuming that this actually was a goal, the odds of your clients being able to maintain or even tolerate such a routine are about zero. I use the analogy of doing the all-celery diet to lose weight—at best, it lasts about half a day and then you overcompensate with French fries because it was so awful. By the same token, the ADHD adult needs to find a lifestyle that both works and can be maintained. This means it will probably be something of a stretch, but it can't be impossible.

Although we all need to accomplish certain tasks, we all also need to give the devil his due, whatever that means to us personally. For example, rather than feeling guilty about stimulus-seeking behavior, the better approach is to learn to choose these outlets wisely (Hallowell, 1995), both the "what" and the "when." If stimulus-seeking behavior is a part of your client's life, she needs to learn to live with it, even if it's different from the way some others may live.

Another helpful suggestion may be to learn to balance activities that emphasize an end product with those that focus on process. Because ADHD folks are weak on reliably creating an end product, they may feel as though they spend too much of their time defending themselves from others' frustrations. By contrast, process activities, like playing music or taking hikes, are inherently rewarding and provide a valuable escape. Knowing this, the ADHD adult should seek a balance between these two types of activities to be more successful overall (Goldstein, 2006, October). Once again, as I reiterate often through this book, the treatment will be most successful when it works to improve functioning and also increase self-acceptance.

For an adult with ADHD, one of the most important protective factors is the choice of the right romantic partner or even the choice not to have one (Nadeau, 2002). Like most of us, many ADHD adults pick partners whose strengths complement their own weaknesses. This can work out well if the ADHD person doesn't allow himself to become overly dependent, leading to resentment from his overfunctioning partner. An impatient and critical partner, whether she starts out that way or becomes that way, will only increase the ADHD person's self-doubt and self-blame, neither of which will make him more productive.

Of course, the opposite scenario also exists in which the ADHD adult finds a partner who is worse off than she is so she can be the more organized, healthier, higher functioning one and thereby avoid criticism. This can be a very exciting relationship but too often, as the crises mount, it can become too exciting.

The best choice of partner is someone who is organized yet still appreciates the ADHD person's good qualities without being overly stressed by the forgetfulness and disorder that come along for the ride (Nadeau, 2002). All romantic partners are a package deal—along with the good qualities, you also get the bad ones. This includes the in-laws. A good sense of humor and the ability to let go of things make any relationship easier, but perhaps especially so when one partner has ADHD. See chapter 7 for a more in-depth look at working with couples in treatment.

Succeeding in the Classroom

Although ADHD creates demonstrable difficulties in every aspect of life, it's often the classroom that creates the greatest angst for those with ADHD. Unfortunately, the traditional classroom environment exacerbates many ADHD weaknesses. Perhaps even more unfortunate, success in later life is often at least partly dependent upon prior academic performance. Most immediately, admission to college is based on grades in high school, even if those grades are not an accurate measure of ability—but they are a good measure of performance.

I often find myself discussing clients' academic performance with them. This can be done retrospectively by helping them understand how ADHD impacted their ability to meet requirements and thereby reinterpret the reasons for their struggles and failures. However, with other clients who are either currently in college or going back after some time away, it's important to speak with them about how to better set themselves up for success. You will need to work with your clients on these matters so that the future doesn't repeat the past's failures. Some schools offer more support to students with ADHD and other disabilities—and some are not supportive at all—so this is worth checking out before even applying. A phone conversation with a disabilities counselor will probably give a more accurate picture of what to expect than the various printed materials will.

Regardless of their age or situation, to be successful, ADHD college students need to do the following (Richard, 1995):

- Understand ADHD and its personal impacts

- Understand and use their best learning styles and strengths

- Understand their rights and become effective self-advocates—this is especially true for college students who had highly involved parents

- Develop strategies for social interactions

- Learn to use effective learning strategies

- Learn and implement methods for time management

- Develop a realistic sense of personal competence and confidence

- Know and use university and community services that provide counseling, health, and academic accommodations

Ultimately, the student needs to learn to do all of the items above by himself, but, initially, there may be more guidance from a faculty advisor or disabilities counselor who takes over the job formerly performed by parents and then helps the student to make the transition to doing these tasks by himself. The role of the advisor/counselor includes offering resources and logistical support, facilitating and monitoring the student's follow-through with plans to obtain and/or provide information from and/or to various sources, and assisting the student in identifying the issues important to decision making (Richard, 1995).

A Smoother Transition into College

I have seen far too many young ADHD adults who went off to college wholly unprepared for the sudden lack of external structure. Not surprisingly, they ran into significant trouble making it to their classes and getting their assignments completed, on time or even at all. Assuming that an ADHD high school student is accepted by a college that he would like to attend, the transition from living at home to living in a dorm can be too much to do all at once, so it can be helpful to break it into smaller, more easily mastered steps.

For example, the student could take some classes at a local college while still living at home and perhaps working part-time. Parents are thereby available to assist with time management, such as sleep and wake times, activities the student engages in, and the timing and extent of studying; temptation management regarding the many enjoyable but nonacademic activities that college students indulge in; and financial management of a weekly, or monthly, budget.

ADHD students will also need extra help with planning a balanced course load, including realistic scheduling in terms of avoiding morning classes or loading up for a long stretch without a break, as well as ensuring that prerequisite and required courses are taken in the appropriate order. All of these issues can be better managed with some assistance from parents living under the same roof, rather than several hours away, thereby reducing the likelihood of disastrous end-of-the-semester surprises. Of course, the goal is that the young adults with ADHD will gradually take over all of these tasks, but in the meantime, it's better to not set them up for what is too likely to be a failure. The trick for the parents is to strike just the right balance between assisting and infantilizing, a line that's often easier to see after the fact.

For those undiagnosed students who made it into college, they may not have made it out with a degree. Rather, they may have taken a wide array of classes, with too many failed or dropped courses. Predictably, this may have led many of them to assume that they can never be successful in school, thus closing off vocational opportunities that require a degree. It's important to work with college-age students and older students returning to school to help them see that, with proper treatment, perhaps the outcome can be different this time; that so many of their inputs have changed that perhaps the results can change too.

For clients who are burned-out on academics, in addition to striving to improve their functioning, it may be necessary to reframe college as a necessary evil, since the classroom is not where ADHD adults can best showcase their talents. Therefore, they just need to survive it, and get their degree without taking their struggles too much to heart. It's just a bad fit, and not necessarily one based solely in the problems of the ADHD adult. As awful as college classes or homework can be, it's only temporary and the better jobs later in life are worth the suffering now. Blunt honesty, rather than sugarcoating, may be called for with these clients.

College may be more palatable if the person works part-time and goes to school part-time. That way she won't be overwhelmed with academic demands, but will also have regular, daily reminders about why she is slogging through her classes. I have a saying that there's nothing like a crummy job to convince someone of the value of an education. Whether a student goes to college directly after high school or attends/returns later in life, her living situation is worth thinking about and discussing. For many ADHD students, the greatest challenge is resisting temptation and staying current with studying, rather than getting lost in socializing or extracurricular activities. Therefore, an off-campus apartment may provide fewer distractions than dorm life would. Also, buying into the college's meal plan will spare the student the additional headaches of shopping and cooking, while also keeping her socially connected.

Older Students

Students who are returning to college or attending for the first time may feel self-conscious about being older than their classmates. The age difference can feel like tangible proof that they are inherently flawed and that they should have earned their degree on time like everyone else. As I have told many clients in this situation, going to college at eighteen is easy; it's showing up later that really takes guts. This is an important reframing. It can also help to point out that once they have obtained their degree, regardless of when they get it, most people will simply assume that they got it at age twenty-two. However, these reframes tend to go over better when there is a certain amount of reality supporting them. Therefore, it can be beneficial to attend a university that enrolls more older students, where your client will feel less out of place.

Finding a Better Career/Job

Work is one of the major activities that adults engage in—and it is one of the major places that ADHD adults run into trouble and thereby seek help. Therefore, you are likely to often find yourself discussing work matters with clients. The discussion may involve the following:

- Seeking a less pejorative understanding of why previous work difficulties arose

- Addressing difficulties that clients are currently experiencing

When ADHD adults run into trouble meeting requirements at work, it's usually because the job doesn't fit their strengths rather than due to incompetence or lack of effort. This is why career counseling, whether official or part of the therapy/coaching discussions, can be especially helpful for ADHD adults; it matches them with positions that are better fits for their strengths and weaknesses (Murphy, 2006). Sometimes, the problem is the career as a whole, sometimes it's just the specific job or workplace.

For example, an audience member at one of my traveling seminars spoke of a client who was a lawyer in private practice. Although well-meaning, his ADHD interfered with his ability to reliably stay on top of his various responsibilities as a self-employed attorney—he was missing court deadlines, forgetting to put clients' money into escrow accounts, and running into other difficulties. After some serious reflection, he decided to work as the in-house lawyer for a large company, a much better fit for him because he did not have as many cases coming at him at once and had better administrative support. He was bright enough to be a lawyer and he enjoyed the work, but he needed to find a better setting in which to showcase his innate talents and acquired skills.

Some environments or careers will never be a good fit for some employees, so they need to take more drastic action than this lawyer did. In these cases, a formal vocational assessment can be really useful, provided it's performed by a professional who understands the specific challenges of ADHD. A thorough assessment should include: interests; strengths and skills; temperament and personality type; and values and needs. A superficial evaluation that doesn't consider these factors sufficiently will be essentially worthless, so if it is to be done, it should be done well. The right job match needs to take into account ADHD-specific factors such as the optimal noise and visual stimulation levels; the physical demands needed to sustain attention and interest; how much supervision and authority can be handled; and coworker or customer interactions (Crawford & Crawford, 2002). For more on career counseling, see chapter 6.

Unfortunately, ADHD adults may not have done as well academically as they could have. Or they may not have completed the course work for desired degrees, which can create barriers to entering the jobs that would better match their abilities and interests. Perhaps as a result of these closed doors, ADHD adults are three times more likely to be self-employed owners of small businesses than other populations. This may be based in a preference for personal autonomy outside of structured work settings that have expectations for performance and achievement and require appropriate interactions with colleagues and people in authority (Young, 2000). This doesn't necessarily reflect the sometimes proclaimed notion that so many ADHD adults are entrepreneurs because they are better at thinking outside the box, so much as it reflects the hard reality that some ADHD adults need to start their own businesses in order to succeed at the level to which they aspire.

For clients who make impulsive decisions or are overly motivated by a desire to avoid difficult or boring situations, you may need to work with them on exploring other options and to discuss whether their initial choices are really worth doing—for example, is better pay worth less security and satisfaction in the long run? You may also have to help them assess potential jobs/careers by comparing how they rank in terms of opportunities for self-fulfillment, money, openness to self-improvement, authority style, and variety (Crawford & Crawford, 2002).

Predictably, many ADHD adults handle their career trajectory in the same way they handle other long-range planning activities, which is to say more reactively and impulsively than would be optimal. They may not have taken the time to really consider what they would be interested in over the long haul. Alternatively, they may not have been willing to invest the time to pay their dues (e.g., by doing the menial work in the less interesting entry-level jobs) and make it to the level that would be satisfactory. For that reason, some of the educational process may involve discussing their academic and vocational history, how they came to be in the position they are currently in, whether that's the best place for them, and what their other options may be.

Conclusion

The purpose of education is to normalize and reframe the client's neurologically based ADHD difficulties, and to remove the unproductive guilt and blame that serve simply to blunt motivation. This is not empty "feel-goodism" that makes the client feel better for a while, until reality comes crashing in. Education provides explanations, not excuses, a crucial distinction. Explanations help the client and family members to better understand how to set up the client for success, rather than repeating strategies that never worked particularly well. The goal is to make the client successful, regardless of or despite his ADHD. As I sometimes tell my clients, "The rest of the world doesn't care about your ADHD; they just want you to meet your obligations." Therefore, excuses that help the client to shirk requirements often carry unacceptable consequences given out by those who are less forgiving—and even the most sheltered ADHD person will encounter some of these people, meaning that it's only a matter of time before trouble strikes.

Having said that, there are indeed times when discretion is the greater part of valor and clients are better served by not pursuing certain paths that simply will stress too many of their weaknesses. However, to make this choice consciously is fundamentally different from making it out of fearful avoidance. It's a matter of self-knowledge and a realistic appraisal of the probabilities. This means finding the middle ground between unsubstantiated optimism and self-protective pessimism. For those whose history includes a lifetime of ADHD struggles, this can be a slippery point on the continuum.

CHAPTER 5

Medications and Other Biological Treatments

Even though most of the people reading this book will be therapists who don't prescribe medications, we still need to know about and understand the effects of commonly used meds and their side effects. We tend to see clients more frequently than prescribing doctors do, as well as perhaps seeing them before they decide to try medications since therapy may be seen as a kinder, gentler treatment. As a result, we are often in a position to answer questions.

Without stepping beyond your limits of professional competence, medication issues such as whether to try them, ambivalence about using them, and compliance are certainly beneficial topics of discussion in therapy. The client's thoughts and feelings about medication are handled in the same way as any other topic; that is, by examining the underlying assumptions and meanings so that the client can make a fully informed decision (Ramsay & Rostain, 2005b). This processing is probably more necessary for mental health conditions than it is for physical ones, in that many people have mixed feelings about taking medication for difficulties that they may feel they should be able to have more control over.

In addition, because we see our clients more frequently than prescribing doctors do, it's important to know when to send the client back to the prescriber during those times when the dose or medication needs to be adjusted or when intolerable side effects are occurring. This may be especially true when the medications have been prescribed by nonpsychiatric physicians who may be less sophisticated about the subtleties of a medication regimen. It's been my experience that these physicians tend to underdose, based on either overcautiousness or on using childhood dosage ranges for adults who weigh significantly more. As a result, the adult may get some benefit but would do even better at a higher dose. However, given the shortage of psychiatrists, we will often be in the position of needing to educate the prescribers in order to advocate for our clients. This may be especially so with primary care physicians; don't assume that they have optimized the client's medication regimen if your observations tell you otherwise. If gentle suggestions based on your experiences with other clients don't suffice to convince the prescribing doctor, then it may be worth suggesting that the client go through the extra effort and cost of finding a psychiatrist experienced with adult ADHD who can develop a more effective medication regimen.

The Medication Controversy

Most of the controversy around the treatment of ADHD involves the biological treatments—the possible overuse of medications or the questionable utility of alternative or complementary treatments. Of course, given all the controversy and hype that has surrounded stimulant medications, perhaps it isn't surprising that ADHD seems to have more than its fair share of natural or alternative treatments on the market, including many that claim to cure the disorder. Although numerous nontraditional treatments are available and touted as effective, there is still much research to be done to validate these treatments and determine if any live up to their promised benefits. The fact that people spend as much as they do on these untested treatments speaks to their suffering and clear desire for relief. It unfortunately also speaks to the success of those who are waging a campaign of misinformation about the diagnosis and its treatments.

The use of medications, particularly the stimulants, for treating ADHD gets a bad rap because of those who misuse the diagnosis as a way to gain an advantage or duck responsibility, as discussed in chapter 1. The notion that medications are the silver bullet for what ails you (or sometimes what isn't actually ailing you, in the case of misdiagnosis or inappropriate use of medications) casts a shadow of doubt on those who truly need and benefit from medication. Restricting everyone's access to medications simply because a small minority is misusing or abusing them is akin to banning the sale of alcohol because some people cannot control their drinking. As a society, we need to find the optimal, but still imperfect, balance between denying those who need medication and prescribing it too easily to those who don't really need it.

THE MORE ACCEPTABLE STIMULANT?

It's interesting that the stimulants evoke so much controversy, yet so many people in our society avidly consume a stimulant every day in the form of caffeine. Despite its clear use as a cognitive-performance enhancer and mood elevator, few people take a moralistic stance toward caffeine the way they do toward the stimulant medications for the treatment of ADHD. After all, no one says to the people standing on line at the local coffee shop that they should just use willpower instead (Brown, 2005).

Let's first get some of the myths and facts out on the table.

Medication Myth	Medication Reality
They are addictive.	They are not addictive when appropriately prescribed and taken.
They cause people to abuse more drugs later.	They actually cause people with ADHD to abuse drugs less.
They cause heart attacks and sudden death.	After a careful review of the data, the FDA decided that this isn't true (Connor, 2006a).
They are performance enhancers for people who want an edge.	They help those with ADHD to function more like those who don't have it.
They are overprescribed.	There are still many ADHD children who are not receiving treatment—and only about 10 percent of ADHD adults are being treated (Biederman, Spencer, Wilens, Prince, & Faraone, 2006).

Medication Benefits

As a psychologist, my preferred mode of intervention is talk therapy. However, I've found that for my ADHD clients, medications just make everything so much easier and can create such a significant improvement in their lives, that I often recommend they at least try them. Medications address the core symptoms of ADHD, which translates into secondary functional improvements in the various domains of life, just as the core symptoms create secondary deficits and suffering.

The benefits of medications have been described in various ways, including the following:

- Creating a sense of clarity

- Calming a busy mind

- Bringing everything into focus

- Being able to think about only one thing at a time

The meds open a small space between thought and thought in the case of distract-ibility or between thought and action for hyperactivity or impulsivity. Where prior to medication there was too little space to really consider whether something would be the best course of action, the medicated ADHD person has the option to make a more con-scious choice. This doesn't mean that she will necessarily decide to do "the right thing," but now, if she would like to, she can.

In the cognitive arena, performance on simple and complex learning tasks, per-ceptual efficiency, and speed of symbolic and verbal information retrieval all improve with medication. Studies with adults have found that stimulants lead to improved atten-tion span and decreased distractibility, restlessness, and impulsivity (Connor, 2006a). Stimulants improve vigilance, reaction time, task persistence, work productivity, working memory, handwriting, and fine motor speed and general coordination (Barkley, Fischer, Smallish, & Fletcher, 2003). Functionally, this leads to improved performance in the following areas (Robin, 2002):

- Planning

- Organizing

- Prioritizing

- Time management

- Sustained attention

- Attention to detail

- Tolerating repetition/monotony

- Resisting distraction

In the social realm, stimulants improve the following (Robin, 2002):

- Frustration tolerance

- Anger management

- Tact

- Patience

- Ability to follow through

- Waiting one's turn

- Listening

- Intimate communication

- Picking up subtle social cues

- Managing restlessness

- General inhibitory control

All of these have significant positive repercussions. Not surprisingly, the appropriately medicated ADHD child tends to evoke fewer negative reactions from caregivers and peers, potentially leading to further secondary gains (Connor, 2006a). Although not as well documented, the same can be said for adults.

It's worth noting that medications for ADHD don't cause anyone to do anything he doesn't want to do; rather they allow him to more easily, reliably, and accurately do what he wants to do. Analogously, wearing glasses doesn't automatically make someone into a better student. However, without glasses, if the student can't see the writing on the blackboard, she doesn't have the option to copy information from it. With glasses, she has the choice to copy the information, but may still choose not to. The medicated ADHD adult still has to do the hard work of changing habits, but he has a better shot at being successful. There is a saying that "pills don't teach skills," but they do make it easier to learn those skills. This is where the other interventions of the integrative treatment model come in. Medications are neither mind control nor silver bullet, but they do help.

Although stimulants are the most widely studied medication prescribed to children (Ramsay & Rostain, 2005a) and there is a wealth of good studies on the effects of medications on children with ADHD, there are many fewer studies on adults with ADHD (Prince, Wilens, Spencer, & Biederman, 2006). However, clinical practice shows parallels in terms of benefits, risks, and side effects, with perhaps one exception. It appears that perhaps adults may not exhibit the same high response rates as children do, although this may be partly due to such extraneous factors as greater heterogeneity of the study population and insufficient dosages to achieve maximum clinical effect (Connor, 2006a). However, regardless of whether the potentially reduced response rate is caused by confounding variables in the empirical data or whether it truly exists, for most clients, medication is still worth a trial.

THE DIABETES ANALOGY

When discussing medications with clients, I often use diabetes as an analogy of a disorder that can be managed in its milder forms by lifestyle changes, such as diet and exercise. However, there is a limit to the gains that can be made with these methods alone in more severe cases and, therefore, insulin is used to control blood sugar levels. Similarly, medication may be necessary to help manage a client's ADHD symptoms and thus allow the lifestyle changes to have a greater effect. I also point out that if the client had diabetes, presumably there would be less resistance, stigma, or feelings of failure associated with taking medication, so perhaps there is less need to feel guilty for taking ADHD medications.

No medication is perfectly safe, including aspirin, so for each client it's a matter of balancing the potential benefits with the potential risks and side effects—but there are risks and side effects with untreated ADHD too, as discussed at length in chapter 3. This side of the equation must also be taken into account to make a fully informed decision. Similarly, no one would willingly undergo the intense side effects and significant risks of chemotherapy if the alternative risks of cancer were not so threatening. Ultimately, it's a personal decision based on the client's level of impairment and suffering, willingness to try to change some of the other aspects of treatment, and desire for improvement.

For example, I had a client who clearly had ADHD but who also had suffered through a manic episode the previous year. Because she had retired from her job and therefore did not need to function at the same level, she decided that she did not want to go on a stimulant, especially since it would have entailed first going back onto a mood stabilizer to ensure that she would not have another manic episode. On the other hand, I have other clients who could not imagine giving up the benefit that they get from their medication.

You may need to discuss with your clients the relative risks and rewards of medications, as well as of remaining unmedicated. For example:

Client: I don't know about this whole medication thing.

Therapist: It's a personal choice, but I usually recommend that clients at least try medication. It can just make everything so much easier.

Client: It kind of feels like cheating, like I'm not trying hard enough.

Therapist: But you've been trying hard your whole life already! ADHD is bigger than good intentions. If you could have mastered this just by trying harder, you wouldn't be sitting in my office now.

Client: I guess. But it still seems like a drastic solution.

Therapist: It is, but sometimes that's what it takes. And besides, meds are no magic potion that makes everything perfect. You still need to do the work, but you're more likely to be successful when properly medicated.

Stimulant Medications

The stimulants are the oldest and most commonly used medication for ADHD. They were first used for behavioral problems in children and adolescents in 1937. They are also the most thoroughly studied ADHD medication. The first double-blind, placebo-controlled clinical trials of dextroamphetamine and methylphenidate were conducted in the 1960s. Over 200 controlled trials have been completed since then (Connor, 2006a), more than 15 of them in adults (Wilens et al., 2006).

Despite claims that stimulants are overprescribed for children, several professional committees have concluded that there is little evidence of this (Barkley et al., 2003). Although there are certainly some children who were misdiagnosed as having ADHD and thus prescribed a stimulant, there are also many children with ADHD who are not receiving any treatment. Despite the fact that critics focus their attention on the use of stimulants, the real problem is one of misdiagnosis in that the person—child or adult—wouldn't be receiving a stimulant had they been diagnosed properly.

Children and adolescents show a robust response rate of approximately 70 percent to stimulants. Unfortunately, the figures for adults may not be as high (Prince et al., 2006). This may partly be due to the fact that adults tend to have more comorbidities because they have had more time to suffer the slings and arrows of living with ADHD and therefore present a more complex puzzle for treatment.

One drawback to using the stimulants has less to do with their mode of action than it does with the logistics surrounding their use. Because the stimulants have the potential to be abused when taken in excess, they have all been classified as Schedule II medications. This means that the prescribing doctor cannot give the client samples or phone in refills, which is particularly unfortunate given ADHD adults' greater tendency to lose prescriptions and run out of medications. For Schedule II medications, the client must present a new paper prescription for each month's batch of pills and the prescribing doctor cannot add refills to the prescription.

Some prescribing doctors, to spare their clients from monthly office appointments, will give them several one-month prescriptions that are postdated—for example, June 10, July 10, and August 10. Although physicians are not supposed to postdate prescriptions, one can understand why they would want to help their patients in this manner.

Commonly Used Stimulants

There are essentially two different types of stimulant currently in common use—methylphenidate (the Ritalin family) and mixed salts of amphetamine (the Adderall family). All of the formulations within each family have the same active ingredient but it's packaged differently within the pill. At the risk of sounding like a product placement, I often use the analogy that of these two drug families, one is like Pepsi and the other like Coke—they're both colas and very similar, but not exactly the same. Also, you can buy each in various sizes of cans and bottles—or buy the pills in various dosage strengths, which last for different amounts of time—but the basic stuff inside is the same regardless of the packaging.

There is a new member of the amphetamine family, Vyvanse (lisdexamfetamine dimesylate), that is likely to be quite successful in the market. Because it was just released at the time of this writing, I don't have much to say about it, but preliminary reports seem promising. It is a prodrug, meaning that it is a precursor to the biologically active form and is activated inside the digestive tract.

Most of the current formulations on the market that would be prescribed to adults are listed in the form Common ADHD Medications that can be found later in this chapter, as well as on my website, www.TuckmanPsych.com.

Two of the formulations deserve special comment. The first notable one is Focalin. Many molecules exist as two similar *isomers*, which are mirror images of each other. Without getting into the chemistry, studies have demonstrated that one of the two isomers of methylphenidate is more biologically active, thereby suggesting that a more powerful effect could be had from purifying the medication to only this one isomer. As a result of this purification process, Focalin is prescribed at half the dosage that the other methylphenidate products are, yet it retains the same efficacy (Prince et al., 2006). Although the manufacturer hoped that this "purer" form would lead to fewer side effects, this has yet to be shown (Connor, 2006a). However, it may be that some people will show a different side effect profile with Focalin than they will to the other methylphenidate products, so it may be worth trying for those who have too many side effects on the others, but it can't be said that, as a whole, Focalin is superior.

The second notable formulation, Daytrana, is the first skin patch developed for the treatment of ADHD. It contains methylphenidate in a gel suspension that allows the medication to be absorbed through the skin. The patch can be worn for up to nine hours and then provides an additional three hours of coverage once it's removed. Although the patch was developed primarily for young children who don't take pills easily, it has the added benefit of being potentially less abusable (Editors, 2006) because it leads to a slower absorption into the bloodstream, and for that reason doesn't produce a high. In addition, the patches can't be shared because they won't stick to the skin again after they have been removed (Connor, 2006a). One potential downside of the patch is that it can take up to two hours to begin taking effect, meaning that the person goes through half of the morning without coverage, although a low-dose short-acting pill can also be taken to kick-start the benefit.

Cylert (pemoline) and Dexedrine (dextroamphetamine, are older stimulants that are no longer widely used.

Mode of Action

Both methylphenidate and amphetamine block dopamine and norepinephrine reuptake, resulting in more neurotransmitter available in the synapse to activate the postsynaptic receptors. However, amphetamine also causes the presynaptic neuron to release additional neurotransmitter, resulting in even more neurotransmitter in the synapse (Prince et al., 2006).

Although methylphenidate and amphetamine are very similar, because they have somewhat different mechanisms of action on the neurons, some people have a differential response to the two (Prince & Wilens, 2002). To expand my Coke and Pepsi analogy further, some people prefer Coke, others prefer Pepsi, and still others like them both. A rough rule of thumb for using these stimulants is that approximately one-third of people show a preference for one, one-third for the other, and one-third show an equal response. This preference is based on both the attainment of the desired effects as well as the severity of side effects. Since we can't predict someone's response to one based on her response to the other, it may be worth doing a trial of both, even if the client got a good response from the first one. However, if someone does not get a good response to one or suffers intolerable side effects, it is certainly worth encouraging her to try the other family (Connor, 2006a).

Dosing

Medication plasma levels, in and of themselves, have not been shown to correlate to response in adults, so dosing is more about response and tolerability than body weight (Prince & Wilens, 2002), although body weight is still used as a general guide for the starting dose. For example, a 250-pound adult will be started at a higher dose than a 60-pound child. Higher stimulant doses tend to yield greater symptom improvements (Connor, 2006a), although they also tend to exacerbate the side effects and cause additional ones. FDA dosing guidelines tend to be overly cautious and should not be used as absolute limits. The prescribing doctor needs to consider a patient's weight, especially in larger adults, and refractory symptoms that may require a higher dose to show improvement. Therefore, the dose should be based on clinical efficacy (Prince et al., 2006).

The prescriber should start the client at a low dose and then increase it every three to seven days until a response is noted or adverse effects emerge. If a client experiences significant side effects with the first administration of a higher dose, she can go back to the previous dose for a few more days to allow additional accommodation before going up to the higher dose, if necessary. In general, because the extended-release formulations spread the dose out over a longer period, a larger dose will be needed to provide adequate coverage. For example, a client may take double the dose of Adderall XR as he does of a single dose of plain Adderall in order to reach the threshold at which the medication is helpful.

Dosage Considerations

There are two factors to consider with dosages: (1) What are the peak blood levels of medication and (2) how much the person takes over the course of a day. Provided that the client doesn't reach problematic levels of either of these factors, he can tailor his regimen to his response to the medication and the demands he faces throughout his day. In addition, because different extended-release formulations have different delivery mechanisms, it makes sense that they may yield different blood plasma level curves over the course of the day and, therefore, some clients may have a somewhat different response to one formulation over another.

Because the shorter-acting formulations have a shorter duration of effect, they need to be taken twice or three times per day to cover the client throughout the day. This is especially true for adults who need to function at work during the day and then at home in the evening. As a result, the advances in the field of stimulant medications haven't been in creating newer, better stimulants, because they are already quite good, but rather in the development of extended-release versions that eliminate the need to take additional doses.

It's difficult for anyone to remember to take a midday dose, but it's especially so for those with ADHD. Therefore, unless cost is a factor, I always recommend that clients use one of the extended-release formulations. Not only do they last longer, they also tend to have a smoother dose curve throughout the day since the shorter-acting formulations can create spikes, and then a rapid clearing of the medication from the body, often causing a "crashing" feeling.

However, even with the extended-release formulations, it may still be necessary or advantageous to add in a small dose of a short-acting formulation of the same medication in the afternoon. This will carry the effect a little further for those who either metabolize the initial dose too quickly or need to function at an optimum level into the early evening. Taking another extended-release version later in the day could carry the effect too far, making it difficult for the client to fall asleep that night. Even with the extra dose, you will want to encourage your clients to do the tasks that require the most focus or accuracy early in the night while they have more medication in their system. For example, it may be better to pay bills early in the evening and to leave folding laundry for later.

The benefits from dosing higher and later to extend the functional window need to be balanced by the side effect of insomnia that can occur if the blood levels are too high when the person gets into bed. There is an even more extended-release form of Adderall slated for release in 2008, which is supposed to have up to a sixteen-hour effect window. This will be marketed to adults who need medication coverage into the early evening, thereby sparing them from having to add the second dose in the afternoon.

Whereas some people will take an additional dose to extend the positive effects of the medication, some people will take it to prevent the side effect of *rebound*. That is, some people experience a negative reaction if the medication blood levels decline too rapidly at the end of the dose curve. This is covered more fully below, but a small amount of a short-acting formulation can help to smooth out the drop in blood levels and eliminate the rebound effect. Some clients may find that extended-release formulations don't provide enough medication at the start of the day. This can be remedied by taking a small dose of immediate-release medication along with the extended release.

There has been some debate on whether tolerance develops to the stimulants, resulting in decreased therapeutic effect and thus necessitating a higher dose to achieve the same result. However, research from the National Institute of Mental Health's Multimodal Treatment Study of ADHD found that the therapeutic benefits continue at a given dose and that tolerance does not develop (Prince et al., 2006).

To the extent that tolerance is found in clinical practice, it may be due to some amount of true biological tolerance, as well as to other factors, such as decreased compliance with the medication regimen, weight gain which would necessitate a higher dose, unrelated life changes that require greater performance, such as a job change or the birth of a child, the development of a comorbid condition, or altered expectations for the person's functioning whereby the person is held to higher standards when her medicated performance has improved (Connor, 2006a).

Contraindications

Although the stimulants are generally quite safe and easy to manage, as with anything there are some contraindications. For healthy adults with no contraindicating psychiatric diagnoses, such as anxiety, bipolar disorder, or psychotic potential, a short-term trial of stimulants is quite safe (Weiss, Hechtman, & Weiss, et al., 1999). For healthy adults, the cardiovascular effects of increased blood pressure and heart rate that can result from the use of stimulants are negligible, although those at risk for hypertension may show greater changes (Connor, 2006a). However, it has been found that if elevated blood pressure is already normalized with medication, then Adderall XR leads to only minor and insignificant increases. If an elevation does occur, it will often return to baseline within a week, so it should be monitored, but medication should not automatically be withdrawn. Although methylphenidate wasn't tested in this study, the results presumably apply equally (Wilens et al., 2006).

Much greater caution should be exercised when treating those with a compromised cardiovascular system; that is, when treating clients who have untreated hypertension, arrhythmias, or known structural heart defects (Prince et al., 2006). Related to these cardiac issues, the concern has been raised over the last few years about a possible connection between stimulants and an increased risk for sudden death. A subcommittee at the FDA issued a recommendation that Adderall XR receive a black-box warning, the strongest warning that can be imposed short of pulling a medication off the market. This was in response to reports of the heightened risk of sudden and potentially fatal cardiac events, based on the sudden death of twelve children and adolescents (Connor, 2006a). In fact, Canada's equivalent of the FDA did briefly pull Adderall XR from the shelves.

BLACK-BOX WARNING

The stimulants carry a black-box warning from the FDA. The methylphenidate products have one warning and the amphetamine products have another, but similar, warning. Both warn of cardiac issues, including structural abnormalities and high blood pressure. In addition, the methylphenidate products have a warning about these medications' possibility of worsening other psychiatric conditions, such as bipolar disorder. Meanwhile, the amphetamine products have a potential for dependence if misused. Although these are legitimate risks, the language used could have been much stricter, implying that the FDA decided that the risks were uncommon and that the potential benefits were justified.

Following careful review of all of the data, including some assumptions that not all incidents would have been reported, it was determined that in all of the small number of cases, there had been undiagnosed or untreated underlying cardiac issues before the administration of the Adderall XR. Or there were other complicating factors, such as heat exhaustion, near drowning, fatty liver, and others. In addition, the incidence of these unfortunate events, out of thirty million Adderall prescriptions written between 1999 and 2003, was not significantly greater than it was in the general population not taking Adderall XR and, therefore, probably not due to the medication (Connor, 2006a).

Without minimizing the tragedy of these events for the families affected by them, these very low probability events must be weighed against the daily certainty of less dramatic difficulties from untreated ADHD. Therefore, for those without a known cause for concern, the benefits tend to be larger than the risks. The analogy I often use with clients is that despite the potential dangers of getting into a car accident, I still get behind the wheel. Of course, I also put on my seatbelt and generally try to drive safely, so this balancing of risks and rewards is universal to all the decisions we make.

Substance Abuse Risks

Some have claimed that using stimulants, even when appropriately prescribed for someone who truly does have ADHD, leads to later substance abuse; but this has not been supported by the research. Rather, research finds that stimulants are not addictive, if appropriately prescribed and administered (Weiss et al., 1999) and can even lead to less substance abuse. The claim that stimulant use leads to later substance abuse is probably based on a flawed reading of the data. What has been found is that those who were prescribed stimulants in childhood are at greater risk for later substance abuse in adolescence and adulthood. In fact, these two are positively correlated, which is where these critics run into trouble—they assume that the correlational relationship is causal, that the stimulants cause the abuse. Unfortunately, they are missing the third factor here, which is that those children with more severe ADHD are more likely to both be prescribed a stimulant and to later abuse illegal substances. It is the severity of their ADHD that drives their later abuse, not the fact that they were prescribed a stimulant.

Interestingly, the research proves exactly the opposite of what these critics claim— longitudinal studies have shown that unmedicated ADHD children are at a significantly increased risk for substance use in adolescence (Faraone et al., 2000), but youths treated with stimulants have a little more than half the risk of later substance abuse compared to those with untreated ADHD, an extremely significant finding (Wilens, 2004). In other words, the use of stimulants actually has a protective effect against later substance abuse.

This isn't surprising, since the medication may help the person to live a more successful life and thus have less need to self-medicate. It can mitigate the effects of ADHD symptoms on demoralization, poor self-esteem, and academic or occupational failure (Wilens, Faraone, Biederman, & Gunawardene, 2003). A thirteen-year prospective study also found that the use of stimulant medication does not contribute to substance abuse in adulthood (Barkley et al., 2003).

Medicating a Substance Abuser

Stimulants do not cause people to abuse substances, but what about those who already have a history of substance abuse? Understandably, many prescribers are leery of giving a potentially abusable medication to those with a history of substance abuse—and especially to those who are currently using. This is due partly to a fear of intentional misuse, but prescribing doctors may also be concerned that the stimulant will give the client a "taste" for illicit drugs again, a fear that may be shared by the client. This is unfortunate, given the relatively high comorbidity of ADHD and substance abuse, because it means that this rather sizeable subpopulation is denied access to the most effective medication treatment. I would like to be able to say that I have never had a client abuse his prescribed stimulant, but, unfortunately, I have had at least two whom I know of who did abuse it and ran into serious trouble with it, so I understand the hesitation of prescribers given the risk of legal liability.

One guideline to use is to require that a client with a history of substance dependence demonstrate at least one to two months of stable sobriety before a stimulant is prescribed (Murphy, 2006). It can also help to have a reliable family member dispense the medication, thus ensuring that it is taken as prescribed. Some clinicians have found that substance abusers

INTENTIONAL ABUSE OF STIMULANTS

There have been media reports, fueled by critics of ADHD as a valid diagnosis, that have tried to make the case that the use of stimulants leads to later substance abuse. This is based on the idea that stimulants can be abused when taken in excess. However, the fact that something can be abused doesn't mean that it is, in fact, abused; at least by most people. Although I certainly don't want to defend the actions of those who do abuse prescription medications, I also wouldn't throw away the baby with the bathwater by saying that all stimulants should be banned simply because a small minority uses them inappropriately.

The fact that some people will fake the diagnosis solely to gain access to the medications speaks more to the need to do a thorough evaluation than it does to anything inherently problematic with the stimulants. By the same token, the fact that underage people will try to drink alcohol should not lead us to ban or condemn alcohol in general, so much as it should motivate bar owners to be more careful about carding their customers. The same goes for those who divert their medications to others who don't have ADHD—they should first be educated about the dangers of giving away (or selling) prescription medication, and then they should be punished if they do it anyway. Once again, this is more about individuals' decisions to subvert the prescription process than it is about the medication itself.

It's important to get an accurate picture of the client's substance use, by asking some or all of the following questions:

- What substances have you used?

- When?

- How frequently?

- How much?

- What was your most recent substance use?

- Have you ever abused stimulants or other uppers?

- Is there any evidence or information from other people to corroborate the history you gave?

use fewer drugs when they are started on stimulants because the medication enables them to lead more successful lives and thus have less psychological need to get high to self-medicate their troubles.

The other option is to be more selective about the type of formulation that is prescribed. Although stimulants as a class are abusable, there are significant differences in the abusability of the various preparations and how they are taken. The high that is sought by abusers results from a rapid spiking in the blood plasma levels of the stimulant. Therefore, modes of administration that lead to faster absorption give more of that high; that is, injecting and snorting result in a more powerful high than oral administration does. In addition, short-acting preparations give more of a high than longer-acting sustained-release preparations do, because the absorption is concentrated into a smaller window of time. The abuse of stimulants is also dose-dependent, meaning that the person must take several times the normally prescribed amount.

Although the stimulants are definitely abusable, the person must intentionally abuse them, because they will not create a high when taken in the method and at the dosage prescribed. Fortunately, the longer-acting preparations are generally less abusable and also preferable in terms of symptom-reduction profiles. In addition, there are some new formulations in the pipeline that will be less abusable. For example, there is a new version of dextroamphetamine called Vyvanse (lisdexamfetamine dimesylate) that is biologically inactive if snorted or injected since it must pass through the gut in order to be activated. Nonetheless, it will still be classified as a Schedule II medication.

Because a relapse, even one that wasn't intentionally initiated, can have drastic consequences, the client with both ADHD and comorbid substance abuse has a difficult decision to make. Each client and prescriber will have her own risk tolerance and willingness to consider various factors, but preferably, of course, it will be a well-informed decision, whatever is decided.

Managing Side Effects

Fortunately, the stimulants' side effects generally tend to be mild and tolerable and often subside within a couple of weeks as the person adjusts to the medication.

Compared to some of the very serious side effects of some of the other psychiatric medications, the stimulants are quite easy and straightforward. With the exception of clients who have a compromised cardiovascular system or a strong history of substance abuse, most feel that the benefits outweigh the side effects. Any side effects that do appear often can be managed by adjusting the dose or changing the timing of administration. As is common with most medications, as the dosage goes up, so do the frequency and intensity of side effects.

If side effects do emerge, it's important to ask about their timing—if they arise an hour or two after taking the medication, then they are probably caused by the medication and can be addressed by changing the dosing regimen or formulation such that the peak blood levels are lower or by changing to the other stimulant family. If they arise at the end of the treatment window, then they are probably due to either rebound, which is addressed below, or to a reemergence of ADHD symptoms as the medication effect wanes (Connor, 2006a).

It's interesting to note that some clients, or family members, will feel that the medication makes the client's ADHD symptoms worse, when, in fact, what it is doing is providing a greater contrast between the treated and untreated symptoms. For example, a client who does pretty well during the day may appear to do much worse in the evening when the medication has worn off, but this is because the family has shifted their frame of reference and take the medicated state to be "normal" and the unmedicated state to be an exacerbation when it's really a return to baseline.

Types of Side Effects

Insomnia. Insomnia can occur if the client takes too high a dose too late in the day, which creates a situation where his blood levels are too high when it's time to go to bed—it's like having a big cup of coffee late in the afternoon. However, many people with ADHD will have preexisting sleep difficulties, so it's important to get a good sense of what the client's sleep pattern was before the medication was administered or what it was during the time when the medication was not taken, to determine what the medications may be contributing to the sleep problems.

There is an imperfect balance to be struck between coverage in the evening versus being able

SIDE EFFECTS? TRY THE OTHER ONE

If the stimulant the client is taking is either insufficiently effective or carries with it too many side effects that cannot be managed with the suggestions below, then there will be no harm in trying a formulation from the other stimulant family. Because their half-lives are so short, most of the medication will have been cleared from the client's system by the morning of the day after it has been administered, meaning that the client can immediately go on to the next medication. This makes it very easy to make quick adjustments and compare the relative benefits and side effects.

to sleep at night (Prince & Wilens, 2002). To the extent possible, it can help to front-load the evening by doing the most demanding tasks early, before the medication effect has dissipated. Interestingly, I have had more than one client who sometimes took a low dose of stimulant to help quiet her mind to enable her to fall asleep.

Appetite suppression. This side effect can be countered by taking the medication after eating breakfast, eating bigger dinners, snacking more, having many smaller meals through the day, and having a large snack just before going to bed (Weiss et al., 1999). This is probably more of a concern in children where reduced caloric intake may have some connection with a possible growth suppression effect. Most adults probably wouldn't mind losing a few pounds.

Edginess, agitation, or irritability. These side effects generally improve with accommodation to an increase in dose, and they are lessened by ramping up slowly.

Irregular pulse, significant tachycardia, or increased hypertension. These can be problematic if excessive, but a mild elevation is acceptable (Weiss et al., 1999). These side effects are generally rare at therapeutic doses (Prince & Wilens, 2002).

Stomachache and headache. These can occur if the medication is taken on an empty stomach, so it's best to take the medication with food, usually at breakfast. A later dose may be taken with a snack (Weiss et al., 1999).

Rebound. This can occur when the medication is wearing off and is marked by irritability, nervousness, or uncharacteristic anger. It is more common with the shorter-acting formulations. Usually, it can be improved by smoothing out the decline in blood levels by prescribing a longer-acting formulation or adding a small extra dose of a short-acting formulation one hour before the end of the coverage period (Connor, 2006a), which makes for an easier transition off of the medication at the end of the day.

Nervousness or jitteriness. These tend to be more likely in premorbidly anxious people. They tend to fade over a few weeks, but can be minimized in the first place if the prescriber starts with low doses and gives the client ample time to adjust to each increase in dosage. It can be helpful to assess whether the nervousness correlates with the blood levels. If it does, the client may be better able to tolerate the discomfort if it is explained that it may be a transient effect of the medication, and that it will dissipate with time. Having a specific and safe biological explanation can reduce some of the attributions that the client might otherwise make of the increased arousal. Ironically, some people feel calmed down and more at peace from the clarity they get from the stimulant (Weiss et al., 1999). In addition to this physiological effect, there is also the psychological benefit of feeling more on top of life's demands and therefore having less to be anxious about.

"Zombie" state.   A zombie-like state can occur if the client is overmedicated, leading her to become overly quiet, withdrawn, and unresponsive. The client may go from inattentive to overfocused and perseverative; from disorganized to preoccupied with arranging and rearranging. Lowering the dose or changing the timing or method of administration to reduce the peak in blood levels should help (Weiss et al., 1999).

Hypomania or mania.   These side effects can occur in those with a tendency toward bipolar disorder—whether it is known beforehand or not. This highlights the importance of doing a thorough diagnostic evaluation to rule out bipolar disorder. If the stimulant does cause an excessive elevation in mood, the stimulant should be stopped immediately and the acute symptoms managed with a mood stabilizer. If the client is willing to continue to take the mood stabilizer, it may then be safe to administer a stimulant again, starting at a low dose and slowly increasing it until a therapeutic level is reached (Weiss et al., 1999), although many prescribers will be leery of attempting this. It may also be possible that once the bipolar disorder has been medicated, the apparent ADHD symptoms may disappear, indicating that the true culprit was the emotional dysregulation and instability arising from bipolar cycling.

Psychosis.   This disturbing side effect can occur in people with schizophrenia or bipolar disorder or upon an overdose (Connor, 2006a) but it is rare at therapeutic doses (Prince & Wilens, 2002). As with manic or hypomanic episodes, those who do experience a psychotic reaction to a therapeutic dose should be withdrawn immediately, and the acute symptoms treated as necessary. Then the client should be monitored closely for a future development of these symptoms, since they strongly suggest a predisposition to these disorders. In these cases, the administration of a stimulant revealed a preexisting tendency.

Tics.   Tics have been commonly cited as a side effect of the stimulants. The data goes both ways on this, but we can probably conclude that stimulants do not cause tics, particularly in adults. It's likely that the presentation of tics is more coincidental with the administration of the stimulant. Alternatively, the tics are noticed more after the person starts the stimulant because family members may be looking for them (Weiss et al., 1999). However, someone with a preexisting tic disorder often will experience an exacerbation of her tics when the medication is in her system. Depending on the severity of the tics and the client's willingness to tolerate them or treat them with something else, such as clonidine or guanfacine, the client may strive to strike a balance between the exacerbation of the tics and the reduction in ADHD symptoms. As with hypertension, this can be one of those dilemmas where neither solution is optimal.

Dizziness.   This side effect may be related to an increase in blood pressure. If the onset of the dizziness seems to correlate with peak blood levels, then cutting the dose or switching to an extended-release preparation should prove helpful by reducing that peak or the speed at which the blood levels rise (Connor, 2006a).

MANAGING STIMULANT SIDE EFFECTS

Although the stimulants are quite safe and generally well-tolerated, you may experience some side effects. Some of these may disappear on their own as your body adjusts to a new medication or a new dosage. Most side effects can be reduced by lowering the dose, but then you may not get as much benefit as you would like, so a balance needs to be struck. The following strategies may be helpful as well. If not, then you may do better by switching to a different kind of stimulant.

Insomnia

- Take your medication earlier.

- If you take a second dose at midday, then reduce that dose.

Appetite Suppression

- Take your medication after breakfast.

- If a big lunch is too much, then eat several smaller meals throughout the day.

- Make up for lost calories by eating a larger dinner or having a healthy snack at night.

Edginess, Agitation, or Irritability

- Start on a low dose and increase it slowly. You can also drop back to a lower dose briefly.

Irregular Pulse, Tachycardia, or Elevated Blood Pressure

- Treat preexisting cardiac issues first before starting stimulant, then adjust as necessary.

Stomachache and Headache

- Take medication with food.

- Change to a different formulation.

Rebound in the Afternoon

- Switch to a longer-lasting formulation.

- Add in a small amount of a short-acting formulation one hour before rebound tends to begin.

Nervousness or Jitteriness

■ Start on a low dose and increase it slowly.

■ Keep in mind that any anxiety feelings are probably just a safe and temporary adjustment to the medication.

Spaced-Out

■ Lower the dose.

■ Change the timing or type of formulation you are taking.

Hypomania or Mania

■ Immediately stop taking the stimulant and contact your medical professional.

■ A mood stabilizer may be necessary to control your elevated mood.

■ Reevaluate whether ADHD is the appropriate diagnosis.

Psychosis

■ Immediately stop taking the stimulant and contact your medical professional.

■ Another medication may be necessary to control your altered state.

■ Reevaluate whether ADHD is the appropriate diagnosis.

Tics

■ Evaluate the degree to which the stimulant is making your tics worse.

■ Reduce the dose to find a better balance between addressing the ADHD and tolerating the tics.

■ Treat the tics with another medication.

Dizziness

■ If you experience dizziness when the medication is at its strongest, then either reduce the dose or switch to an extended-release formulation.

Withdrawal

■ Withdrawal symptoms are unlikely to occur at normally prescribed dosages, but any symptoms should be temporary as your body readjusts.

Withdrawal symptoms.   This effect is not a concern at therapeutic doses, contrary to what some media reports might say. However, withdrawal symptoms can occur for those who have been on high doses for an extended period of time. Likely symptoms will be transient and include fatigue, hypersomnia, excessive eating, dysphoria, and depression (Prince et al., 2006). Obviously, withdrawal symptoms are much more likely to occur among those who abuse stimulants and far exceed the normally prescribed dosages.

Drug interactions.   These are usually mild and not a source of concern. The major exceptions are the old MAOI antidepressants, which can cause serious hypertensive reactions (Prince & Wilens, 2002), but it should be noted that the problem lies with the MAOIs, which have almost completely fallen out of favor because of their potentially fatal interactions. Excessive caffeine intake potentially may reduce the benefits and exacerbate sleep difficulties (Prince et al., 2006) and feelings of jitteriness. Interestingly, though, I have had many clients who found they did not crave caffeine to the same extent they did prior to treatment once they were appropriately medicated.

Nonstimulant Medications

These medications are often seen as less controversial and less problematic than the stimulants because they are not abusable. Unfortunately, they are also often less effective for most clients. As a result, the stimulants are by far the most commonly used medication for ADHD, with a smaller percentage taking Strattera, a handful taking Wellbutrin, and almost no one taking a tricyclic antidepressant. Each of these nonstimulants is covered below.

Unlike the stimulants, which have a specific and limited duration of effect that begins shortly after ingestion, the nonstimulants need to be taken daily for four to eight weeks to achieve full effect. The downside of this is that the nonstimulants don't give the same quick benefit stimulants do, meaning that they require some patience, which is not typically an ADHD hallmark. This delayed response also makes it harder for clients to notice improvements that take place slowly. Taken together, these two factors make it more difficult to titrate the dose precisely. It also means that these medications can't be taken on an as-needed basis and that the client needs to be consistent about remembering to take it every day. However, the nonstimulants provide twenty-four-hour coverage once their effect is showing, which is a distinct advantage over the stimulants.

Strattera

Strattera (atomoxetine) started life as an antidepressant, although it was never marketed as such in the United States. Unfortunately for its manufacturer, it was not found to be sufficiently effective. However, as is sometimes the case in pharmacology, it was given a second chance when it was discovered that it had some efficacy for treating ADHD. It was the first nonstimulant to be approved by the FDA for ADHD and the first medication of any class to be approved for adults with ADHD.

Strattera's mode of action is that of an SNRI (selective norepinephrine reuptake inhibitor)—it selectively blocks the norepinephrine reuptake pump. Based on animal studies, it is also thought to increase dopamine in the prefrontal cortex (Prince et al., 2006). It's assumed that the increase in norepinephrine winds up creating an increase in dopamine in neurons downstream. However, because it doesn't lead to euphoria, there is no potential for abuse (Wilens, 2006). It may be a good choice for clients with comorbid anxiety, mood disturbances, or tics (Prince et al., 2006) who cannot tolerate a stimulant. It can be especially helpful in the fairly significant population who have ADHD and comorbid substance abuse/dependence because, as already stated, it is nonabusable, unlike the stimulants (Spencer, 2006b).

Common side effects include: dry mouth, insomnia, decreased appetite, constipation, decreased libido, dizziness, and sweating. Males may also experience difficulty attaining or maintaining erections (Prince et al., 2006). As with the stimulants, it can kindle a manic episode in those who have that tendency. Twice a day dosing may be helpful in improving the benefits later in the day and reducing side effects (Spencer, 2006b). If the side effects are intolerable, in most patients it's safe to do a rapid tapering off from the Strattera (Prince et al., 2006).

> ## BLACK-BOX WARNING
>
> It should be noted that Strattera carries a black-box warning, the strongest warning that the FDA can put on a medication without taking it off the market. The warning concerns reports of potential liver toxicity, so the prescriber should be contacted immediately if the client develops jaundice, excessive itching, dark urine, right-upper-quadrant tenderness, and/or unexplained flu-like symptoms. Most likely the medication will be discontinued immediately. Despite this rare possibility, routine laboratory tests do not seem warranted. Strattera should also be used cautiously in adults with hypertension and other cardiovascular risks (Prince et al., 2006).

The bottom line on Strattera is that it just doesn't seem to be as effective as the stimulants. For some clients it works very well, but not with the same frequency that the stimulants do. An informal survey of therapists and psychiatrists whom I know supports my experience with the medication in that it is just not as likely to be of significant benefit. Therefore, in my opinion, it should be considered a second-line medication unless there are specific reasons why the stimulants should not be used.

The Antidepressants

As much as Strattera is a second-line medication for ADHD, the antidepressants are a third-line choice, but they do seem to have some benefit for some clients. They can be helpful if the patient has mild ADHD with comorbid depression or anxiety and the prescribing doctor is hoping to kill two birds with one stone. They can also be of benefit for clients with cardiac abnormalities or significant current/past substance abuse where a stimulant is contraindicated.

Wellbutrin, Wellbutrin-XL, and Wellbutrin-SR (bupropion) inhibit the reuptake of both dopamine and norepinephrine (Wilens, 2006). The typical adult dose range is 150 to 450 mg/day. Its side effects include excitement, agitation, increased motor activity, insomnia, tremor, tics, and a potential for increased seizures in those with a vulnerability (Prince et al., 2006). Wellbutrin has been marketed as a safe option for clients with a bipolar tendency in that it is less likely to prompt a manic or hypomanic episode, which would be great for those clients with comorbid ADHD and bipolar disorder. However, it may be that Wellbutrin is not quite as bipolar-neutral as we may have thought, meaning that prescribers should exercise some caution with these clients.

Effexor (venlafaxine) inhibits the uptake of both serotonin and norepinephrine. More study is needed to determine optimal dosing and whether there is an actual benefit for ADHD, but it is sometimes mentioned as a possibility (Prince et al., 2006). Therefore, it should probably be considered a last resort for ADHD at this time.

Stimulants	Nonstimulants
Benefit lasts less than 12 hours	Benefit potentially lasts 24 hours
Can be taken as needed	Must be taken daily
Begins to work within an hour	Can take several weeks or more to achieve effect
Potentially abusable	Not abusable
Quick and easy to titrate dose	Slower and more difficult to titrate dose

Two useful forms are included below (Common ADHD Medications and the Medication Monitoring Sheet). They can also be downloaded from my website, www.TuckmanPsych.com, at no charge.

COMMON ADHD MEDICATIONS

The Stimulants

The stimulants are the most frequently prescribed and generally the most effective medication.

	Methylphenidate family Typical adult dose range is 20–80 mg/day*	Amphetamine family Typical adult dose range is 10–60 mg/day
Short-acting formulations (4–6 hours)	Ritalin Methylin Focalin Metadate	Adderall
Medium-acting formulations (6–8 hours)	Ritalin LA or SR Metadate CD or LA Methylin ER	
Longer-acting formulations (10–12 hours)	Focalin XR Daytrana Concerta	Adderall XR Vyvanse

* Focalin and Focalin XR are prescribed at half the dose of the other methylphenidate products.

The Nonstimulants

These tend to be less frequently prescribed, but can be beneficial especially when the stimulants are contraindicated. In theory, they provide twenty-four-hour symptom coverage.

Strattera (40–100 mg/day)

Wellbutrin (150–450 mg/day)

MEDICATION MONITORING SHEET

You can use this sheet, one per day, to record how a new medication or dosage is working. This can help you and your prescribing doctor find the right medication regimen. This monitoring sheet is short enough so you can fill it in quickly, but it still covers enough important areas to help you judge the benefits that you are receiving from the medication.

Name: _____ Day: _____ Date: _____

Was this a typical day in terms of the demands placed on you? If not, then how was it different?

Inattention Symptoms	Improvement (0 = none, 4 = significant)				
Distractible	0	1	2	3	4
Disorganized	0	1	2	3	4
Poor Time Management	0	1	2	3	4
Forgetful	0	1	2	3	4
Careless Mistakes	0	1	2	3	4

Hyperactive/Impulsive Symptoms	Improvement (0 = none, 4 = significant)				
Feel Restless	0	1	2	3	4
Tendency to Blurt Things Out	0	1	2	3	4

Are you experiencing any side effects? If so, write down those effects below to keep as a record for your therapist and your prescribing doctor.

_____

_____

_____

_____

_____

Other Medications

Other medications have been tried over the years, with limited success. If a medication is not mentioned above, you can assume that no significant benefit has been found and that it should not be considered for the treatment of ADHD, although it may still be necessary for the management of comorbid conditions.

Provigil (modafinil) is used to increase wakefulness in clients with excessive sleepiness due to narcolepsy, obstructive sleep apnea-hypopnea, and shift work sleep disorder. It blocks norepinephrine reuptake and perhaps it also blocks dopamine. After some studies found it to be beneficial for ADHD at higher doses (Connor, 2006b), its manufacturer tried to get an FDA indication for ADHD under the trade name Sparlon. Their application was eventually turned down due to a rare but potentially dangerous side effect, although there was disagreement about its existence in the one subject who displayed it. Although it appears at this time that its manufacturer will not appeal that decision or pursue further applications, it may still be used off-label in the medical community.

Catapres (clonidine) and Tenex (guanfacine) are old antihypertensives that have a calming effect on some people. They can be beneficial for the management of aggression, hyperactivity, overarousal, impulsivity, and sleep difficulties (Connor, 2006b), but not for the inattention symptoms (Brown, 2005). However, since these symptoms tend to fade as an ADHD child enters adulthood, it makes sense that these drugs are used much more commonly with children than with adults.

Polypharmacy

There is a growing trend in psychiatry to use more than one medication simultaneously to treat the same condition. The research behind this is rather limited, which isn't surprising given the many permutations of using more than one medication at more than one dose. Be that as it may, clinical practice often precedes empirical validation, particularly when clinicians are faced with treatment-refractory clients who need more benefit than they can get from a single agent. For example, although it has not been sufficiently studied, combining a stimulant with Strattera seems to be safe, well-tolerated, and effective (Prince et al., 2006).

Encouraging Compliance

If the client does decide to try medication, finding the best regimen will involve working closely with the prescriber by reporting both the benefits and side effects from each new dose or medication. Just as ADHD can affect everything else in the client's life, so too can it affect this process. For example, this population isn't the best at consistency, so ingraining the new habit of taking a pill every morning and possibly every afternoon, as well, can be difficult, which can lead to inconsistent dosing. As a woman from my adult ADHD group joked, "The biggest problem with the meds is that they don't work if you don't take them."

Additionally, this population isn't the best at self-awareness, so it can be helpful to include family members in the medication checks. As one man from my support group said with a smile, "Sometimes my wife asks me if I've taken my meds and it really bugs me, because she's always right." Fortunately, given that the stimulants take effect so quickly, it is often easier to find a good medication regimen than it can be with other psychiatric medications where weeks must pass before the client can see their effect.

Because therapists have more frequent and extended contact with clients than the prescribing doctor does, it often falls to us to help clients maintain their medication compliance, both when it comes to unintentionally missing doses and more resistance-based noncompliance. I emphasize the importance of consistently following the regimen to get the maximum benefit, especially when first trying out a new medication. I also encourage clients to get an inexpensive plastic weekly pill case to help them remember to take their medication as well as to show whether they did, in fact, take the medication this day—no dose and a double dose are both problematic.

Taking a pill, especially when done every day, becomes a completely unmemorable event, making it too easy to remember yesterday's dose as having occurred today or forgetting that they already took today's dose. I encourage my clients to place the pill case somewhere that they can't miss seeing it. Putting it in a drawer dramatically decreases the odds of remembering to take their medication. As will be elaborated further in chapter 6, the coaching chapter, the converse of "out of sight, out of mind" is "in sight, in mind," so clients should be encouraged to leave the pill case out on a kitchen counter or somewhere easily visible. I also recommend that clients should keep a few extra pills at work, in the car, or on a key chain so the day isn't wasted if they realize after leaving the house that they forgot to take their morning dose.

Unlike the antidepressants, which require four to eight weeks of daily dosing to show their full benefit, the stimulants begin to take effect within an hour or two and can therefore be taken as needed, if desired. For example, some clients only take their medication on days that they really need to focus. This rapid onset of action is fortunate, given the impatience common to many with ADHD. The downside of this rapid onset is an equally rapid clearing of the medication, such that most people are no longer receiving therapeutic benefits by the end of the day, meaning that they are probably unmedicated at night and certainly by the next day. As a client once told me, quoting his wife, "Your coworkers get medicated Tom but I don't." The lack of carryover to the next day means it's important to remember to take the medication each morning.

Despite the potential benefits to be gained from medicating ADHD, some clients may resist the idea, for a number of different reasons, usually based more in psychological defensiveness than anything else. Some may see taking medication as a sign of weakness; that is, as a tangible admission of their being flawed. Others may feel that it's better to live with the struggles than to risk disappointment if the medications don't work. Still others may hesitate to engage in the difficult process of facing a lifetime of pain and failure in order to strive for something better. Although these reasons are certainly understandable, they sell out the future to avoid some discomfort in the short-term. This doesn't mean that everyone should try medications, but the decision not to try them should be based more in well-reasoned personal reflection than in defensive maneuvering.

Managing Expectations

Some clients will unrealistically expect the medication to change everything and are disappointed when that doesn't happen, giving the medication poor marks even when it is, in fact, helping. Medication is not a silver bullet, but rather an aid to help those with ADHD apply their efforts more effectively—but they must still apply their efforts. Moreover, if the client has comorbid conditions, such as depression or a learning disability, the ADHD medication will not provide much direct benefit for that, except to the extent that the ADHD is exacerbating the other difficulties.

Other clients will lose patience with a slow titration upwards and bail out prematurely, or not be willing to try a second or third medication if the first doesn't hit the bull's-eye. Still other clients believe that nothing will help or they don't really want to change anything so they take the medication solely to appease a spouse, boss, or parent, in the hope of earning a reprieve from the complaints when the medications fail. Because they aren't looking for benefits, they may not notice them or may even downplay the positive effects the medication is having.

There seems to be some growing evidence that women may experience differing responses to medications during different times of their menstrual cycles as well as when they enter menopause, related to fluctuating hormone levels. This needs to be studied further, but it may be worth keeping in mind with your female clients, especially those who are going through menopause (Brown, 2005).

Nontraditional Treatments

There has been a growing interest in complementary, alternative, holistic, or Eastern treatments across all of the medical and mental health disciplines. ADHD has more than its fair share of these nontraditional treatments, perhaps based in the largely unfounded fears surrounding the use of stimulants. In addition, a general lack of understanding or overly simplistic explanations of ADHD symptoms and etiologies have led some people to believe the quasi-logical rationales behind some of these proposed treatments. Despite the grand claims made by some of these variously marketed materials, there is absolutely no cure for ADHD—like diabetes, treatment means lifelong management.

As for the various proposed treatments, I've seen little that really works in double-blind, placebo-controlled studies. The research that does exist for most of these treatments could be called "pseudoscience" at best, or "junk science" at worst. It's possible that some of these interventions may work for a few people but the results can't be generalized because the intervention didn't address the ADHD so much as it affected something else that looks like or exacerbates ADHD. For example, getting a good night's sleep can help anyone be more attentive at work, whether they have ADHD or not, but I would hardly call that a treatment for ADHD.

Some will say there is no harm in trying these nontraditional treatments, but there is, if it delays more established treatments, wastes financial resources that could be better spent, or causes the person to become pessimistic about more established treatments when the nontraditional approach provides no benefit. All of these choices may lead to unnecessary suffering. My advice to clients is to go with what we know works, then experiment with some of these other interventions if they feel they want to give some alternate options a chance.

In this section I mention some interventions by their trade name. I do this intentionally because I feel that, as clinicians, we have a responsibility to share with our clients what we know works, as well as what we know doesn't. They come to us for our expertise, so to hold back for fear of sounding critical gives the client only half the story. Provided you stay within the boundaries of what the research has found—and not found—then you will be on safe ground.

It's certainly easy to understand that people want relief from their various ailments and that the providers of these nontraditional treatments are stepping in to fill this need. I assume that most of the people touting these nontraditional treatments mean well, and that only a minority are con artists. However, good intentions do not remove the burden of proof or the need to show efficacy. Let's review some of these proposed interventions more specifically.

The Feingold Diet

The basic premise of the Feingold diet is that hyperactive children are sensitive to a variety of food additives, colorings, and artificial products. I'm certainly not defending junk food and, of course, I encourage everyone to eat a healthy diet, but this doesn't mean that the Feingold diet should be used as an intervention for ADHD. Removing these offending substances from the diet supposedly will lead to an improvement in symptoms. However, few studies have found real success in this area and those that did suffered from major methodological or statistical problems. Some well-designed studies found perhaps very small effects of sugar on behavior but only for a very small percentage of ADHD kids (Ingersoll, 2006, October). There are some real sacrifices involved in this diet that are not justified by the small potential benefit (Schab & Trinh, 2004).

Megavitamins and Supplements

Although many nutrients are necessary for good health in the correct dosages, mega-doses have not been found to have any benefit and, in fact, can be dangerous at high levels (Goldstein & Ingersoll, 2005). The idea is that "if a little is good, then more is better," which isn't necessarily true. Our bodies function best when in balance—and they work really hard to maintain this very complicated homeostasis. Too much of something can foul up this balance by affecting other body processes. Taking neurotransmitter precursors like L-dopa or other amino acids like tyrosine and phenylalanine hasn't shown much lasting benefit (Prince et al., 2006). There have been no studies that demonstrate herbal supplements have any efficacy.

Essential fatty acids seem to be the newest contender in the race to find a nutritional cure for ADHD, but more study is needed as to whether there actually is any benefit and at what dosages (Ingersoll, 2006, October). Given the increased prevalence of processed foods with less nutritional value, my general advice to everyone is to take a good multivitamin and an essential fatty acid supplement. This is especially true for ADHD folks whose poor planning makes them more likely to eat on the run, which means that they eat more junk and less good stuff.

Neurofeedback

Neurofeedback, also known as EEG biofeedback, is basically a version of biofeedback wherein clients are connected to sensors that measure brain waves and display the results on a computer screen. Each type of brain wave corresponds to a certain type of brain activity. By receiving this feedback, clients gradually learn to adjust their brain activity accordingly. People with ADHD tend to display a certain pattern of brain waves, as do people with various other conditions, so the neurofeedback practitioner sets up the feedback to guide the client to change the targeted brain waves. As the brain waves change, so too should the symptoms.

Very dramatic claims have been made about neurofeedback's effectiveness with ADHD and many other conditions. Although the enthusiasm of its practitioners is impressive, I would go so far as to say that its greatest supporters have also been its greatest problem—their grand claims unfortunately lump them with the proverbial snake oil salesman. A bit of restraint would give them more credibility. Solid empirical studies to prove these claims are still lacking.

In spite of an abundance of published research on neurofeedback, most of it, unfortunately, has been either flawed by confounding variables that raise doubts about the study's results or overly limited by the use of case studies or small groups that don't allow sufficient generalization (Riccio & French, 2004). Sadly, the quantity of studies is not a substitute for quality. A few solid placebo-controlled, double-blind studies would put these doubts to rest. In the meantime, however, we can say that the theory behind neurofeedback is consistent with our general understanding of ADHD etiology, so it is certainly plausible that it could be beneficial.

Typically, neurofeedback involves twenty to forty sessions or more, usually two or three times per week, which can be a significant investment of time and logistically difficult for many clients. Fees tend to be similar to those of standard therapy sessions, but because insurance reimbursement for this service is often lacking at this time, a course of treatment can add up quickly. Proponents of neurofeedback claim that after treatment, most clients will be able to reduce or go off of their medications entirely since they will have trained their brains to function better. Although this would be great, and there is some face validity to these claims, more research is needed to really answer the question of how long the benefit lasts, whether booster sessions are needed, and if so, how often.

It is relatively inexpensive to set up shop as a neurofeedback practitioner, with some systems costing less than $5,000. There are also training programs that certify, at least by their standards, practitioners in less than five days. While this ease of entry can be a good thing to the extent that it enables more practitioners to offer this potentially beneficial service, it also can be a bad thing to the extent that it enables nonclinicians, with limited training, access to an intervention that can be dangerous when applied incorrectly or used with clients for whom it shouldn't be used. Therefore, as with anything else, even if neurofeedback in general may be helpful, that doesn't mean neurofeedback with a specific practitioner would necessarily be helpful.

The Biofeedback Certification Institute of America offers certification for practitioners in EEG biofeedback. To qualify, the applicant must demonstrate certain didactic training and supervised hours and then pass a test. (More information is available at www.bcia.org)

Although it seems that neurofeedback can be helpful in addressing the core deficits of ADHD, as the medications do, it's important to remember that it is still not the full treatment picture. Just as pills don't teach skills, neither does neurofeedback, even though some unscrupulous practitioners call it a cure for ADHD. For that reason, even after a successful course of neurofeedback, the client will still need to learn the life management skills that she never got along the way, as well as perhaps having to deal with some of the emotional fallout that resulted from the many difficulties she has had.

Working Memory Training

Working memory is one of the key executive functions affected by ADHD. Therefore, there's been interest in trying to improve working memory in an effort to ameliorate the secondary effects that come from these working memory deficits. Although the replication studies are still in the works, the Cogmed system, a computer program, seems to offer some promise. By employing a variety of continually adapting working memory tasks, clients are exposed to trials that are just at or beyond their abilities, forcing them to stretch themselves to perform successfully. This custom tailoring is responsible for the good results the system shows.

However, although it's important to demonstrate that clients score progressively better over time while using the system, it is far more important to show that they are performing better in their daily lives—since that is what actually matters. The designers of the Cogmed system have shown that after completing the training program, ADHD children also showed significant improvements on visuospatial and verbal working memory, response inhibition, complex reasoning, and parent ratings of ADHD symptoms. These improvements have been found in the initial studies to persist for three months at follow-up (Klingberg et al., 2005).

As with neurofeedback, there is a significant investment of time necessary to achieve these results—typically, five forty-five-minute sessions per week over five weeks. However, the training is done on the internet and for that reason can be done at home, once the child and parent have been shown how to use the system. Although most of these studies used children rather than adults as subjects, there is no reason to think that the results would not be the same or perhaps even better for adults. Additional studies are still necessary to be able to endorse this system with confidence, but the theory is sound and the initial results are heartening.

Other Interventions

There have been other computer programs for sale that claim to train the brain in a way that is beneficial for ADHD, such as Play Attention and Brain Gym. All are sold privately and have almost worthless data behind them, assuming that that data has even been made public, which it often is not (Ingersoll, 2006). There is definitely a need for solid studies on these attention-training programs before anything good can be said about them (Riccio & French, 2004). They are probably as effective as they are fun, which is to say not much. What separates the Cogmed system from these other programs is that it constantly adapts to the user's performance, a feature that appears to be of key importance.

The Dore Program involves vision, balance, and sensory exercises for "cerebellar developmental delay," a generic term that could mean virtually anything but sounds impressive in the company's marketing materials. Despite the website's claims, there is absolutely no data to suggest that these exercises accomplish anything other than enriching the company that operates the centers (Ingersoll, 2006, October).

No benefit of any sort has been found for optometric vision training, applied kinesiology, interactive metronome, auditory training, anti-motion-sickness medication, or treatment for *Candida* yeast (Ingersoll, 2006, October). Since none of these fit the current theories of ADHD and brain functioning, it's unlikely that any evidence will ever be found to show any of these as effective treatments.

Nontraditional Treatments Conclusion

Anything that is generally helpful when it comes to improving performance and functioning is helpful for adults with ADHD, maybe more so because they are more vulnerable to performance decrements. For example, proper sleep, regular exercise, healthy eating, and stress reduction are a good idea for everyone. It would be hard to argue against ADHD clients striving to do better with these, but we would be even more hard-pressed to claim that the benefits are ADHD-specific or sufficient to overcome the core deficits of ADHD. However, some of these nontraditional treatments offer nothing more than mild and general benefits that have nothing to do with ADHD, yet their proponents mistake not only the degree of benefit but also the mechanism.

More research is needed to see if there is anything to these nontraditional treatments. Neurofeedback and working memory training show the most promise and now need further validation. As for the remainder, there is very little to be excited about—or even mildly interested in. Therefore, I urge caution in using them and recommend that clients employ tested treatments instead and certainly first. Note that this advice is less about personal opinion than it is about what the data say. If the proponents of these other interventions would like a seat at the table, let them produce the double-blind, placebo-controlled studies to earn their place.

Conclusion

It is interesting that medication is both the best-known treatment for ADHD as well as the one that draws the most criticism. I take a middle ground—for most clients with moderate or severe ADHD, I recommend that they at least try medication, unless otherwise contraindicated, simply because the research so strongly supports its effectiveness, and I have seen what a difference it can make. However, I also encourage them to not rely solely on medication, since the other three parts of the integrative treatment model are also important. Education and medication set the stage and then coaching and psychotherapy bring it home.

It may be that as ADHD continues to gain credibility as a legitimate diagnosis, and as the critics become less numerous and vocal, some of the hysteria surrounding the stimulants will fade as well. In the meantime, they are the best we have, although this may change as new medications with different mechanisms are developed.

CHAPTER 6

Coaching: More Than Obvious Advice

Coaching has become a buzzword over the last several years, with all sorts of people donning the title and working to build a practice. In this book, when I use the term coaching, I'm referring only to ADHD coaching, that is, working with ADHD clients to come up with very specific and practical strategies to help them deal more effectively with the daily life management challenges they're currently facing. Note that, even within the subspecialty of ADHD coaching, other authors and practitioners will have different definitions of what coaching is or how it should be practiced, just as different therapists have different theoretical approaches. What I bring to the table in this chapter are mostly the techniques I've found helpful with my clients. Some of these techniques came from my understanding of what sorts of strategies are most likely to be helpful for someone with typical ADHD deficits. Others I've incorporated from readings and discussions with clients and other professionals.

As a result, the techniques included in this chapter are very much biased toward those that can be successfully integrated into a therapy relationship. Those practitioners who do only coaching may have a different spin on these techniques and may employ other techniques, as well. Some people may even call these interventions "directive psychotherapy" rather than coaching. Labels aside, these strategies are a crucial aspect of working with most ADHD adults.

At its most basic, coaching is a collaborative problem-solving process. The coach and client work together to solve the tangible problems the client is currently experiencing. The coach uses an active approach to identify and clearly define the problem, and then brainstorms potential solutions with the client. Sometimes this involves teaching skills, including those that don't come naturally or are difficult to apply consistently. This requires a solid understanding by both the coach and client of ADHD in general, and the client's strengths and weaknesses in particular, in order to devise strategies that are most likely to prove helpful. For example, consider the following discussion with a client who has difficulties dealing with her mail.

Client:	I keep getting late payments on my bills because I keep losing them.
Therapist:	Where do they wind up?
Client:	Like all over the place in my apartment. Then I find some after they were already due, and I feel like an idiot. Some I never find.
Therapist:	Where do you put your mail when you bring it in?
Client:	I don't know. Various places.
Therapist:	Is there one place that you could put it all?
Client:	On the kitchen counter.
Therapist:	Is that the first place that you go to when you come home?
Client:	Not necessarily. I sometimes stop in the living room or put down my keys and stuff.
Therapist:	What about setting up a place right near the front door where you can put all the mail as soon as you walk in?
Client:	I guess it won't get scattered throughout the apartment that way.

Although the kitchen counter makes sense as a repository for her mail, it won't work consistently if she gets waylaid before she gets there. To get the mail to the kitchen, she has to keep it in mind as she goes through the apartment and resist the temptation to put it elsewhere "just for a couple minutes." Good intentions aside, her ADHD makes it too likely that her mail will wind up elsewhere.

Kevin Murphy (2006, p. 700) has defined coaching as:

> … a supportive, pragmatic, and collaborative process in which a coach and an adult with ADHD work together (usually via daily 10 to 15-minute telephone conversations) to identify goals and strategies to meet those goals. Because most adults with ADHD have difficulty persisting in effort over long periods and often cannot sustain ongoing motivation to complete tasks, coaches can assist them in staying on task by offering encouragement, support, structure, accountability, and at times gentle confrontation.

Coaching tends to focus on actions and measurable outcomes. Another way to put it is that it focuses on what, when, where, and how—but not on why (Ratey, 2002). Coaching is much more than just giving obvious advice to clients, like "Get to appointments on time," and "Don't forget to mail in your mortgage payment." ADHD folks already know many of these things but they have trouble carrying them out consistently. This describes both the frustration of ADHD and the trick of coaching. As one client insightfully pointed out: "If I could follow the tips, then I wouldn't need to follow them, because I wouldn't have ADD in the first place" (Hallowell, 1995, p. 158; Editor's note: ADHD was formerly called ADD).

For most untreated ADHD adults, to-do lists might as well be called never-done lists or wish lists. No amount of therapeutic delving into passive-aggressive, self-destructive, dependent, or entitled dynamics will be able to do enough to improve their performance on these tasks. Some therapists feel that coaching is simply dumbed-down therapy, but there is a real benefit for ADHD clients when it's done right, a benefit that can complement and enable therapeutic gains very nicely. It's also not easy to do, requiring just as much building of rapport and creativity as therapy does.

Referring Out Versus Doing It Yourself

Coaching can be provided to clients within the context of psychotherapy or it can be performed by a designated ADHD coach. I don't make a distinction between them in this book because some of the same techniques are used by both therapists and coaches. I've had therapy clients who were simultaneously seeing someone else for coaching; I've met people who are working only with a coach; and I've had many clients where our work combined elements of both.

Nonetheless, coaching and therapy are not the same thing and not all of the techniques mix so easily, even though there is some overlap between them. Coaching is hard to mix with traditional psychoanalysis, but any therapeutic orientation that tolerates a more active therapist can be adapted. On the one hand, some of what I call coaching in this book is similar to the more directive techniques already employed by many therapists. On the other hand, specific coach-training programs teach more than I've included here, so this shouldn't be considered a chapter on how to do coaching in general. Rather, this chapter focuses exclusively on techniques therapists can use in their work with ADHD clients. If you prefer to leave these techniques to a separate coach, then this chapter will help you understand the sort of work that person will do and how such work can complement the standard therapy work that you do.

The following table summarizes some of the differences between therapy and ADHD coaching:

Therapy	ADHD Coaching
Often considers how the past impacts on the present	Stays focused on the present
Generally less directive	Generally more directive
Seeks understanding	Seeks tangible accomplishments
Explores complex intrapsychic and interpersonal experiences	Focuses on pragmatic strategies

However, both therapy and ADHD coaching have certain similarities, as outlined below. They both:

- Require a strong understanding of ADHD

- Require good rapport-building

- Assist the client in finding greater happiness and success

There's something to be said for the efficiency of one-stop shopping, assuming that you are comfortable blending coaching into your therapeutic work, that it works for your particular therapeutic style, and that it fits with what the client is working on. If the client has a therapist, a coach, and a psychiatrist all working on his ADHD, he may feel as though his life is all about being a full-time client.

For some clients, it can be preferable to refer out the coaching so that it doesn't interfere with the therapy process; for example, when daily "firefighting" uses up too much session time, thereby taking time away from addressing important dynamic issues. This would be most helpful for those clients whose crises are driven primarily by their chaotic ADHD lifestyle, rather than for more psychodynamic reasons, such as a defensive avoidance of getting into deeper issues. There are no hard-and-fast rules on this, so it all comes down to the individual client's needs and the availability of appropriate professionals.

In addition to the client's needs, the other consideration here concerns the therapist's scheduling. Different coaches work in different ways and, more so than with therapy, there are more options for setting up the logistics of the working relationship. For example, some coaches meet clients face-to-face in weekly sessions, much like a standard therapy schedule. Others work exclusively by phone or e-mail but provide more frequent, sometimes daily, contact.

It's hard to say that one is definitively better than the others, since it all depends on the client's needs. As a therapist, it can be difficult to deal with the logistical issues of doing something other than the standard therapy hour, since a five to fifteen minute phone call may make it impossible to schedule a full session during that hour, thereby potentially costing the therapist the difference in income from these two services.

Of course, there is always paperwork to deal with and other phone calls to make, so the time could be used for that, but it can be a setup for frustration and negative countertransference, so it bears some serious thought beforehand. Speaking for myself and probably many other therapists, my schedule doesn't easily accommodate clients who need daily check-ins to help them stay on track or who need on-site help at home or work, so in cases like those, especially, I will refer out to someone who can better provide that service.

One convenience coaches have that therapists don't is they are not limited to clients within a commutable radius. If they do their work over the phone and/or by e-mail, their clients can be located on the other side of the world. In addition, because there is no state-by-state licensing process, there are no concerns about potentially practicing in a state where they aren't licensed. The ethical and legal issues involved in doing therapy over the phone, especially across state lines, have yet to be defined, and few practitioners would like to be the test case that clarifies the issue for the rest of us; so most therapists don't do it and those who do tend not to talk about it. For good or ill, coaches don't have to deal with this complication.

One consideration for some clients will be the cost of these services and the related issue of the potential for insurance reimbursement. Because they are not licensed health care professionals, coaches are not reimbursed by insurance companies, although they generally charge less than licensed professionals do. Although life coaching does not qualify as health care, I do feel comfortable billing insurance companies for the ADHD coaching that is provided in fifty-minute sessions in my office. As I explain further in the section below, Coaching as a Clinical Intervention, I believe I can make a good case for saying that the coaching work I do is a form of cognitive behavioral therapy for a legitimate clinical diagnosis, so I bill it as I would any other session. Of course, this can be a slippery slope, so you need to be clear with yourself about what services you are providing and to what degree they meet the criteria the insurance company sets. Although I am no fan of most insurance companies' arbitrary rules and decisions, I certainly don't advocate fraudulent billing practices.

There are a number of books available that teach therapists how to make the transition into coaching. Although most of these books tend to deal with life or executive coaching, they may have techniques that can be useful with or adapted for an ADHD client. For example, David Skibbins recently published *Becoming a Life Coach* (New Harbinger, 2007).

Coaching Certification

Coaching as a field is still very much in its infancy. Individual coaches and some groups are working to create the field as they go, just as the pioneers in every developing profession have done. Perhaps it's because the field is so new that many practitioners from other, more established disciplines look at coaching skeptically. However, the rapid growth in the number of coaches, if nothing else, indicates there is a need in the marketplace not being satisfactorily met in other ways, so coaches are stepping in and trying to meet that need.

Time alone will tell how the discipline as a whole evolves, but in order to put themselves on an equal footing with other professionals, coaches will have to do two things to establish the field's credibility. First, they will need to create some consistency and standards for training and credentialing. As the matter currently stands, anyone who can print up business cards can call herself a coach and hang out a shingle. Unlike many other professions, such as psychologist or certified public accountant, "coach" is not a protected title that requires some specific, state-sanctioned credentialing process before someone can call himself one. This can cause quality control problems but, in fairness, incompetent practitioners slip through the credentialing processes in the better regulated professions, too, although hopefully in lower numbers.

The second matter that must be attended to for the field to gain wider credibility is the publication of some solid empirical research on the effectiveness of various coaching interventions. To date, this has not been done, perhaps because independent practitioners are not financially able to undertake unpaid research nor are they able to acquire and implement grant funding. Until that time, clinicians and prospective clients will be left to judge the face validity of coaching, based on their tolerance for risk and ambiguity. To be fair, every other professional field faced these same barriers when they began and practitioners established themselves over time—as with childbirth, the end result may be great, but the process can be difficult and messy.

For would-be coaches, there are many training programs out there with various philosophies, approaches, and requirements for graduation. In an effort to create some consistency in the field, the International Coach Federation offers the accreditation of Master Certified Coach (MCC). The Federation certifies training programs, as well as individuals. You can get more information at www.coachfederation.org. However, it should be noted that this training focuses on general life coaching and does not specifically address ADHD issues, which means that someone with an MCC may understand only half the picture. Just as a therapist must really know about ADHD to work effectively with this population, so too must a coach; so simply having strong general skills is not sufficient to work optimally with these clients.

Just as you would assess a psychiatrist or therapist before referring a client to her, you would also want to know that a coach is competent and a good fit for your client. A good way to assess this is to look for a related credential or certification. Unfortunately, at the time of this writing there is no specific certification or credential for ADHD coaching, although such certification is in the works. The Institute for the Advancement of AD/HD Coaching was started in 2005 and is currently working on establishing these standards. Its mission is "to advance the field of AD/HD coaching through the development and delivery of credentialing and certification for AD/HD coaches worldwide, in pursuit of excellence in our profession." More information can be found at www.adhd coachinstitute.org.

Also, there is now a nonprofit association that represents ADHD coaches and seeks to advance the profession, the ADHD Coaches Organization. Their goals are to establish professional and ethical standards, promote awareness of ADHD coaching, provide resources to members, and serve as an informational link to the general public and other professionals working with people affected by ADHD. You can find more information at www.adhdcoaches.org. Their website also includes a searchable database of member coaches. There are other private accreditation organizations, but not all of them are worth much—as in every field, some of these vanity credentials seem to have as a primary qualification the ability to fill out a check correctly.

Some questions to ask a coach whom you are considering referring clients to include the following:

- What manner of coach training have you had?

- What manner of training about ADHD have you had?

- What did you do before coaching, to the extent that it provides some foundation of transferable knowledge?

- How many ADHD clients have you coached?

- What professional organizations do you belong to?

- What other professional activities, mentoring, or peer-supervision groups are you involved with?

- What sorts of continuing education activities do you engage in?

- How do you tend to work with ADHD clients?

- What do you do in the event that more serious psychological issues come up?

- What is your opinion about medications?

Assuming that a coach has the necessary skills, training, and experience, we can say that coaching probably can be helpful for ADHD clients. However, coaches with insufficient clinical knowledge or poor boundaries can find themselves in over their heads with clients who have a history of sexual abuse, hypomania, personality disorders, substance abuse, or other serious mental health conditions, and not know how to contain the situation or when to refer out. Training provides not only the knowledge of what you can do, but also what you can't.

Coaching as a Clinical Intervention

Helping ADHD adults to change their behavior through coaching has a powerful effect on changing their inner world (Weiss, Hechtman, & Weiss, 1999). Success in the present can go a long way toward undoing much of the damage to their self-esteem and sense of self-efficacy because it helps them to feel more effective in their lives. I like to say that "you can't leave the past in the past if it's still happening in the present." One vindication for past failures is to learn to overcome them in the present. You may not be able to change the past, but perhaps you can create a different future. Ultimately, this is more beneficial than simply lowering standards or expectations for the ADHD adult, because at some level that confirms she is damaged and shouldn't be held to the same standards of personal responsibility as other adults.

In contrast, coaching provides tangible successes and improvements, so she has some legitimate reasons to feel good about herself in her therapy. Granted, she will be climbing uphill to learn those habits that don't come naturally, but she can indeed make improvements if she works at it. I sometimes tell clients exactly that. I say, "This is stuff that won't come as easily for you as it does for some other people, but that doesn't mean that you can't do at least somewhat better." Of course, this entire process is easier if the client is properly medicated—to play on the phrase I quoted earlier, "pills don't teach skills," but "skills do come easier with pills."

Beyond the effect that it has on the rest of their lives, typical ADHD difficulties such as disorganization, chronic lateness, and forgetting important events can also affect clients' ability to get as much as possible from the therapy experience (Weiss et al., 1999), especially if they miss appointments or arrive significantly late. The irony is that the very symptoms that they are looking for help with are also the symptoms that will interfere with their getting the help they want. For that reason, some coaching may be necessary simply to get the client into your office for the full session.

In their lives outside of therapy, ADHD adults do worst on the sorts of maintenance activities that offer no reward for doing them—tasks like laundry, grocery shopping, paying taxes, showing up on time, and so on. But there is a punishment for not doing such activities or for doing them late; bosses don't give out plaques for showing up on time, but they do write up employees who frequently arrive late to work. Therefore, many ADHD adults need to find rewards elsewhere to keep them motivated to stay on top of these kinds of tasks. A coach can provide that enthusiasm and external motivation, in a way that runs counter to the years of critical comments that the client has probably endured. Without being Pollyannaish about it, the coach can provide more positive comments for the client to internalize.

Nancy Ratey, often credited as the inventor of ADHD coaching, describes the five areas where ADHD coaching can be especially helpful (Ratey, 2002):

1. **Coaching maintains arousal**—it helps clients work on abstract or long-term goals by keeping them in the forefront of the mind and thereby eliciting enough anxiety to kick clients into gear.

2. **Coaching modulates emotions**—it prevents shame, guilt, and fear from paralyzing the client by identifying the triggers that set off these negative emotions, exploring more effective ways to modulate those emotions, and identifying strategies to move forward on goals. (Author's note: This sounds a lot like therapy to me, which makes me nervous about coaches without a clinical background moving into these areas. To Ratey's credit, though, she does recommend referral to another professional when necessary.)

3. **Coaching maintains motivation and sustains the feeling of reward**—it does this by breaking large projects into smaller pieces and cheering the achievement of partial successes, which makes it easier for clients to continue moving forward.

4. **Coaching acts as the "executive secretary of attention"**—the coach keeps the client focused on priorities and helps to drive away distractions.

5. **Coaching supports the client's ability to self-direct actions and change behavior**—the coach provides daily reminders and helps break down into smaller parts the necessary steps to take, thereby modeling how to deal more proactively with challenges.

The Process of Coaching

Every practitioner will put her own spin on what coaching looks like and how it is integrated with the rest of the interventions she uses. In this section I describe how to engage in the coaching process. Later sections will list specific suggestions for various ADHD difficulties—for example, strategies to cope with running late. The first subsection below describes my overarching theory of coaching, followed by a general discussion of how to address the core deficits of ADHD, with the hope that you will be able to generalize from this to the specific situations you find yourself in with your clients. The following subsection provides more detail about how a coach works, adding flesh to the skeleton first outlined.

A General Coaching Theory

At the simplest level, folks with ADHD run into problems when they don't do the right thing at the right time. This can happen because they do the right thing at the wrong time, don't do the right thing at all, or do the wrong thing. Coaching aims to help in two ways:

1. **Prevent problems** by helping clients do the right things more often at the right times, as well as do fewer wrong things. Perfection would be nice, but really, we're just hoping to improve their batting averages.

2. **Clean up problems** after they occur, since situations can either go from bad to worse or bad to better depending on what the person does after the fact. Given that even a fully treated ADHD adult will still make the occasional mistake, it's worth working on fixing those occurrences. Most lists of ADHD coping skills tend to focus on preventing problems, which is certainly a worthy goal, but they neglect this equally important second aspect for those times when the inevitable happens.

Preventing problems usually entails helping the client set himself up for success beforehand, because he can't reliably trust himself to do the right thing in the moment.

For example, he might set an alarm before he starts to check his e-mail to remind himself when it's time to leave for a meeting. A more generic example I often use with clients is that you shouldn't bring home a box of donuts if you don't want to be tempted to eat them—the more powerful choice point occurs when you're standing in the supermarket aisle contemplating their purchase, not when you're standing in your kitchen.

The theory is for the ADHD adult to act at the moment when the goal is on her mind, rather than waiting for later when the goal is more likely to have slipped away. To succeed, the client may need to learn new skills or habits and consciously push herself to use them. Some of this may also involve environmental management—for example, reducing clutter to prevent important items from getting lost in piles of paper or putting up a whiteboard in a conspicuous spot to write reminders on.

Some other strategies have a social aspect in that it's helpful or necessary to get significant others or coworkers on board with the changes. This can take several forms, as discussed below:

- **Direct assistance.** This works by recruiting others; for example, to take on certain tasks or provide reminders or updates in exchange for something the ADHD adult will agree to do. Note, however, there are limits to what others will do without beginning to feel that the relationship is unbalanced.

- **Expectation management.** This works by recognizing the limitations of direct assistance and, for that reason, may be more important. Since the majority of adults do not have ADHD or related difficulties, most people assume a certain level of performance by others and they make assumptions about the person's intentions and character if she falls short. Therefore, she can save herself and others a lot of trouble from the get-go by being up-front with them about what they should and should not expect from her. For example, if she knows that she has difficulty remembering to return phone calls, she can tell the people she will be working with, "I'm really bad at remembering to call people back. I'm working on it, but I still kind of suck at it. So if I forget, please don't take it personally and don't assume that it's not important to me. Just give me a call if you don't hear from me. Feel free to bug me—I won't be annoyed."

Obviously, it would be preferable for an adult with ADHD to be able to remember to return calls consistently, or whatever, but if that's not likely to happen, then eliciting assistance or being up-front about the need for assistance is the second best course to take. It's certainly better than dropping the ball and letting the other person come to his own conclusions about the ADHD person's failure. This requires the ADHD adult to have a pretty good acceptance of her deficits—without defensiveness—and be able to rebalance the scales to keep the relationship fair, when necessary.

In addition to training the people with whom they interact, ADHD adults also benefit from preselecting those with whom they must interact by choosing people who are more open and understanding to begin with, if such choices are at all possible. These actions could be called *social environment management*. Since so much of our success and happiness depends on our interactions with others, this is an important focus of treatment.

Addressing the Core Deficits

If we now look at the core deficits of ADHD—inattention, hyperactivity, and impulsivity—we can create some general guidelines for how these deficits can be addressed to prevent problems. Any individual client's specific trouble spots will involve customized solutions, but most clients will probably follow these guidelines. Keeping this general theory in mind will enable you to better understand the rationale behind the specific strategies and tools mentioned later, as well as better enable you to create your own strategies customized for your clients' situations. Ultimately, every specific strategy is really a variation on these basic themes. With this mind-set, you don't need to completely reinvent the wheel, no matter how unique a client's circumstances seem to be.

Inattention

The key to dealing with inattention is to reduce the odds of getting off track and thereby increase the chances of doing the right things at the right times. This is done by:

- **Reducing extraneous stimuli.** This is accomplished, for example, by reducing clutter, noise, visual stimuli, or reminders of tasks they shouldn't be engaging in. I once had a client who often needed to look up online information for his job. Unfortunately, he had designated a sports website as his homepage, thus creating too many opportunities to get sucked into checking scores rather than seeking out what he needed for work. The solution we chose was to set his homepage to open as a blank window, which meant that he had to make a conscious choice to look up the scores, as opposed to getting drawn in before he even realized that he was off-task.

- **Amplifying relevant stimuli.** This works, for example, by putting up a whiteboard in an easy-to-see place and writing reminder notes on it. Thus, rather than allowing these reminders to fade into the background, the notes bring those tasks forward, front and center.

This is why distractible children are seated at the front of the class—not only so they can't see their classmates, but also so the teacher looms larger in their attention. We can increase the relative intensity of the relevant stimuli by both decreasing the strength of undesirable stimuli and increasing the strength of the desired ones.

Hyperactivity

The key to dealing with hyperactivity is to:

■ **Seek out situations that allow for the safe expression of hyperactivity.** Many ADHD adults will self-select their environments; for example, preferring to watch movies at home where they can move around more freely rather than feeling constrained in a theater. Others may need to counterbalance the mental efforts and demands for restraint at work with more active or discretionary pursuits at night and on weekends. Of course, there are better and worse ways to spend free time, so it may be worth discussing the costs and potential risks of various activities so that the client can choose safer options, if necessary. Such discussions may be especially helpful with young adults.

■ **Minimize or avoid situations that require more restraint than the person can muster.** For example, someone who has difficulty sitting still should not take a job that demands long stretches of inactivity, or doesn't permit exercising at lunchtime, or even allow taking several short walks while running errands around the workplace. To the extent possible, you can work with your clients to increase their psychological tolerance for repetitive or mundane activities, although there will be some limits to this.

Impulsivity

The key to dealing with impulsivity is to:

■ **Create barriers to problematic actions by reducing tempting stimuli or avoiding situations that make it more likely that the person will leap before looking.** This is the "lead me not unto temptation" approach. For example, if someone knows that she is far too likely to spend too much money in certain stores, she shouldn't even go into those stores in the first place, because whatever good intentions she has when she enters will be quickly lost.

■ **Set up cushions to reduce the potential damage done.** For example, if this same woman must go into one of these risky stores, she could bring a specific amount of cash with her and leave her credit cards at home. This forethought will make it easier for her to stay within her limits at a time when her impulses would push her to do other than planned. Although working on self-control and thinking about consequences in the moment should also be treatment targets, this type of insightful forethought is likely to have a greater impact.

Setting Goals

The first step in coaching, as in most treatments, is to identify the problems to be addressed. Because the deficits have an impact on other people in the ADHD adult's life, the goals the client initially reports may be driven to a large extent by the wish to make someone else happy, such as a romantic partner or boss, which can diminish the ADHD person's motivation to really work on those goals (Ratey, 2002). Therefore, it may take some digging to ensure that the stated goals are ones that the client is really invested in, rather than those he thinks he should be invested in because of the idea that the other person's goals are what it takes "to be normal like everyone else."

Once the client's true goals have been identified, the client and coach work together to brainstorm possible strategies and how best to implement them. When it comes time to work on those goals, keep in mind that the client's difficulties will probably represent a combination of:

- Neurological dysfunction

- Skills that were never acquired, such as the ability to create and maintain an effective organizational system

For that reason, it may take some sleuthing on your part to tease these interacting causes apart (Weinstein, 1994). At the risk of oversimplifying, it can probably be said that whatever deficits are ameliorated by medications are neurologically based—although we can't necessarily say that those deficits not treated by medications are therefore based in skills deficits because it simply may be that the medications do not fully address the neurological dysfunctions. So, once the medication regimen has been settled on, and the client seems to be getting whatever benefit she is going to get, you are left with a smaller pool of difficulties to try to explain and deal with.

Fortunately, the medications should make it easier for your client to learn those weak or missing skills in a way that wasn't possible without the medications, just as wearing glasses will enable a student to get more out of what's written on the blackboard.

As a general rule, it's best to assume that any remaining difficulties are based in a lack of skills and to work on teaching those skills, but with the expectation that a failure to fully master those skills is probably based in neurological factors. This spares your clients the experience of being told yet again that they could do something—if only they tried hard enough or wanted it bad enough. Once you hit the limit where a client is no longer progressing in acquiring or improving those skills, then switch to teaching work-arounds to minimize the impact of the neurological deficits.

Coaching's Short-Term Goal

Coaching has two goals. The short-term goal is to offer the client and possibly the family specific solutions with the hope that they can build some momentum immediately.

Particularly because they will most likely enter treatment when matters are not going well and they are feeling especially discouraged, clients will need some quick bang for their buck if they are to remain invested in the process. This is especially true for impatient ADHD folks. To that end, it's best to start with a few small problems where immediate success can be achieved—for example, this is not the time to work on increasing overall marital happiness, even if this is the problem the client presents. A more manageable goal may be to help the client not begin every morning by tearing the house apart in a frenzy because he can't find his keys. Some of this early coaching may seem similar to the education discussed in chapter 4 and it is, except that it will be a little more customized to the client's specific needs.

Coaching's Long-Term Goal

The longer-term goal of coaching is to teach clients a process of creative problem solving that can be used to deal with future difficulties. Essentially, this is the experimental method—identify the problem, brainstorm possibilities, try some strategies, evaluate the results, make small or large corrections as necessary, stay focused on the goal over time, and then use the strategy until it needs to be changed. As the old adage goes, "teach a man to fish...." Part of this work involves encouraging patience and persistence as clients slowly climb up the learning curve. This is especially important given the inertia resulting from clients' past failures and pessimistic expectations.

It takes energy on the coach's part to counterbalance that pessimism and maintain an inspiring and infectious hope that things can be different this time around. This can be easier to do if the coach and the client utilize a strong understanding of ADHD to select those strategies more likely to be helpful. The coach also acts as an historical archive for the client and keeps reminding him of the goals he is working toward. This may involve keeping the client focused in the moment by reminding him of past patterns and their consequences, as well as his desire to reach future goals. The coach acts as the ADHD person's missing internal monitor, thereby enabling the client to stay the course long enough to build on his accomplishments (N.A. Ratey, personal communication, December 2, 2006).

Providing Structure

The coach also provides structure to clients to help them pursue their goals more consistently and not become sidetracked. Most ADHD folks have a love/hate relationship with structure and schedules—they know they need them, but they still hate being constrained by schedules, routines, plans, reminders, rewards, and punishments. Therefore, part of the work involves helping the client to see that the benefits outweigh the subjective costs, which becomes more apparent when some reinforcing successes have taken place.

Because too many of your client's experiences with structure will have been imposed by others or unsuccessfully shoehorned to fit an ADHD person's way of functioning, a strategy can be an easier sell if you suggest structural elements that take into account your client's preferences, life situation, strengths, and weaknesses (Ratey, 2002). A one-size-fits-all approach only further confirms to the ADHD adult that there's something wrong with her when she can't make it work. The client will be far more willing to stick with a suggested structure that is a better fit for her.

Less Helpful Structure	More Helpful Structure
Go through the mail every day and open every bill to ensure that there is nothing that needs immediate response.	Weed out the junk mail and put the rest in a designated place. Go through the mail and attend to bills on a designated day of the week.
Get all your work done first before taking a break.	It's okay to take occasional breaks, but it may help to set an alarm to ensure that the break doesn't last too long.
Get everything put away and organized to create an efficient work space.	Get everything generally put away and organized enough. Perfection would be nice, but we're looking for functional.
Get everywhere fifteen minutes early.	Things often take longer than we think they will, so make a habit of adding fifteen minutes to your travel time.

Technology and Systems

Perhaps more so than most people, those with ADHD can benefit from external aids to help them maintain a higher level of functioning. It's therefore helpful for the therapist/coach to keep abreast of new technologies and tools that can help clients stay on top of their responsibilities, such as computer software, various reminders, and time-management systems (Nadeau, 2002). There are lots of possibilities. It's all about matching them to the particular client's situation, trying them out to see what works, and adjusting as necessary.

Standard systems that help non-ADHD folks may not work well for those with ADHD—although people without ADHD do tend to benefit from ADHD-friendly tools and tricks, if they need them. The basic idea is to use technology to provide or supplement the functions in which the client is weak. For example, for those ADHD clients who have difficulty remembering to start getting ready for bed early enough, an alarm can be helpful if this is something their internal clock cannot reliably provide for them.

Some clients may view such aids as tangible symbols of their shortcomings and thereby refuse to use them. Unlike the neurologically and habit-based difficulties they may have with reliably incorporating such aids into their lives, this other resistance is far more psychological. The fear is that these aids will shine a spotlight on them, highlighting their differences from everyone else. Ironically, of course, using the aid actually allows them to perform more like everyone else, by making their functional differences less obvious. After all, what's a more obvious defect—using a personal digital assistant with multiple alarms or forgetting to show up for a meeting?

The sales pitch is that these days no one can keep up with everything, so using an electronic aid says only that you have a full life and that it's important to you to stay on top of it all. We all use tools when we can't do a task by ourselves. For example, wrenches make it possible to get nuts tighter than if we did it by hand; writing down appointments in schedule books prevents foul-ups because no one can remember it all.

This section presents a sampling of the aids, tools, and gadgets available and offers suggestions on how they can be used. Feel free to come up with your own, no matter how strange it might seem. The only thing that matters is that it works for the client to whom you recommend it.

Calendars

A simple wall or desk calendar can make a big difference in an ADHD adult's life, if it's used consistently and properly. (Planners, which include a calendar, are more complicated and are discussed in detail in the next section.) So, when we talk about technological aids, it certainly doesn't have to be anything complex or expensive. Sometimes the simpler, the better.

For an ADHD adult, it's especially important to put the calendar somewhere highly visible—if it's stored in a drawer, it may as well be stored in the garbage can, because it won't be used. Anything that requires the ADHD person to specifically remember it is much less likely to be helpful. "Out of sight, out of mind" very much applies, so the client can benefit from the converse—in sight, in mind. Therefore, some conversation should be devoted to the not-so-simple topic of where exactly is the best place to put the calendar. For maximum benefit, it should be placed somewhere that it will be seen frequently, without the client needing to intentionally seek it out.

Obvious places include putting it on the fridge or in a hallway, but that's not always as easy as it sounds. I had a client who felt self-conscious about having her calendar in public view in her kitchen, yet she didn't want it in her bedroom, so it took some discussion and compromise for her to put it in her kitchen, but in a less conspicuous location. This wasn't the optimal place, but it was better than the other alternatives.

The key to using a calendar effectively is to use it frequently. There is a momentum effect here, in that the more the client uses it, the more valuable it becomes and the more likely he is to use it again. This means writing down tasks and events on the calendar, as well as occasionally checking it to see if anything is coming up. Of course, the act of writing also provides some incidental checking, creating yet another opportunity to look at the calendar that the client doesn't need to seek out intentionally.

It can be helpful to use different colors to connote different events or important dates for different people in the family, making it easier to scan the calendar quickly yet still get the necessary information. Especially for clients who have children with complicated schedules, it can be helpful to impose a rule stating that nothing counts unless it's written on the calendar—just as we therapists are sometimes advised regarding our clinical notes, "if it isn't written down, it didn't happen." This can reduce the number of situations where one person swears he told the other, who swears she was never told anything.

Planners

Most ADHD adults have had a difficult relationship with planners. At some level, they know they need to use them, but that doesn't mean that they like to. Partly this is because, for many ADHD adults, the process of actively using a planner—remembering to write important dates and events into it, checking it regularly for upcoming events, not losing it or losing interest in it—doesn't come naturally. There is a certain element of walking uphill to using a calendar in that, for many clients, it takes additional conscious effort to force themselves to use it consistently.

In addition, especially before clients were medicated or knew about their ADHD, they may have racked up many failure experiences with various planners that were used briefly before being abandoned, forgotten, or lost. For that reason, it's worth spending some time exploring the client's past experiences with planners and recognizing the pain, shame, criticism, frustration, and hopelessness she has felt before. However, with your guidance as part of an overall treatment program, plus some work on her part, the outcome can be different this time (Robin, 2002). Here's an example of how the discussion might go:

Therapist: What sorts of planners have you used in the past?

Client: All sorts. Cheap ones, expensive ones. I should've saved myself some money and only bought the first month since that's all I ever used!

Therapist: Maybe that's why they don't sell them that way! The thing is, a lot of times when a planner doesn't work, it's because it wasn't quite the right tool for the job. You have to find the one that will be right for you.

Client: I guess. I either got overwhelmed at the store and bought the first one I could grab or I just bought whatever someone else was using and hoped that it would work for me too.

Therapist: That makes sense. I mean, if you don't really know what you're looking for, then it's a good idea to copy others who seem to be doing well.

Client: Of course, then I just felt like a bigger loser because I couldn't make it work.

Therapist: That kind of makes sense, too, if you didn't know about your ADHD, but I think this time can be different. Now that you know about your ADHD and are doing all this stuff to get on top of it, I think we can find you a planner that will work better for you.

Client: I hope so, because I really need some help here.

Of course, it's likely that most ADHD adults were given at least some of their past planners as gifts with the implicit, or quite explicit, message that the recipient needed to get his act together. Therefore, part of the clinical work is to convince clients to take an active role in selecting the planner as a way of overcoming those negative experiences when they were passively on the receiving end of an emotionally loaded gift.

Taking the time to enter phone numbers, upcoming events, various reminders, and other useful information will increase the value of the planner and perhaps make it more likely it will be carried along and not forgotten. Of course, the process of entering that information is likely to be tedious, so it may be worth discussing whether it will be less painful to do it all at once or to break it up into more tolerable pieces. Regardless of the client's decision, setting a deadline together may move that process along. A failure to make the deadline then becomes just another learning opportunity to see how things can get fouled up and, more importantly, how that foul-up can be countered.

Once he has chosen a likely product, the client needs to work on ingraining the habit of checking the planner often enough, based on how much he has going on in his life and how well he can accurately remember the details in between calendar checks.

A reasonable place for most clients to start is to shoot for checking at the beginning, middle, and end of each day. It can help if you set this up as homework for the client to practice, even if he knows he doesn't have anything specific written down, just to get him into the habit of checking the calendar.

Setting a reminder alarm (see below) or putting up reminder notes in high visibility places can also be helpful during this habit-acquisition phase (Robin, 2002). Realistically, however, total compliance is unlikely, but even partial success can be a significant improvement and should be framed as such. It's important to not give the impression that you are expecting more than the client can reliably do—he will likely be sensitized to disappointing people, so you need to actively ensure that this dynamic isn't created with you, while also holding him sufficiently accountable that he makes progress.

For clients who have a tendency to overcommit themselves, it can be worth suggesting that they self-impose a rule that they will commit to nothing unless they have their planner in front of them. Of course, for this to work, they have to be in the habit of entering things into the planner. This may include tasks that don't necessarily have a specific time, such as doing paperwork, other maintenance activities, or tasks with soft deadlines. This means that they can't schedule other events and activities into every moment of the day, or these lower profile, but nonetheless important, tasks will never be completed.

Some clients may want to use the planner as a to-do list as well. When that is the case, you can work with them on how to form the habit of entering items into it, as well as how to assess whether they are scheduling a realistic number of tasks, given the amount of available time and the likelihood that unpredictable events will cause some tasks to take longer. This may involve actually writing down the predicted time allotted to each of the tasks and taking a second look to see if each allotment is realistic; that is, figuring out whether they add up to more time than the client has available. Another good habit for the client to develop is to review her old to-do list and create a new one at either the beginning or the end of each day (Robin, 2002).

Of course, a to-do list has value only if the client actually does the things on the list, so it should be checked regularly and adjustments made when necessary. For the list to be manageable, the client should limit the number of items that she writes on it. In a rush of enthusiasm, clients may enter aspirational items as well as necessary tasks—for example, "Read *War and Peace*" should not be on the list unless the client has been assigned a paper on the novel. There are two dangers to overloading the list: (1) it can be demoralizing to see the list grow longer instead of shorter; and (2) overloading can cause the most important tasks to get lost in the mass of less important items.

When discussing the items on the to-do list, it may be worth checking that all the necessary materials will be available at the time the client needs them (Robin, 2002). For example, will the store be open when the client plans to shop? Will the coworker on the group project be available for questions at the time the client plans to work on it? It should not be taken for granted that your client will have considered all these elements.

Another key to effective to-do list use is to prioritize the items, such that the most important and/or timely items are completed first. Of course, this will probably not be the order in which the items were written. If that is the case, the client can either go through the list and number the items in the order they should be completed or he can mark the items with numbers in the order of their importance; e.g., 1 means "Must do today," 2 means "Should probably do today," and 3 means "It would be nice to do today." In this way, the client can focus first on the number "1" items, then "2," and then "3," if time permits. This process may be easier for some clients to handle than deciding which of two tasks is more important in a sequential rank ordering. If the client fails to follow the priorities assigned to the tasks or still runs into difficulty getting things done, it's worth exploring exactly where the process breaks down. That can be accomplished by asking the following questions:

- Did she put everything she needed to do on the list?

- If so, did she prioritize appropriately?

- If so, did she follow those priorities?

- If so, was there simply more to do than time allotted to do it, given predictable interruptions and inefficiencies?

Obviously, the intervention offered to the client will depend on exactly where the chain broke and why.

Paper Planners

The advantage of paper planners is that they tend to be simple and inexpensive, at least compared to electronic planners, although there are more complicated paper versions available as well. Also, most people have some experience with using paper planners, so the basics shouldn't take much time to learn. The downside, however, is that the loss of a paper planner can be disastrous because most likely there's no backup for the crucial information. One way to guard against such a loss is to write your contact information prominently on the cover or inside the planner and to include a notice of a reward if it's found and returned. (If someone were to find my schedule book, she would very quickly earn herself $200, and I would happily pay every penny of it.)

Despite the proliferation of electronic options, there is still something to be said for plain old paper planners. Although some of the electronic versions are very impressive, sometimes they can be too powerful for the job or can add unnecessary complexity to a simple process. For that reason, I often recommend that clients stick with paper, if that suits their lifestyle or preferences better. The gadgets can be fun, but they aren't always necessary.

Personal Digital Assistants (PDAs)

PDAs have become increasingly popular over the last decade because they offer some features not to be found in nonelectronic versions, which can be lifesavers for some ADHD adults. Moreover, they are great for gadget lovers who will find it enjoyable enough to keep using one; the downside of PDAs is there are many technophobes who could never imagine mastering one.

Depending on the desired functions, PDAs can cost less than $100 or closer to $1,000. Even the simplest units include the basic features of contact information, to-do list, schedule, and memo pad. It's likely they will also have the ability to set multiple alarms, including prior to or at the time of a scheduled event. More advanced versions allow users to view and edit various documents, send and receive e-mail, browse the Web in a limited way, and much more. However, clients should consider carefully whether they will actually use the various features they will pay more for.

Furthermore, just because a device can do something doesn't mean that it does it well or that the client will actually use it for that purpose. For example, browsing the Web on a three-inch screen may be technically possible but it's not nearly as efficient or satisfying as doing it on a larger screen. Therefore, your clients may find it worthwhile to discuss with you what their needs really are, before they find themselves standing in front of overwhelming and tantalizing display cases. As the angry spouses of some of my clients can attest, this is especially important for impulsive clients.

Beyond the PDA itself, there are extra options. The first is to get a combination PDA and cell phone, which can mean one less thing to keep track of and possibly forget—but an even bigger disaster if the item is lost. For those clients who find data entry on the PDA cumbersome, they can buy portable keyboards that make it seem more like working with an ordinary computer.

Perhaps the single biggest advantage that PDAs have over paper planners is that the data can be backed up, even if the hardware disappears. This can be crucial for ADHD clients or anyone who believes their data is worth more to them than the cost of the physical item. Most of these devices will automatically synchronize when plugged into a computer, creating an identical backup on the hard drive. Of course, the client will have to plug it in occasionally for this feature to work, but at least she will lose only the changes made since the last synchronization. However, some more advanced, and thereby expensive, versions that also function as a cell phone can be set to synchronize on their own.

Alternatively, even the most basic cell phones contain at least a rudimentary calendar function with an integrated alarm that can be set to go off a designated amount of time beforehand. This approach may be especially helpful for younger clients who never part from their cell phones. It also probably works best for clients who don't have a great many events to track or who schedule intermittent events, like appointments, and would benefit from an additional reminder.

Clocks, Alarms, and Reminders

If the client has trouble paying attention to the passage of time or the arrival of a specific time, it can help to scatter clocks liberally throughout the house or workplace, making it easier to notice what time it is. If a client's internal clock is faulty or ticks too quietly, then he should make up for it with external clocks. For more specific problems, such as not noticing that it's time to leave for an appointment, setting an alarm can remind her and thereby help her break away from the current activity. By setting the alarm at a moment when she is thinking about it, she doesn't need to rely on her imperfect prospective memory to alert her at the relevant moment. Alarms come in many different shapes and sizes, and since most of them are fairly inexpensive, clients don't have to limit themselves to just one.

Most people are familiar with watches that have multiple features, such as programmable alarms, countdown alarms, stopwatches, and repeating alarms. These are often called "sports watches." Although they tend to not be great fashion pieces, they are generally unobtrusive enough that most people can get away with wearing one in the workplace. After all, frequently running into meetings late is likely to be far more noticeable than wearing a clunky watch. Beyond the standard issue watches to be found at the mall, there are souped-up versions available that offer more features, including the ability to beep or to vibrate for more private warnings. Users can set many different alarms to go off at various times of the day, including at regular intervals to provide reminders that they should get back to more productive work if their attention has wandered. Some of these are worn as wristwatches (WatchMinder and VibraLITE) and some are worn like a pager (Invisible Clock)—you can get more information at www.watchminder.com, www.globalassistive.com, and www.invisibleclock.com, respectively.

A less complicated alternative might be standard, quickly set kitchen timers. Although they don't travel as easily as watches do, they are so inexpensive that clients can buy several of them to place around the house where they are needed—for example, at the computer, TV, or any other places that clients tend to get stuck for too long. There are the old-fashioned twist timers that can be set for up to an hour, as well as digital ones with multiple alarms that can be clipped onto a belt or pocket. Their ease of use makes it more likely that they will be used, especially by technophobes who would otherwise be intimidated by more complicated alarms.

Finally, many people with ADHD have great difficulty getting out of bed in the morning. It's unclear whether this is due to a primary sleep disorder, a neurologically based slower awakening, or poor time-management habits that lead to later bedtimes.

Regardless, getting out of bed late sets a negative tone to the morning that can cascade throughout the whole day. One solution is to set an alarm to go off at night to signal that it's time to go to bed, thereby making it easier to get out of bed on time the next morning.

Software

There has been an increase in the number of specialty programs available that can be helpful for those with ADHD, whether they are specifically designed for them or not. Some of these programs are used on a computer, others are for use on or synchronized with a PDA. Although hardly an inclusive list, some examples include the following:

- **Life Balance** provides a powerful to-do list, complete with sophisticated prioritizing and outlining abilities. More information is available at www .llamagraphics.com.

- **Visual Mind** and **MindApp** provide a graphical interface for to-do lists and project planning that may be more useful than a straight text format for some users. More information is available at www.visual-mind.com and www.mindapp.com, respectively.

Digital Voice Recorders

These small devices are available at most electronics and office supply stores. They function the same way a digital answering machine does, in that distinct messages can be recorded, skipped through, played, and deleted. For some clients, depending on their life circumstances and information-processing preferences, it can be easier to dictate a note than to write it down. These handy little recorders can also be used to capture thoughts on the fly that might otherwise be lost, such as when in the car.

The least expensive models cost less than $30 and provide plenty of recording time, often an hour or more, whereas the more expensive models can record much more than an hour's worth of messages and come with many more features, such as multiple folders to store messages and the capability to download the recordings onto a computer. Some of these recorders are certified by the various voice-recognition software programs, such that the downloaded files can be automatically transcribed into an editable word processing file. For example, one of my ADHD clients found it much easier to dictate a large creative project than to sit down and type it out.

The potential downside of using these recorders is that, unlike written records, there is no indication when just looking at the device as to what is recorded on it. Therefore, the user has to remember to check the messages, especially if the recorder is used to record tasks to be completed. But, once again, given their relatively low price, if they are used for those tasks where they are helpful, they may be worth the small investment.

A Four-Part Coaching Model

There are many possible solutions to typical ADHD difficulties. The trick is to match the strategy to the client's specific strengths and weaknesses, life circumstances, obligations, and willingness. This sizable section lists many of these solutions, partly to give you a variety of choices to choose from when you are looking to assist a client, and partly to provide you with some samples so that you can create your own strategies.

For the sake of clarity of presentation, I've broken down these strategies into four different categories: memory management, time management, stuff management, and goal management. There's some overlap and some artificial distinctions made between these four, but it's helpful to use these categories as a framework for the purpose of discussing them. I intentionally put them into this order because, generally, they build on each other in this way—for example, you can't work on pursuing your goals if you can't manage your time effectively. The general layout of this section will specify a common problem area and then provide a bulleted list of strategies that you can offer to your clients. This will make it easier to refer back to in the future, as well as to digest in the moment.

As much as lists like these can suggest that these interventions are very cookbook, the real magic comes from creative collaboration with your clients and possibly their families. Use these lists as a jumping-off point. As with therapy, it's personalization that leads to the best success. Wacky doesn't matter, if it works. For example, I had a client who far too often forgot where he'd parked his car in the two giant parking lots at work, which left him wandering around searching for his car, feeling like an idiot. The trouble was, when he tried to remember where he had left his car that morning, sometimes he would inadvertently remember where he had parked it earlier that week and fruitlessly look in that location.

My suggestion in the moment was to find one area in one of the two parking lots that would pretty much always be open when he arrived at work. Then, he should always park there, even if that meant he would have to walk past many empty parking spaces. If he followed this plan, at least he would always know where his car was. I've never seen this problem listed anywhere and I've never had another client mention that specific problem since, but the solution is very much in line with the strategies I have seen or created with other clients.

You can download client handouts for each of the following problem areas and their solutions from my website, www.TuckmanPsych.com, at no charge.

Memory Management

ADHD adults often complain about their faulty memory problems—and perhaps their families complain even more often. In fact, the client discussed above was referred to me for help with his memory problems. Regardless of whether the true dysfunction lies in executive functions, attention regulation, or only in working memory but not other forms of memory, the functional effect is that adults with ADHD look as though they have memory problems, loosely defined. This means both remembering the past, such as something that they were told, as well as remembering for the future, such as remembering to call the plumber when they get to work. This latter ability, which is called prospective memory, is integral to staying on top of most adult responsibilities; ADHD folks pay a big price for their weaknesses in this area. Success in life is all about remembering and then doing the right things at the right times.

Difficulty Remembering What One Was Told

This difficulty concerns episodic memories such as, "my wife spoke to our neighbor about getting some tree work done at the property line." *Episodic memories* are memories of events that took place at specific moments in time. Unfortunately for adults with ADHD, many things that happen in these individual episodes carry forward into other episodes, leaving the person out of touch if she can't remember what others remember. This is the scenario where one partner swears he told the other partner something who swears she never heard it.

Here are some strategies for improving ADHD adults' recall of such moments:

- Break the habit of delivering or receiving messages yelled across the house or when someone is rushing from one thing to the next.

- Ask for reminders, in an appropriate way, if the person to be asked is amenable and it will help—for example, your client can have his girlfriend leave a message on his voice mail at work to remind him to call the bank rather than just reminding him at breakfast.

- Always carry note cards and a pen and leave note cards and pens stashed in various places (Hallowell, 1995).

- Use a digital recorder to capture important information to be retrieved later.

- Use a memory notebook to record things (Weinstein, 1994).

- Use active learning techniques, such as rehearsing, relating new information to old, thinking about how the information will be retrieved, and processing the information further, thereby increasing the odds that the piece of information will be remembered (Nadeau, 1995a). These are variations on the old trick of repeating someone's name after meeting at a party or paraphrasing what you were told to make it stick better in your memory.

- Ask the speaker to slow down or repeat what was said (Weinstein, 1994), rather than pretending to have heard and remembered it all.

- Resist the temptation to impulsively fill in, either mentally or aloud, what the speaker is about to say, to prevent yourself from guessing wrong and then remembering your wrong guess (Weinstein, 1994).

- After a meeting or conversation, briefly summarize what was decided, what will be done next, and who will do what, to make sure everyone is on the same page. This can be done verbally right at the end of the conversation or later by e-mail.

Difficulty Learning New Things

This difficulty refers to *semantic memories* such as, "Columbus discovered America in 1492," which are facts not tied to a specific moment in a person's life.

- Use flash cards and repetition (Wells, Dahl, & Snyder, 2000).

- Repeat someone else's actions rather than relying on remembering written instructions (Wells et al., 2000). This is especially helpful for those who learn better by doing rather than by hearing or reading.

- Reduce external distractions (Wells et al., 2000) in order to make the relevant information stand out more. However, note that for some people, music or television can help to quell internal distractions and keep them focused.

- Break the work into several shorter sessions based on mental sharpness (Wells et al., 2000) or the time of day during which the most intense learning can take place based on the best alertness or medication coverage.

- Use active learning techniques (Nadeau, 1995a).

Prospective Memory Difficulties

Unlike the situations where the ADHD adult has no memory at all of something that she was told, with most prospective memory problems, she probably has a memory of it but fails to recall it at the relevant time. For example, remembering at work that she needs to buy milk on the way home doesn't really do her much good. Neither does remembering it when she's pulling up to her house. The only time that the memory counts is when she's approaching the turnoff to the supermarket. If she was asked about the milk, she would remember that she had to buy some, but she has difficulty self-generating the memory at the relevant moment. In neuropsychological terms, this is the difference between *free recall* and *cued recognition*.

Therefore, given that ADHD adults have difficulty generating those cues internally, the trick is to keep it in their thoughts until the relevant moment, or to create external cues at a moment when they are thinking about it, such that they will be reminded at the relevant moment.

- Place objects where they will serve as their own cues—for example, tell clients to put DVDs to be returned right in front of the door they'll have to go through to leave the house so they won't be forgotten. Remember, the corollary to "out of sight, out of mind" is "in sight, in mind."

- When setting a reminder alarm, respond to it immediately to prevent quickly forgetting it again (Nadeau, 1995a). A useful variation of "Speak now or forever hold your peace" is "Do it now or forget it forever." At a minimum, if the client can't do the task immediately, then he should set the alarm to go off again so he'll have another chance.

- Post a family calendar in a very visible place and meet occasionally to discuss the items on it.

- Use post-its, whiteboards, and pads of paper as reminders. The client should sprinkle them liberally throughout his home and workplace.

- The client can leave herself a voice mail or send herself an e-mail to better remember what she needs to remember at the place that she needs to remember it. For example, she can call her home voice mail while at work and leave herself a message to pay bills that night.

- Reduce the number of external distracters in the environment so that the relevant reminders stand out more. This may involve reducing the amount of overall clutter.

- Develop routines for doing the same things in the same order on the same schedule to prevent skipping steps (Weinstein, 1994).

Time Management

Time management involves using time effectively and staying on track through the day—something that is far easier said than done, but certainly a goal worth striving for.

Inefficient Use of Time

ADHD clients often complain that they just don't get enough done in a given stretch of time, despite their best intentions. It may also be the case that family members, coworkers, and bosses complain even more about this than the ADHD adult himself does.

■ The inefficient use of time is often related to the person's chaotic disorganization of his possessions because a lot of time is wasted looking for things, so it may help if clients can get their stuff organized. See the subsection below for more details on how to do this.

■ Clients can reduce distractions when trying to get things done, by turning off the phone and e-mail alerts or moving into a quieter environment.

■ They can use daily goal-setting to keep priorities at the front of the mind (Wells et al., 2000).

■ Clients can strive to limit the number of balls they have in the air at one time. Tempting as it can be, coach them not to start something before finishing something else. Following this "rule" provides an incentive to finish the first tasks.

■ Use a beeping or vibrating alarm to regularly alert clients to the passage of time and also to remind them to consider whether what they're currently doing is what they should be doing.

■ Make hard choices ahead of time to limit the number of activities they're involved in so they won't get stretched too thin and accomplish too little.

■ Use social pressure positively, by having the client make a commitment to someone else to get a certain number of things done in a given time period.

■ Work with someone else present—even if she is not directly involved in the process, her mere presence can serve as a reminder to stay on task.

Distractibility

Getting off track is a very common way for ADHD folks to wind up losing time and thereby not having enough time to do the things they were supposed to get done. Some of this wasted time occurs in big chunks, but clients can also dribble away small amounts of time that can add up to quite a bit. To the extent possible, it's generally best to set up these strategies beforehand, when they're on the client's mind, rather than relying on her to do the right thing in the moment.

■ Use reminders to keep ADHD folks on task, whether large or small notes taped onto a wall or large whiteboards (Wells et al., 2000). There's an anecdote about the 1992 presidential campaign that says Bill Clinton taped up a huge sign in his campaign headquarters that said "It's the economy, stupid!" as a way to keep him focused on the issue he thought would have the most resonance with voters.

- Related to this, clients can work to ingrain the habit of frequently asking themselves, "What should I be doing now?" (Nadeau, 1995a). They can cue themselves to do this by using a repeating alarm that forces a small break in the progression of time so that they can observe what they are doing and then make a conscious choice as to whether it's the best use of their time.

- Clients should do their work in a quieter and less visually stimulating environment or they can use a sound machine or fan to provide white noise to screen out other sounds. Alternatively, if the client doesn't become distracted by the sounds or images, music or television can provide a kind of white noise (Wells et al., 2000). They can also buy noise-canceling headphones that are relatively inexpensive these days. Foam earplugs cost virtually nothing, but they may block too much sound.

- ADHD folks should try to keep an orderly work space, but if their work space is currently messy, rather than making organizing it the major project of the moment, it's probably best to merely clear some of the mess to one side and schedule a later time to deal with it (Nadeau, 1995b).

- When clients discover themselves off on a tangent, they should go back to the original task and finish that before moving on to the next (Nadeau, 1995b). A certain amount of meandering is to be expected, so there's no point in beating themselves up about it. Instruct them to just go back to the previous task.

- Clients should use their ability to hyperfocus (Wells et al., 2000) for good instead of evil by immersing themselves in a project and completing a big chunk of it.

- They should break work sessions into smaller segments with short breaks in between to reduce wandering attention or to prevent crashing and abandoning the work altogether (Nadeau, 1995a). However, to give the devil his due, they should set an alarm to cue themselves to return to work so their breaks don't become longer than their work sessions.

- Clients can employ active learning or active processing techniques to stay involved in what they're doing (Nadeau, 1995a).

- For people with ADHD, there's a careful stimulus balance to strike—too much and they'll feel overwhelmed, too little and they'll become bored and sleepy. They should learn their ideal balance and strive to create that balance in their work environments (Nadeau, 1995a) depending on what they are working on and what their energy is at that moment. One person's ideal work environment is another's recipe for disaster.

■ If feasible, ADHD folks should work with a partner or in a group (Nadeau, 1995a), but only if this will not arouse any resentment in teammates who may be only partially willing to work this way with your client. The concept of informed consent applies here, in that the client should be up-front with his teammates if his ADHD symptoms will cause them undue stress or annoyance.

■ The client can set aside specific interruption-free periods of her day for tasks that require extra focus (Nadeau, 1995b). She can preserve this solitude by closing the web browser, turning off the phones, and turning off the new e-mail alert. If necessary, she can explain to coworkers or family members that she would prefer them to come back later unless there's an emergency, and then she can put up a sign to remind them. As one of my clients discovered, a closed door not only keeps other people out—it also kept him in.

■ If a new idea for a project keeps popping up, the client should take a small moment to write it down so that he can return to it later rather than pursuing it immediately (Nadeau, 1995b). Alternatively, he can dictate it to a digital recorder. Many ADHD people feel that if they don't immediately act on a good idea, it will disappear forever, so it may feel necessary to at least capture the thought briefly before being capable of giving the original task their full attention.

■ If a client tends to lose focus when speaking in meetings, he can write himself some brief notes beforehand (Nadeau, 1995b).

■ If the client's job involves getting assignments from a number of different people, she may be better off in a job with only one boss (Nadeau, 1995b) or where she has fewer projects to juggle at one time.

■ If the client is simply too distracted by internal stimuli at work, then maybe he needs a new job (Nadeau, 1995b).

Procrastination/Avoidance

Although some procrastination and avoidance difficulties may be based in the primary symptoms of ADHD, such as by becoming distracted while working on other tasks, these are also secondary psychological characteristics of the disorder. Avoided tasks are either too boring to inspire the person into action and/or there is something about them that arouses anxiety. Therefore, these issues may need to be addressed in therapy to help the person take a more proactive approach to dealing with school or workplace demands with less interference from negative thoughts and feelings. This may also involve working with the client to learn to rely less on others in a dependent or entitled fashion and/or to feel more worthy of success. These issues are covered in more detail in chapter 7, Adapting Psychotherapy for the ADHD Adult, but in the meantime there are some more circumscribed strategies that you can use to get your clients moving.

- Keep in mind the potentially high price paid for procrastinating—e.g., the stress and fallout from missing the deadline.

- If the problem is based in not knowing how to do something well, then encourage the client to learn the necessary skills so she can do the task more easily and quickly.

- The client can learn to break big projects into smaller pieces so the project feels less overwhelming, then he can give himself small rewards for meeting interim deadlines. However, because of their working memory or executive function deficits, many ADHD people have difficulty visualizing whole projects and how the pieces fit together, so they may need some help to learn how to break big jobs into smaller parts from a coach, therapist, romantic partner, friend, or coworker.

- Clients can make a commitment to someone else to complete the task (Nadeau, 1995b)—thus using the perceived social pressure from that person to their advantage.

- Teach clients to intersperse boring and enjoyable activities. The more enjoyable activities may be only slightly less boring than the primary activity, but at least they can provide a break of sorts.

- If the thought of a long stretch of working on the dreaded activity is too much to bear, then the client should make a commitment to do ten minutes and see how it goes. If it's going well, she then agrees to do another ten minutes. Often these activities are not so awful once they are actually started. It's getting over the initial hump that's the hardest.

- Severe procrastination may be a signal to the client that she would be better off doing something else, having someone else do that particular task for her, or finding a new way to do it.

Hyperfocus

The main trouble with hyperfocus is that it is very difficult to catch oneself and stop it once it has begun. Therefore, the best point of intervention is usually ahead of time, before the client gets locked in on a specific task. Here are some ways to head off hyperfocusing:

- The client can set an alarm before she gets hyperfocused to serve as a reminder.

- Enlist others to provide reminders, if they are willing to do it. For example, have the client say to a coworker, "I get really focused on my work, so do me a favor and swing by my cubicle to pick me up on the way to the meeting."

- Sometimes the client just needs to give the devil his due, so she can allow herself some time to do that. For instance, I had a client who allowed himself some free time on the weekends just to wander through his day and do whatever struck his fancy. Knowing that this reward was coming made it easier for him to stay focused during the long workweek.

- If the client notices that he has hyperfocused on something for too long, then he can take a moment to reassess and figure out what the best course of action would be, rather than putting himself down or impulsively jumping into another activity that may not be the best use of his time, especially under the new circumstances.

Running Late

Running late refers to the tendency ADHD folks have to arrive late for their appointments, meetings, and other obligations. This can have significant occupational and social consequences because when this tendency is perceived as excessive, the ADHD people can lose jobs and friends.

- Coach clients to create a schedule ahead of time for what should get done and when. They should count time backwards—for example, "To get there by 2:00, I need to park by 1:50, leave home by 1:20, and start getting ready by 1:00." They can write down the "backward" schedule, if that will make it more tangible and easier to stay on schedule.

- Clients should avoid best-case scenario planning and build in time for unexpected events, transitions, and breaks. Then they should pad the plan with a little more time if it's something really worth being on time for.

- Clients should time how long different tasks take and write down that information. Then refer back to what was written later when scheduling any activities (Tudisco, 2005, February). A client can make this process more fun, and therefore more likely to be done, by making bets with herself and/or others and seeing how she does.

- The client can set an alarm for when he needs to stop a task or start getting ready; for example, he can use an alarm clock in a reverse fashion by setting it to signal the time to get into bed (Nadeau, 1995a).

- To avoid starting the day late and allowing it to snowball, the client can learn to make a point of getting to bed on time and then getting out of bed on time. Many morning problems really start the night before by going to bed too late or not doing what's needed to be ready to roll. Keep the morning routine as simple as possible and do whatever can be done the night before, such as fixing lunch if the client takes lunch to work.

- Clients can learn to avoid distracters like the television, radio, and newspapers when trying to get out on time (Nadeau, 1995a).

- They can also learn to avoid starting an engrossing activity too close to a transition time (Nadeau, 1995a).

- Clients can build slack time into their schedules to absorb unexpected overflow from various activities (Nadeau, 1995b).

- They can plan to be early to appointments or meetings and bring something to work on or read if there's extra time (Nadeau, 1995b) to avoid the dreaded boredom of having nothing to do.

- Tell clients, "Don't even think about starting those tasks that 'will take only a minute.' Nothing takes only a minute."

Missing Deadlines

Even with the risk of exaggeration, it's fair to say that many ADHD people alternate between feeling haunted by deadlines and being oblivious to them. Unfortunately, the world is full of deadlines, so they are a necessary evil that ADHD adults must learn to deal with. You can teach clients to:

- Break large projects into several parts with mini-deadlines to create a greater sense of urgency earlier. Put these mini-deadlines into the schedule and plan accordingly.

- Avoid overcommitment and learn to say no—no amount of creative time management will fit twenty-five hours into twenty-four.

- Recognize the risks and additional stress, for themselves and others, inherent in waiting until the last minute to do things.

- Carry their schedules at all times and not commit to anything without looking at it. When adding a new task, actually put it into the planner—either at a specific time or on the to-do list if it isn't time-specific (Nadeau, 1995b). This forces clients to see what else they need to do and whether they will have enough time to do it.

- Learn additional skills that may need to be mastered to make certain tasks go more easily or efficiently, such as what does and doesn't need to be saved for taxes.

- Talk to their boss about setting up more regular meetings to review their progress on various projects and prevent last-minute surprises. They can do the same at home with their romantic partners to discuss what needs to be done at home.

Difficulty Controlling Impulses Regarding the Use of Time

As with the strategies to manage hyperfocus, these strategies also are most effective when implemented before the impulse strikes. It's far more difficult to rein oneself in than it is to avoid the temptation in the first place. ADHD adults can learn to:

- Eliminate potentially exciting impulse stimuli before they occur, such as by unsubscribing from e-mail alerts.

- Give the devil his due—the client needs to accept that a certain amount of time each day will have to be spent on relaxing and recharging her batteries. She can learn to build that time in so that it doesn't happen at less convenient times (Hallowell, 1995).

- Post visual reminders to counterbalance his impulses and keep him on task. This can be written, like Clinton's sign "It's the economy, stupid!" or it can be less direct, like a picture of the vacation spot that he's working toward visiting.

- Use self-talk, such as "slow and steady, one step at a time," to stay focused, at least during the times that the client is consciously thinking about it (Wells et al., 2000).

- Switch gears mentally by purposely thinking of something else when she catches her mind starting to wander. If she's in a tempting situation, she can switch gears physically by leaving the tempting situation (Wells et al., 2000).

Stuff Management

Managing stuff means keeping track of the important possessions and having the right stuff at the right time. Many ADHD adults have an all-or-nothing relationship with keeping their stuff organized—their possessions usually wind up in a chaotic state before they finally get fed up or someone gets on their case about it, which may spark a frenetic organizing spree. Such a spree, although perhaps admirable in its intensity, doesn't necessarily follow a systematic process nor does it result in a more logical, easily maintained system, thereby setting up clients for further difficulties. For those reasons it can be helpful to discuss with the client how to assess what's scattered about and how it got there, and from that basis move to creating better ways to manage those possessions (Robin, 2002).

Most ADHD adults will feel some degree of hopelessness when it comes to getting organized. My tack is always to focus first on functionality; that is, the gains they will make in efficiency and the reduction in their general stress level. From there, I speak about the esthetic gains, but only if esthetics are of value to the client. Some will suffer from the sense that they should be "neat and organized" like everyone else supposedly is. This heightened sense of discrepancy only makes them feel even more hopeless and defective. Therefore, I encourage clients to find their own personal comfort level when it comes to neatness. The homes pictured in the design magazines look very impressive, but they may be neither comfortable nor realistic, so they should not be aspired to.

I will also say that people at the extreme end of being obsessive-compulsive have problems of their own. I often tell clients that if they really wanted to, they could probably achieve and maintain the picture-perfect neatness of their superorganized friends and family members, if someone were to give them a million dollars to do it. But then I ask them whether the energy required and the other activities that would have to be forsaken would be worth it without that enormous financial reward. Most of them say no, and then they feel perhaps a little less inferior as a result.

I frame neatness as a preference and a choice that, like any other choice, involves both rewards and costs—it then comes back to preference. This fits my general treatment approach which is to improve skills to the extent possible, while also accepting certain limitations without guilt or shame.

It can help to have the client write out the rewards for generally being more organized, as a way to maintain motivation during a boring or painful process. Posting this rewards list can also help to keep it fresh in their minds. This list can be supplemented with a second list of rewards to be earned for each step proposed and then accomplished toward achieving the larger goal. Note that the reinforcing power of the rewards may be greater if someone else administers them, thus preventing shortcuts or unearned rewards (Robin, 2002).

General Messiness/Chaos

Staying organized is a continual process, not a one-time event—it's like saying, "I've taken showers before, but I never seem to stay clean, so I don't bother anymore" (Nadeau, 1995a, p. 210). The client needs to accept the necessary evil of setting aside a certain amount of time each day or week to keep the chaos in check. Just living life tends to create chaos, so it requires a regular input of energy to reestablish order.

Often the disorganization of objects is partly caused by the disorganization of time because the person doesn't have enough time to sort through things and put them where they belong. It's not always this simple, though. Some people could have endless time and still not get everything organized because they lack a good system for putting things away. You will need to work with these clients on creating a better organizational system by discussing what sorts of things they don't have good places for, where they tend to run into trouble, what they've already tried, and so on. Some of this might be better handled by a professional organizer who can go to the client's house or workplace and really dig into everything—see more on this subject below under the heading Professional Organizers.

Regardless of whether the client doesn't have enough time to organize or doesn't use that time well, many ADHD adults find themselves living in chaotic conditions because they simply have too many things to organize effectively. This may be partly due to not making the time to go through their belongings and papers to weed out the unnecessary or obsolete items. However, sometimes it's more complicated in that they have great difficulties in deciding what to keep and what to toss. This form of pseudohoarding is partly an information-processing issue, in that they may have difficulty retaining the master organizing scheme that would enable them to see how individual items fit into their big plan. As a result, they play it safe and keep more than they need.

For other clients, this pseudohoarding can also be emotionally based—they try to defend themselves from ever being caught empty-handed by keeping much more than they need. Everything has some value, they reason, so they should keep it all. But that's not the relevant fact. It's not about whether the item has some value in absolute terms, it's about what its value is relative to their other belongings. Some items with little absolute value will have an insufficient relative value to justify keeping them, especially if they will get in the way of finding other more important items. For example, keeping every single receipt you acquire can be helpful if you need to return some purchases, but it's less helpful if it takes an hour to go through all the receipts to find the right one, or if the right one is hopelessly lost in the clutter. In such cases, saving all the receipts doesn't do any good if the one you need can't be found.

You will have to work with these clients to accept that although their anxiety is legitimate, their way of dealing with it is ultimately counterproductive, and perhaps becoming more selective would serve them better. This will mean making hard choices about letting go of some things. Clients could set a cutoff point below which the items will get recycled, donated, or thrown away. To help with this process, have your client visualize her responses to the following scenarios:

- If you were going to move and had to pay the movers to move it, would you keep it?

- Imagine having to pack it up and then carry it out to a moving truck on a scorching August day. The truck is almost full and some choices must be made—does it make the cut?

- Or imagine yourself frantically digging through all your stuff to find something really important—say, your passport or your grandmother's wedding ring. Would you be happy to have all this other stuff then?

To point out the price paid for keeping too much stuff, really play up the drama of these scenarios. You can also work with clients in the following ways:

- Work with the client to actively restrict the flow of new stuff into his world, such as mail, e-mail, magazines, newspapers, and the stuff he buys. Some of this stuff comes in all by itself, so he will need to actually expend energy to keep it out. It's like bailing out an old, leaky rowboat—we do our best to plug the holes, but there will always be more bailing to do.

- Increase the outflow of possessions to at least equal the inflow, unless she needs to go on a "junk diet" to reduce the total amount of stuff, in which case more stuff needs to go out than comes in.

- Create a better organizational system—often things aren't put away because they're "homeless" and lack a designated place to be stored. Alternatively, their place may be out of the way or not easily accessible. Creating a better, easier organizational system can help with this issue, and will make it more likely that stuff gets put away.

- Things should be put away or filed based on how they will be retrieved—and how often. If it's unlikely that the client will need to track down a particular item, then it's probably not worth keeping it superorganized. For example, when I accepted insurance reimbursement for my clients, I would place new explanations of benefits in a folder, behind the old ones. On the rare occasions when I needed to find a specific explanation, I knew it would be in generally chronological order, and I could usually find it in a few minutes. I could have separated them by insurance company, but the extra time expended wouldn't have been justified by the time saved. So, don't spend more time organizing than is saved by being organized.

- Sometimes ADHD adults have trouble finding filed papers because they don't remember how they were filed. It may be better to file by category, such as financial, personal, medical, legal, and so on, and then have subfolders within each of those (Nadeau, 1995a). A good filing system is easily remembered, which is more likely if it's personally meaningful, rather than adopted from someone else's system.

- You might suggest that the client take photos occasionally to track her progress, or lack thereof, in getting the chaos under control. Progress can be motivating and lack of progress can relight the fire.

- If organization and follow-through are your client's weak points, try to get him to work with someone else to better stay on track, if that's feasible (Nadeau, 1995b).

Not Having Important Things at the Right Times

This is partly related to the chaos described above because it can contribute to a general lack of awareness or loss of the memory of where relevant items have gotten off to. Work with the client to put things where she can't help but see them at the relevant moment. For example, place the bills to be mailed right next to her keys so she can grab them all before heading out the door. Since many ADHD folks can't count on themselves to remember reliably, it's best to set these things up immediately when they think of it.

- Have the client put up a whiteboard on his path out of the house so he can write reminders to himself—and then make a daily habit of checking the whiteboard. To increase the salience of each note, he should limit the number of items he writes on the board and erase the old ones. Using different colored markers can keep everything from blending together and disappearing.

- Have the client duplicate all important but easily lost items, like keys and glasses (Nadeau, 1995a), and make sure she keeps them in several convenient locations.

- Work with the client to build in some time when getting ready to leave the house, rather than rushing out the door, which makes it too easy to leave things behind in a flurry of activity.

Goal Management

Good goal management involves both creating and pursuing long-term goals. However, as a rule, it's easier to come up with goals than it is to stay on track with them. Achieving those goals really depends on having some basic mastery of the three areas discussed above: memory management, time management, and stuff management. They are the building blocks that allow the person to move forward successfully in life. "Goals function as a kind of guard against aimlessness, drawing the individual through time toward a desired place" (Hallowell, 1995, p. 149). Because planning for the future and holding to a goal to guide behavior is a more difficult cognitive task, you can expect your clients to have a harder time staying on track in the way either you or they may want.

Some of this discussion of goals will focus on upcoming difficulties or transitions—such as starting a new job, moving, or the birth of a child. It can be helpful to brainstorm likely problems together and then generate solutions in advance before something becomes a problem. It's often easier to think of better solutions when not in the heat of the moment. Even if the client does quite well overall, she may still return for booster sessions to deal with new challenges or to get back on track with the old ones (Weiss et al., 1999).

Difficulty Staying Focused on Short-Term Goals

Managing short-term goals tends to be easier than longer-term goals because it involves a smaller window of time in which the ADHD adult must stay focused. However, it still may require a certain amount of white-knuckling, as the person uses a strong force of will to stay on task and resists becoming sidelined. The client can use the following instructions to stay focused on short-term goals:

- Use the techniques for distractibility (the second section under Time Management above), since there's likely to be some overlap between the solutions to these two difficulties.

- Take the first fifteen minutes of the day to plan the day's activities and set priorities (Nadeau, 1995b). This may work better if he puts a sign up to remind himself to do this, rather than getting sucked reactively into other activities.

- Build in small rewards for completing tasks (Nadeau, 1995b).

- Encourage the client to think about her priorities before she dives into a new task. Have her ask herself, no matter how tempting the new thing may be, "Is this what I should be doing now?" For example, I had a client who went out into his backyard to give the grill a "quick clean" before company came over. He wound up spending more than an hour making it look like new, certainly not a worthwhile goal with company on the way.

- Tie short-term goals to larger ones, so there will be a feeling of progress with each small step that is accomplished.

Difficulty Staying Focused on Long-Term Goals

Long-term goals are especially difficult for most ADHD folks since they do not loom as large in their consciousness as more immediate concerns and distractions do. It is not that they are unaware of these goals or do not want to pursue them, but rather that working on them is continually pushed from the present into some future moment— later, tomorrow, next week—and thereby potentially postponed into oblivion. So the trick is to find ways to keep these future goals in mind in the present. Here are some suggestions for accomplishing that:

- Post a picture of the desired goal to serve as a reminder.

- Have the client put up a conspicuous note to herself, like Clinton's sign to himself about the economy, described above.

- Break long projects into smaller pieces and set deadlines for each part. This may also entail setting up more regular check-ins with a boss or romantic partner to ensure that the client doesn't get carried too far afield.

- Work with the client to spend some time on a regular basis tracking his progress on long-term projects to make his successes more tangible and to see where he needs to do better. Make adjustments as necessary.

- If her job involves a lot of long-term projects and she keeps running into trouble with them, the client may be better off in a job with shorter goals (Nadeau, 1995b).

Difficulty Tolerating Repetitive Tasks

Repetitive and boring tasks are the bane of most ADHD folks. Such tasks can feel like torture, yet they are still a necessary part of managing our lives. The majority of the suggestions below come from Wells and colleagues (2000).

- Set deadlines to create structure and stay on task.

- Use last-minute pressure to get energized and stay focused, if there isn't too much danger of disaster striking.

- Delegate parts of the task away, if possible.

- Do it in small bits.

- Work with someone else.

- Create variety by rotating through several activities. The variety is less boring and the time is still spent productively.

- Set up rituals to create consistency.

- Set a timer to spend a specific amount of time on the task before taking a break.

- Keep in mind the cost of not following through.

Hyperactivity/Motor Restlessness

Fortunately, the most obvious aspects of hyperactivity that were present in childhood will have faded for most adults. However, we also expect adults to be much better at sitting still, so the bar has been raised. The trick is to find more productive, or at least less destructive, ways to manage that excess energy so that clients can pursue their goals more effectively. If possible, the following suggestions by Nadeau (1995b) should be explored:

- Work at a job that provides or allows a lot of physical movement, such as movement from room to room, frequent interpersonal interaction, or travel from one job site to another.

- If the client's job requires prolonged desk work, she can take frequent brief breaks that allow movement, such as going to the water fountain, delivering mail, and so on.

- The client can bring lunch to work so he can spend the lunch hour walking or exercising without having to take the time to buy something to eat. The more sedentary the job, the more important it is to exercise, so he should walk before or after work if he can't do it during the day.

- Try to avoid jobs with lots of long meetings or sedentary, detailed desk work.

Low Frustration Tolerance

Some of this low frustration tolerance comes simply from brain wiring that leads to strong but transient emotional reactions and impulsive actions. However, some of it is also an outgrowth of the greater stress that many ADHD adults feel because of their difficulties with organization, time management, relationship balance, and so on. Medications can be helpful for addressing the brain wiring, so the following techniques provide other ways to lengthen that short fuse.

- Examine the situations that cause the most distress or that the client has the least patience for—is there a better way to do it? (Nadeau, 1995b).

- Work with the client to monitor her frustration level and counsel her to leave a situation or take a break before she blows (Nadeau, 1995b). It also helps for her to think ahead about situations that are likely to test her limits and to have some strategies prepared before going into them.

- To the extent possible, avoid intense situations that are likely to be overloading.

- Teach the client relaxation techniques that can be used in various situations (Nadeau, 1995b), such as deep breathing, progressive muscular relaxation, and visualization. For more information on these exercises, check out *The Anxiety & Phobia Workbook, Fourth Edition*, by Edmund Bourne, Ph.D., published by New Harbinger Publications (2005).

- Work with the client to exercise regularly, sleep well, eat well, and generally take care of himself to give himself a longer fuse. See the Creating an ADHD-Friendly Lifestyle section in chapter 4.

Eliciting Support from Others

Because ADHD is a disorder that affects other people in the adult's life, it can be helpful to teach the ADHD adult how to appropriately elicit support from those others in his life (Hallowell, 1995). This involves working with him on how and when to ask for help, striving for balance in the relationship, living up to his obligations without making his problems other people's problems, and not promising more than he can deliver.

Ambivalent Dependency

Many ADHD adults have ambivalent feelings about getting help from others. On the one hand, they can display an overdependency and sense of entitlement wherein they expect others to rescue them from their poor planning—others are made responsible for keeping them on track or completing tasks that they "can't" do. On the other hand, they can exhibit a strong counterdependency in which they strongly resist any perceived efforts to "control" them, even when the other person's influence is intended to be helpful—such as, "Your cell phone is going to get cut off if you don't pay the bill by tomorrow." I see this particularly among my college students and young adults with ADHD, either in relation to their parents or their romantic partners. It's almost as if the normal dependency/counterdependency of adolescence takes longer to mature into an adult's independence/interdependence.

Obviously, this flipping between extremes can be quite confusing, even maddening, for others who don't know how best to manage the relationship. For those reasons, it may be useful to discuss when and how your client could ask for help from others. The couples therapy section in chapter 7 discusses further how to restore balance to relationships where one person is overfunctioning.

Self-advocacy is an important skill in most domains of life. As I sometimes tell clients, "Most people are really bad at mind reading, so you may need to come out and tell them." It can be helpful to work with clients on building a solid understanding of their own strengths and weaknesses, including how their ADHD impacts these, and then on how to convey that information to others in a useful way. This may involve role-playing and practicing a brief canned speech, asking for what they need, and answering likely questions (Murphy, 2006).

To Tell or Not to Tell

When is it a good idea for clients to share their diagnosis with family, friends, coworkers, or bosses? It depends. Disclosing in the workplace can bring its own problems, even if it's impossible to directly tie subsequent negative events to the disclosure, so it's usually best not to disclose it to an employer. There are rarely legal complications when disclosing to friends and family, but it's still a question that deserves some serious thought. There are three problems that may arise when clients disclose their ADHD diagnosis:

1.   Once the cat is out of the bag, they can't get it back in.

2.   They may not know what the other person knows about ADHD—he may have some gross misconceptions that would need to be corrected.

3.   They can't guarantee that the person will respect their privacy and keep that information confidential.

However, none of these is insurmountable, nor should it mean that clients should never disclose. Rather they are worth keeping in mind just to ensure that the ADHD person doesn't set herself up for unexpected trouble. The decision to disclose is one that should be made with forethought, never impulsively in the moment. Some solutions to the problems outlined above are found below.

Because something can't be unsaid, my recommendation is to talk about symptoms before talking about diagnoses. For example:

■   "I have trouble remembering things that are told to me on the fly, so could you remind me in an e-mail?"

■   "I often get totally caught up in my work and have trouble remembering to stop for a meeting, so can you remind me when you're leaving for the meeting?"

■   "Sorry, I'm just really bad at keeping track of things, so please don't take it personally that I lost your CD."

Because talking about symptoms may not be enough, and the client feels it necessary to disclose the diagnosis, and the person to be told is trustworthy and open to learning more, then the client can share the diagnosis. Truth is earned, so there is no moral obligation to give someone information that he might misuse.

If there is some concern that the person to be told may not really understand ADHD or, worse, has serious misconceptions about it, I recommend to clients that they first find a way to ask the person what he knows about ADHD and then gently correct some of the misconceptions. If the person is willing and able to hear this, then it may be safe to disclose to him. If so, then I recommend that clients educate the person further about ADHD, either verbally or by providing helpful books, magazines, or websites. The appendix at the back of the book has a listing of such resources.

The third point in the problem list above concerns confidentiality. My philosophy is that people who don't treat personal information with respect, either by sharing it inappropriately or by using it against the person, set themselves up to be lied to or withheld from. So, I recommend that clients not tell people who are unable to keep private information private. This is not a reflection on the client or anything about ADHD, it's just that telling a loose-lipped person is a setup for disappointment. Even if a person is trustworthy, nevertheless the client should ask her to keep the information private, rather than just assume that she will keep it to herself.

There was a member of my adult ADHD support group who, perhaps recognizing his tendency for impulsive acts, made it very simple for himself. He had two rules about telling people about his ADHD: "(1) Never tell anyone you have ADHD. (2) Even if you forget rule number one, never tell anyone you have ADHD." Obviously, this got a good laugh from the group, perhaps from the recognition that good intentions beforehand sometimes get lost in the moment.

There are people who believe that those with ADHD should announce it to the world without shame. Although I certainly agree that ADHD is nothing to be ashamed of, I also recognize that there can be social consequences for disclosing this information to the wrong people and/or at the wrong times. It's a personal decision that I hope will be well thought-out, regardless of what the adult with ADHD ultimately decides.

Involving Family Members

Part of coaching involves working with the client's family, romantic partner, friends, and coworkers—either directly by including them in the sessions or, more likely, indirectly by coaching the client on how to get these people to alter their behaviors. The sales pitch to these other people is that everyone benefits from the ADHD adult functioning better. The complex dynamics that can occur in romantic relationships where one person has ADHD are covered more fully in the couples therapy section of chapter 7, but here are a few specific strategies more in keeping with those in this chapter.

Work with your clients to teach the other people in their lives to:

■ Give clear, concise directions that are easy to follow and understand.

■ Write down important directions.

■ Break down tasks into small, achievable steps rather than set general goals.

■ Give reminders, as appropriate.

For example, one of my clients put up a whiteboard on the fridge where his wife could write notes to him of what needed to be done around the house, rather than relying on him to notice these tasks himself—experience had taught us that this did not happen with the frequency that she was hoping for. By having it up on the whiteboard, he knew exactly what to do when he had some spare time. This is an example of the expectation management mentioned above in the section A General Coaching Theory. By altering his wife's expectation that he would simply notice these tasks himself, which he really wasn't able to do, she was able to adopt a better method.

Professional Advocacy

Sometimes the client will need a professional to assist in the advocacy process. This should be a last resort, but some situations are not workable otherwise. The advocate could be a therapist, psychiatrist, coach, educational advisor, or lawyer. She should have a solid understanding of ADHD, the client's strengths and weaknesses, and whether it's a battle worth fighting. In high-stakes situations where the client is attempting to gain accommodations for testing, school, or work, especially when the decision maker isn't friendly to the diagnosis, it can be helpful to have someone else provide some intellectual muscle and credibility. Examples of these situations include special-education meetings, writing reports that seek special accommodations, meeting with supervisors/professors to explain the diagnosis and the rationale for the requested accommodations, participating in disciplinary meetings, and providing a professional opinion on decisions about job modifications and placement (Murphy, 2006).

Other Professionals

In this section, I cover two other types of professionals who may be helpful for your ADHD clients: professional organizers and career counselors. Obviously, these two specialists aren't coaches, but because they offer pragmatic strategies, I am including them in this chapter. However, just as with therapists and medication prescribers, these professionals must have a strong understanding of typical ADHD deficits if they are to be effective working with ADHD adults. There is a licensing requirement for career counselors, who will have degrees at the masters level or greater, but there is no licensing requirement for professional organizers, so it's harder to know what you're getting with them.

Professional Organizers

The proliferation of stuff, to use the most generic term, has made it more difficult for most people to stay organized. There just seems to be a lot more stuff to keep track of. Whereas this is merely an annoyance for most people, for those with ADHD and some others, it can be disastrous and ego-sapping. The field of professional organizing has sprung from this growing societal trend, promising to impose order on the chaos.

An organizer can help clients dig themselves out from under an accumulated mountain of disorganization that has grown far beyond their ability to climb alone (Nadeau, 2002). Beyond merely babysitting clients while they put stuff away, or putting it away for them, a good organizer can also help clients create customized organizational systems to better manage their belongings and thereby make it easier to maintain their stuff. This is not a trivial task, since many ADHD adults are disorganized not just because they hate organizing and don't spend enough time doing it, but also because they're not good at creating these larger systems, so they wind up moving stuff around without really making things better. If each item doesn't have a designated place, it's likely to get shuffled about in an unproductive way. Alternatively, items are put away in less than optimal ways, creating inefficiencies that can add up over time. The organizer can help find places for the homeless items, as well as move things around so everything makes better sense to the client.

One common problem among disorganized people is that they hang on to too many things, which makes everything worse. The extra clutter makes it harder to find the important items and adds to the feeling of chaos. An organizer can help the client go through everything and make the hard choices about what to keep and what to toss, often freeing up a surprising amount of space. The remaining items may then be easier to organize.

Hiring an organizer periodically may be money well spent (Nadeau, 2002). If the client has the money to do it, then it becomes a personal choice of whether it brings enough happiness to justify the expense. Even if they can easily afford it, though, some clients may feel guilty about bringing in an organizer to do something that everyone else seemingly does easily. My response to this is that I could change the oil in my car myself if I had to, but the hassle isn't worth saving twenty bucks, so I have the garage do it for me. So, for some clients, perhaps the cost of the organizer is less than the headache of doing it themselves. Beyond whatever personal benefit the ADHD client gets from the organizer, there is also the potential benefit for the romantic partner, if there is one, if the disorganization is a source of conflict.

The National Association of Professional Organizers (www.napo.net) is the national nonprofit organization that represents organizers. They provide a searchable directory as well as classes for organizers. Ideally, an organizer should be a member.

For those who don't need a complete reorganization, a plain old cleaning service can prevent much unhappiness. As the saying goes, "A housekeeper is much cheaper than a divorce." However, as with any financial matter, the decision to bring in a cleaning service can become less simple than it should be. A member of the audience at one of my seminars on adult ADHD told a story of a client with severe ADHD whose husband refused to allow her to hire a cleaning service. His opinion was that she should be able to do it herself, despite the fact that she had never successfully managed to keep the house clean and orderly over all the years of their lengthy marriage. Obviously, the dynamics in this relationship created a situation where a simple solution isn't so simple.

Career Counselors

According to Nadeau (1995b), career counselors help their clients find careers that are a better fit by evaluating their:

- Interests

- Strengths and skills

- Temperament and personality type

- Values and needs

It's important to do a thorough evaluation if career counseling is to be at all helpful. For example, evaluating only the client's interests without assessing whether he has the necessary ability may be a setup for disappointment or even failure. After all, many people would like to be a rock star or professional athlete, but very, very few of them actually have what it takes. For those clients with ADHD or a learning disability, one facet of goodness of fit that the evaluation must consider is the impact of their ADHD deficits since they may rule out some possibilities.

Evaluations, whether career or diagnostic, are usually performed when the person or professional is feeling lost and is looking for guidance as to the best next steps, all of which makes them especially vulnerable to bad advice. When informed by a solid understanding of ADHD, though, the evaluation can be very helpful for ADHD adults who have felt adrift during their many academic and job struggles, and have been unable to find a niche they enjoy and are good at. Ideally, the evaluation should also include recommendations for reasonable accommodations to ask of employers, compensatory strategies to be undertaken by the client, and suggested areas for remediation (Nadeau, 1995b).

If a client is having difficulties in his current position, it's generally better to seek accommodations before an employer is at the end of its rope and to seek them in a constructive way (Nadeau, 1995b). The sales pitch is that the relatively minor accommodations will enable the employee to do a better job, which is ultimately to the employer's benefit. Of course, for the employer to buy into this, it has to get back more than it gives, or it's no bargain. No matter how accommodating an employer may be, ultimately the lion's share of the work falls to employees to improve their performance or to find a job that's a better fit.

Employees will probably get a better reception if they state their needs in a positive light, by making their requests in the spirit of dedication to their job and a desire to improve their work performance, rather than from a hackle-raising position of entitlement. Note that using ADHD as an excuse after a reprimand for unacceptable performance is the absolute worst way to disclose the diagnosis.

If the evaluation includes an assessment of abilities, or if the client already knows that certain skills are weak, then remediation may be called for—for example, speech and language therapy, tutoring to improve writing skills, computer training, and so on. If these skills cannot be learned in a self-directed manner, then tutors/job skill coaches can teach the specific content and help process the information that the employee might have missed along the way.

At other times, it may be easier to change some aspects of the job. For example, eliminating or reassigning unessential tasks, like proofreading, filing, or documenting, may enable the employee to perform better on higher level or more important tasks (Weiss et al., 1999). Other employees will benefit from increasing the structure on the job; for example, by breaking big projects into smaller pieces with interim deadlines; holding more frequent meetings with supervisors or project-mates to ensure the employee is on track; or empowering others to act as the employee's external executive functioner.

A splendid example of this was provided by ADHD advocate Rob Tudisco (2005, February). Due to his ADHD, he had a lot of difficulty getting out of the office on time to pick up his son after school. Finally, one day, after unintentionally keeping his son waiting at the school for an hour, he told his secretary that she was not allowed to leave the office at the end of the day unless she took him with her. She was not to accept any of his excuses or believe his claims that he would only be another two minutes after she left, since those two minutes too easily became half an hour. By making an honest self-assessment and giving his secretary the authority to override his excuses, he never picked up his son late again.

Sometimes restructuring the environment will enable the ADHD person to become more functional (Weiss et al., 1999), for example, moving the employee's desk to a less distracting location that isn't next to a door or the copy machine. In these cases, the person has the skills to do the job well but has difficulty managing the extraneous distractions that are part of the workplace but not inherent to the job itself.

Work accommodations should be the minimum necessary. Unless someone is absolutely irreplaceable or a genius, most employers aren't interested in doing more than they have to since they have enough to deal with already. Employees aren't owed an ideal work situation, whether they have ADHD or any other disorder. Rather, the onus is on the employee to make herself as desirable and employable as possible, even if that means skill building outside of work hours. Although employees with ADHD qualify to receive protection under the Americans with Disabilities Act, invoking legal rights or involving a lawyer should always be a last resort due to the difficulty, time, expense, and probability of receiving accommodations through this avenue. Pragmatically, who would want to work in a post-lawsuit environment? In these cases, it may be better to walk away and find better employment elsewhere—although justice may not be served, happiness is more likely to be. Therefore, it's much better to work out accommodations informally.

Conclusion

Coaching is an important part of treatment for ADHD adults and it's the part that was missing from many of these clients' former therapies. Success in the present cuts the chains of failure binding them to their pasts—and makes it much easier to overcome those struggles in the present. This more active and directive style may be a stretch for some therapists, whereas it may give permission to others who have already been doing it, but may have felt vaguely guilty about it. I wouldn't recommend coaching for every single client who walks through my door, but I don't think there is anything that I would recommend for every client. The key is to give each client what she needs, no matter how different from the client before her. Coaching is just one more tool in our toolbox to help us get our jobs done, and done well.

CHAPTER 7

Adapting Psychotherapy for the ADHD Adult

The challenge for the therapist working with ADHD adults is to sort through the layers of personality traits, intrapsychic conflicts, and neurologically based patterns, and then approach each in an effective way. This requires a broad perspective rather than use of a single theoretical lens through which to interpret all behavior (Nadeau, 2002). Some of the client's problems are neurologically ADHD-based, but the client is more than his ADHD. He will potentially have all the same problems we all have, plus perhaps some that are specific to those with ADHD.

You need to help dispirited clients start feeling more motivated to try to improve their functioning and happiness. Their pessimism is well-founded, in that they've often received well-intentioned advice and embarked on self-directed campaigns of self-improvement, to little avail. Therefore, part of your job is to convince them that this time around, the outcome can indeed be different. Obviously, more of the same tends to lead to more of the same, but that's exactly why there is reasonable cause for optimism now—knowing what the diagnosis of ADHD means and using that knowledge to engage in a targeted treatment program, plus a fair bit of hard work, can lead to a different outcome this time.

As much as the functional successes and performance improvements to be gained from the other three parts of the integrative treatment program will provide tangible reasons for the client to begin to feel better, so too will the therapy help the client to take a more active approach to employing the strategies from the other three parts of the program.

EXCUSES VERSUS EXPLANATIONS

ADHD is viewed by some as nothing more than an excuse for poor performance. Effective reframing goes beyond excuse-making. Excuses allow someone to get out of his obligations. They lower the bar for what is expected of him. Those who make excuses expect most of the changes, flexibility, or accommodations to come from other people. In contrast, explanations first offer a solid understanding of how and why things can go bad and then provide strategies the ADHD adult can use to increase the odds of success.

Explanations also mean owning up to likely failures and taking active steps ahead of time to prevent them, which may include instructing the client not to put himself into no-win situations. Explanations place most of the onus for improvement on the person himself, whether it's to directly improve the situation or to make amends afterwards. Also, explanations assume that we cannot easily change the rules for individuals, at least not without paying an unacceptable price, be it academically, financially, occupationally, relationally, or psychologically. For example, a client can't call the electric company to say he has ADHD and therefore probably won't get most of his bills paid on time.

Basic Concepts

Before I go into more specific aspects of doing therapy with ADHD adults, I will lay a foundation to guide your work with these interesting clients.

Reframing Past Struggles

Adults with undiagnosed ADHD are very much in touch with the price they've paid for their struggles. Until the day they received a diagnosis, though, they'd found various other explanations for the behaviors that had caused their difficulties. Most of these explanations tend to be along the lines of the book title *You Mean I'm Not Lazy, Stupid, or Crazy?!* by Kelly and Ramundo (2006). Therefore, a big part of what we do with these clients is reframe the difficulties they'd experienced in the past because this has important implications for their odds of success in the future, and their willingness to apply themselves in the present. I'll sometimes use the following joke with clients or during presentations to point out how easy these misattributions can be.

Johnny and Sally decide that they are now old enough, so they should be allowed to curse. After all, they hear Dad cursing sometimes. They decide that they will each curse at breakfast and see what Mom does. As they walk into the kitchen, Mom asks, "What do you guys want for breakfast?" Johnny is the first to speak, saying, "What the hell, I'll have pancakes." Mom whacks his butt and sends him up to his room. She then turns to Sally and asks, "Okay, what do you want for breakfast?" Sally looks Mom in the eye and says, "I don't know, but it sure as hell won't be pancakes."

The humor in this joke comes from the misattribution—Sally mistakenly assumes that Mom was upset about being asked to make pancakes, rather than the cursing. Similarly, those with undiagnosed ADHD attribute their struggles and failures to being lazy, stupid, or crazy, rather than to an untreated neurological condition. Therefore, part of our work involves going over common and/ or significant events in the client's life and reinterpreting them in the light of this new information. This may include the effects of secondary psychological consequences like anxiety, depression, substance abuse, addictions, pessimism, and decreased academic interest. We build solid self-esteem and hope for the future by reinterpreting the causes of past failures as currently treatable and manageable, such that the future can be different than the past.

Reframing has four parts (Crawford & Crawford, 2002):

1. Recognize the disability of ADHD.

2. Accept the ADHD, as well as other strengths and weaknesses.

3. Understand the implications of having ADHD.

4. Make a conscious choice to address the limitations that ADHD brings.

We can't rewrite history, but we can change our interpretations of what happened and therefore how those old lessons carry forward into the present and future.

Addressing Comorbid Diagnoses

Adults with ADHD often suffer from anxiety, depression, substance abuse, and other comorbid conditions, whether to a degree that fully merits a second diagnosis or subclinically. In fact, going by the prevalence rates, you should initially assume the presence of a comorbid condition until proven otherwise. If you do find evidence, it can be helpful to determine to what extent the ADHD is primary to the other condition and then normalize the connection, since some clients may feel as if they have too much wrong with them. For example, you could tell a client:

- **The personalized approach:** "No wonder you feel depressed, considering all the problems you've been having at work because of your untreated ADHD."

- **The objective approach:** "Most ADHD adults also suffer from anxiety or depression after having struggled so much, so you're pretty normal in that regard."

Fortunately, just as the untreated ADHD exacerbated these other conditions, so too does treatment lead to gains in these other areas, and it's often worth telling dispirited clients this. However, it may be that the degree of depression or anxiety impedes the client's ability to move forward on the ADHD treatment. If this is the case, then that will need to be addressed directly first, so that the client has a fighting chance to deal with the ADHD. However, when addressing these secondary conditions, it's still helpful to tie the feelings back to the psychological blows the client took to her self-esteem and self-efficacy following her lifetime of ADHD struggle and failure. Therefore, normalize the feelings, based on the experiences that she's had, but also offer the possibility that things can be different this time around now that the presence of ADHD is out in the open.

Managing Substance Abuse

Given the prevalence of substance abuse among adults with ADHD, you should ask specifically about clients' frequency, intensity, and duration of use and address it early in the treatment if necessary. Many clients who drink to excess may not think to mention it because it may not feel noteworthy or relevant, particularly if their peer group engages in the same level of alcohol use. Excessive substance use is an attempt to minimize internal or external sources of stress, but actually it just creates more stress (Kilcarr, 2002), and can undermine other therapeutic work you may be doing. You may want to refer clients to AA or NA as a support, especially in the beginning, even if you think that they may not be true alcoholics or addicts.

However, you also may need to educate clients ahead of time that there are people at these meetings who are decidedly antimedication, particularly regarding the stimulants. Although presumably well-intentioned, this rigid attitude is usually counterproductive, so it may be helpful to first discuss with your clients whether they should disclose at these meetings that they are taking medication. If they do disclose, they may need to educate other attendees about what medication does and doesn't do. Your clients may also need to know how they can counter charges that taking medication is the equivalent of "still using" and/or that they "just need to work the twelve-step program harder" to do better.

For clients who are more problem users than true alcoholics or addicts, meaning that they have some control over their use but it causes problems in their lives, they may find that progress in treatment leads to less desire to use. As their overall mood improves and they begin to feel more optimistic about making continuing gains, the escape offered by substance use may become less necessary or appealing.

Empirical Foundations

Unfortunately, there has been very little controlled research on psychosocial treatments for adult ADHD (Murphy, 2006). Some solid studies have begun to come out over the last few years and there is a building momentum. The last several years have also brought some highly structured, session-by-session cognitive-behavioral treatment programs specifically tailored for adults with ADHD. In my opinion, however, these programs suffer from the typical pitfalls of overly structured manualized treatment protocols: limited generalizability to the full range of clients seeking the services of therapists under nonresearch conditions; difficulty dealing with comorbid conditions; and insufficient flexibility to deal with situations that deviate from the schedule advocated in the protocol. For this reason, I've intentionally focused this book on providing numerous and varied strategies that you can use as you see fit in your work with different clients.

Those of us in the trenches must rely on our general clinical judgment, experience, and knowledge of ADHD to guide our work with ADHD adults. Pragmatic, skills-based self-management strategies are most helpful with this population (Murphy, 2006). This is not to say that ADHD adults don't have the kinds of intrapsychic conflicts that psychodynamic or insight-oriented therapies focus on, but rather that it is often more helpful to address these more tangible struggles first.

Special Considerations

The field of therapy is becoming increasingly specialized, with more and more treatment approaches being tailored to specific populations, rather than employing a single theoretical orientation with every client who walks in the door. ADHD adults present certain specific challenges that therapists must be aware of if they are to provide real help to these clients.

Reframing Limited Benefits from Past Treatments

Lack of progress is frustrating to both therapist and client. As a rule, with ADHD adults, you won't address this inertia in the same way that you would try to convince an oppositional client that he is shooting himself in the foot by taking the path of most resistance. ADHD people know they should do things differently but are as confused as everyone else about why they can't or don't. Therefore, you will need to join with them in finding those better ways of getting the job done.

This can be difficult since many adults with ADHD have had negative—or at least unsatisfactory—experiences with therapy and/or medication that wasn't specifically directed toward their ADHD (Weiss, Hechtman, & Weiss, 1999), so you will need to convince them that perhaps this time can be different. Interpreting neurologically driven behaviors psychologically—such as by labeling them as self-defeating, oppositional, or defensive—only endorses the client's feelings of shame and self-blame; the implication is he could change, if only he addressed his psychological issues (Nadeau, 2002). This can retraumatize the client, even when such a statement is made in a well-intentioned and friendly way. We wouldn't interpret a wheelchair-bound person's inability to walk as resistance to walking, yet, if you ignore the neurological underpinnings of ADHD, it is analogous to thinking the wheelchair-bound person is resisting advice that might help her to walk.

For those adults with ADHD who have sought treatment previously, treating only secondary anxiety and depression while ignoring the ADHD is like painting over the water stains on the ceiling without fixing the leaks in the roof above—a short-term solution at best. Antidepressants will treat depression and anxiety, which may help somewhat with poor concentration or impulsive self-soothing behaviors that are driven by anxiety or depression, but will not directly address the ADHD itself, except to the extent that these comorbid conditions are exacerbating the ADHD symptoms. Unfortunately, this partial treatment response can give the impression that the client is simply suffering from treatment-resistant anxiety or depression, and thus can lead the clinician to settle for this partial success without looking for alternative explanations.

It is crucial to acknowledge clients' deep feelings of distress caused by the undiagnosed ADHD and to frame those feelings as a normal response to a lifetime of unexplained struggle. This allows clients to let themselves off the hook of guilt, shame, and self-blame. However, with the new knowledge of the diagnosis also comes the responsibility to use that information effectively, by actively taking charge of their lives. A therapy that is informed by the presence of ADHD will do both; that is, it will allow the client to reframe her past as well as activate her to take charge of her own life, whereas a therapy that isn't informed by the implications of ADHD will probably do neither sufficiently.

The feeling of being truly understood is crucial for newly diagnosed adults with ADHD after their lifetime of inexplicable difficulties. This crucial experience may not happen even with a great therapist if she doesn't understand and address the ADHD piece of the puzzle. The moment of receiving the diagnosis often involves a sense of relief, of finally being understood and understanding oneself. It's as if all the random pieces suddenly fit together; now the adults with ADHD understand why they've always felt different. In my diagnostic evaluations, I make a point of leaving time to educate clients about ADHD in general and to tie together the events in their lives with the diagnosis; for example, "No wonder you did so badly and got depressed when you were promoted up to team leader—there were way too many details for you to manage effectively because of your ADHD."

I also give them a list of online and local resources to help them learn more (see the appendix for ADHD resources). I explain the four-part treatment program and why it will lead to better outcomes than past treatments did, and then I give them a handout that reinforces this (Integrative Treatment for Adult ADHD). Copies of both of these are available for download at no charge on my website, www.TuckmanPsych.com. If they are interested, I also give them the names and numbers of local psychiatrists who do a good job with ADHD medication. Note that the worst thing that you can do is to drop the diagnosis in their lap and send them on their way without a clear plan for the next steps.

Celebrating clients' successes in life despite undiagnosed ADHD can also be very important in helping them feel a sense of competence and hope. I once had a client who never finished college, despite several attempts, but managed to run a successful lawn service business that was a pretty good situation for him in many ways. He still felt bad about not yet having a college degree, but I pointed out to him that, given his undiagnosed and untreated ADHD, it was hardly surprising. I also stressed, however, that he should give himself credit for being smart enough to create a work situation that was a good fit for him and enabled him to be successful without a degree. Celebrating successes may also involve smaller achievements, like forming the habit of always putting their keys and wallet in the same place at home, or other good strategies that clients may have already come up with on their own. These achievements will seem too trivial if the ADHD is left out of the equation, since it simply will be assumed that clients can do them.

ADHD Traits That Interfere with Therapy

Clients bring their ADHD to your office, just as they bring it everywhere else. Although this creates additional challenges, you can minimize the impact by using the following strategies:

- **They may prefer action over talking.** Some ADHD people prefer action to talk and just want you to tell them what to do without really thinking about the rationale for your instruction (Weiss et al., 1999), which limits generalizability. Make your points succinctly so you don't exceed their attention span. Encourage them to think things through themselves, but then also give them specific strategies to practice between sessions.

- **They may feel an entitled dependency.** Some people with ADHD have a lifetime of experience in getting others to do things for them through charm, endearing naiveté, or incompetence and may try to pull you into this role too (Weiss et al., 1999). Resist the pull to rescue them; encourage them to learn and implement these important skills themselves.

- **They may be prone to impulsive decision making.** Impulsive adults tend to operate by the adage "Ready, fire, maybe aim if I get to it," even with major life choices, like moving in with a romantic partner. For that reason, you need to work with them on ingraining a new tendency to stop and think before acting. They must learn to ask themselves, "What are the consequences of this action and what else could I do?" (Young, 2002, p. 153). This is the heart of therapy, but it is neither easy nor interesting for impulsive adults to do this.

- **They may be reactive decision makers.** Many ADHD adults will go through life without a coherent plan, for example, winding up in jobs and even careers merely by chance and circumstance. They may take the same approach to dealing with their ADHD, allowing circumstances to dictate what they work on and what they don't. You can counter this tendency by helping them create a plan and then actively work toward achieving it.

- **They may interpret rules loosely.** Following rules can be difficult, uncomfortable, or boring for some adults with ADHD, which can cause problems with starting and stopping sessions on time, regular payment, and other boundary issues. It helps for you to be clear on this from the outset and then address the transgressions as they occur (Weiss et al., 1999). In the first session, I tell clients that I charge for no-shows and late cancellations. Without being an ogre about it, I maintain that boundary because this is the way the rest of the world works. You may want to explore why a client was late or missed an appointment, as an example of how things get off track, then brainstorm ways to deal with that situation in the future. Frame it as an opportunity to learn, rather than a punishment.

- **They may be nag-resistant.** ADHD adults are used to having people nag them and may have become good at drowning it out, which, of course, causes an escalation in the nagging. This can occur with a therapist too (Weiss et al., 1999). You shouldn't care more than your client about what he does. This may require mastering your own anxiety, obsessive-compulsive tendencies, sense of responsibility, and need to adhere to rules. It's better to put the onus on them, as in the following: "You say that this is something that you want to change, but we're not making any progress. So, are you not really interested in changing it or do we need to approach it differently?" Avoid getting pulled into a chase dynamic where you're trying too hard to convince the client that she really should want to work on a specific issue.

- **Some may be fidgety.** Some ADHD adults listen best when they are physically active, which can include tapping their feet, cracking their knuckles, or fiddling with their hair or a cell phone, which can be distracting for the therapist, but may be best for the client (Weiss et al., 1999). It's best to learn to ignore this and not take it personally. For very hyperactive clients, you may need to add some physical activity to the sessions, such as by taking a walk while you talk together.

- **They may go off on rambling tangents.** It's easy for ADHD adults to tell long rambling stories that quickly move away from the main point, making for interesting but less productive sessions. Without becoming a police interrogator, sometimes you may need to rein them in (Weiss et al., 1999).

- **They may present with very poor memories.** ADHD adults who complain of memory problems may have difficulty maintaining continuity from session to session unless you can provide some guidance. For this reason, it can be helpful to record sessions so the client can listen to the tapes/CDs between sessions. Or you might want to encourage the client to keep a dedicated notebook for taking notes in and out of session and for recording homework assignments and progress (Nadeau, 2002).

- **They may be noncompliant with homework assignments.** Just as with school homework, ADHD adults will often forget to do therapy homework assignments, do them halfway, or fail to bring the requested materials to the next session. You can increase compliance by summarizing the homework at the end of the session and ensuring that it gets recorded on paper, digital voice recorder, PDA, or voice mail. You will also need to check in on assigned homework at the start of the session to show the client that the work is important. If the client doesn't do the homework, then explore whether he understood the assignment, was committed to it, and had the appropriate resources and time to complete it. Take noncompliance as a learning opportunity and in that way try to reduce the unproductive shame it may evoke, especially since it will remind clients of the many, many experiences of noncompliance that they've had over the years.

Transference and Countertransference

Although the treatment model espoused in this book tends more toward the cognitive-behavioral, there is still value in being attentive to potential transference and countertransference issues that may arise. Adults with ADHD develop good masquerading skills (Weiss et al., 1999) to make it look as though they are more tuned in than they really are. They may not admit that they have missed things and may not really understand what is being talked about, even when it's a conversation with just one other person. They get tired of having to ask people to repeat things too often. Moreover, they may fear sounding stupid, or even be afraid of angering someone for not having heard it the first time. They may also have trouble with other conversational deficits like overtalkativeness or constant interrupting.

You can use the therapy relationship to point out these tendencies, especially if the client is unaware of them. Clients bring to therapy the same learning, attention, memory, language, and communication deficits that cause them problems elsewhere; so the therapy relationship can be a safe place to address these issues. Your own feelings of boredom, tuning out, frustration, not getting the point of what the client says, or feeling not listened to can be very helpful in understanding the client's impact on others. Alternatively, the sessions may be very entertaining but not address the important topics (Weiss et al., 1999). It's often best to point out the effect of the client's actions on your countertransference in very concrete ways, such as, "It's hard for me to concentrate on what you're saying when you're flipping your pen around" (Weinstein, 1994).

Some clients may approach therapy with the expectation that you will fix them, as if they were coming in to have a hangnail removed. This is especially true for those who have a pattern of externalizing responsibility. Therefore, you may need to educate these clients about the importance of their being actively involved in the sessions, as well as the importance of practicing homework outside of session.

Other clients will come into treatment with the mind-set of a victim and work harder to gain accommodations rather than to improve their functioning. Predictably, this helpless sense of entitlement can alienate others, including possibly yourself. It may be helpful to frame this as a less productive strategy for coping with the seemingly uncontrollable deficits of ADHD and try to shift the client toward more active approaches (Ramsay & Rostain, 2005a).

As with any treatment, a balance must be struck between holding clients responsible for their actions, while also taming their self-critical voices. However, given the preponderance of their experiences with others, clients may assume that you too will be critical and disappointed in them, leading to premature termination. Therefore, it's worth addressing these matters directly, by exuding an attitude of acceptance while simultaneously encouraging clients to actively address their difficulties (Ramsay & Rostain, 2005a).

Adapting Standard Therapy Models

Typical therapeutic techniques that work well with non-ADHD clients may have limited benefit with ADHD adults. In general, any therapy with ADHD adults should possess the following qualities (Ramsay & Rostain, in press):

- Active involvement of the therapist

- A strong therapeutic relationship

- Reasonable ground rules

- Psychoeducation

- Problem-solving focus

- Case conceptualization that incorporates the neurological factors of ADHD

- Strategies for living with ADHD

Now, let's take a look at how to adapt traditional therapeutic orientations.

Psychodynamic

Widely ranging free association for an ADHD adult may be based more in neurology than in defensiveness (Weiss et al., 1999). Unlike the more open free associations that are used with non-ADHD clients, ADHD adults need you to act as a guide through their thoughts and associations, to help them prioritize their thoughts so as to stay focused on the most productive elements. This may mean that some interesting associations get lost, but too much time can be wasted on random associations (Hallowell, 1995). Once the client has created some stability in his life using more pragmatic strategies, it can be helpful to address any intrapsychic conflicts.

Cognitive/Behavioral

Although the most studied therapeutic models for working with ADHD adults are based in cognitive behavioral therapy, there have been some important adaptations from typical techniques. ADHD clients may have particular difficulty complying with traditional cognitive homework assignments like writing down lists of cognitions or bringing thought diaries to session (Weiss et al., 1999).

Impulsivity in particular is resistant to typical techniques. For example, self-talk may not be helpful since by definition impulsive acts precede that kind of processing (Weiss et al., 1999). Covert verbal mediation will be helpful only if it is engaged in before the impulse strikes and during the full length of time that the client is at risk for leaping before looking. Although you shouldn't expect miracles with self-talk, the occasional success may justify trying it. Examples include "One thing at a time," "Focus, focus, focus," or "Listen to what she's saying." Relaxation techniques can be used to calm a racing mind or physical restlessness (Morgan, 2000) with some clients, but others won't tolerate the inactivity or get much benefit from it.

Behavioral programs work very well for children with ADHD when they are administered by their parents, but it's completely different when it is self-administered (Weiss et al., 1999). Having a romantic partner administer the program brings other potential problems that are often best avoided.

Adjusting to the Diagnosis

Some clients will be more motivated than others to really work on their ADHD. This is important to assess, in that your approach will likely differ based on how invested the client is in the process. Perhaps more than some other conditions, ADHD impacts other people too, such as family, romantic partners, employers, and friends, so they are more likely to push the ADHD adult to seek treatment. As a result, some of these clients may be unwilling participants and will need some convincing to see that treatment is not only potentially helpful, but also relevant. This is most common among young adults who are receiving strong pressure from frustrated parents. You can win over these clients by:

- Increasing acceptance of the diagnosis by reframing it as based more in neurology than in character, thereby reducing unproductive guilt and shame for past failures

- Offering hope by explaining the four-part integrative treatment model

- Increasing compliance by explaining that how much clients gain from treatment depends on how hard they work at it, just as with exercising

- Increasing feelings of self-determination by emphasizing that ultimately clients control how much they get out of treatment, regardless of whether someone else is pushing them to come in for it

Once clients accept the need for treatment, I've noticed they tend to go through the following four stages of adjustment to their new diagnosis of ADHD. It's important to keep these stages in mind to help the client adjust, and to prevent early termination in the third stage.

Getting Excited

Upon first receiving the diagnosis, many clients will react excitedly with "This explains everything!" They finally have an explanation that isn't pejorative—as the book title says, "you mean I'm not lazy, stupid, or crazy?" However, for others, the diagnosis confirms their feelings of being defective (Brooks, 2002). Regardless of their initial reaction, clients may also experience intense feelings of anger and sadness for all the wasted time, lost opportunities, and unnecessary struggle. As one client put it, "I spent most of the weekend crying, pissed about how hard things were and how bad things got sometimes. I was mad at my parents for not realizing and then mad at myself. Finally, I was able to come to some peace with it."

This is the time when clients gather their treatment team, buy too many books (which they don't finish), join support groups, and get involved. They may see everything through the ADHD lens and use ADHD to explain everything that happens in their lives, even when it's a bit of a stretch.

Getting Down to Business

After the initial rush fades, clients get down to work. The motto during this stage is "Okay, now I know what I can do to make my life better." The rush of discovery is replaced by a more sober attitude of responsibility. They start trying some of the tips and tricks they've learned, work to get their medications adjusted right, and explore the psychological manifestations generated by a life of ADHD. Although this can be a very positive time, this may also be the calm before the storm, so you should keep an eye out for signs of a potential crash in motivation. It can be helpful to temper the excitement with frequent comments to the effect that big behavior change requires both time and hard work.

Getting Overwhelmed

The initial rush of enthusiasm and optimism of the first two stages often runs into the hard reality that, even with a good medication regimen, it takes a great deal of hard work to make the desired changes. The motto here is "Damn, there sure is a lot to do. Maybe life was better without the diagnosis." They may feel frustrated that everything doesn't magically fall into place. They got their hopes up once again, only to be disappointed. In some ways it's worse now since they know better what their problems are. At this point, they will have more problems than solutions.

Despite their greater understanding of ADHD and awareness of how it impacts their daily life, the functional improvements may not be as great as they would wish (Ramsay & Rostain, 2005b). They discover that the medication is not a cure-all or that it has side effects, potentially requiring a switch to a different medication. Real life intrudes on behavior change plans and strategies, causing some slipping back to old habits. At these times, to counteract hopelessness and potential early termination, I often tell clients that they've already addressed all the easy problems in their lives, so, by default, they're left with the harder problems which we will work on together.

Clients at this stage may struggle with "the acceptance and acceptability" of their ADHD, learning to see it as neither stigma nor excuse (Ramsay & Rostain, 2005a, p. 80). This may evoke anger about the injustice of the universe. Validate their anger as normal but also get across the message that life isn't fair and that everyone has his own limitations, issues, sacrifices, and annoyances. Awful things sometimes happen to good people. ADHD is one of the lousy cards that they were dealt, but presumably they were dealt many good cards, too. You may need to work with them on accepting that they need to do things differently than most people in terms of their cognitive strategies, medications, and therapy (Weinstein, 1994). With acceptance comes a greater ability to gain some degree of mastery.

Getting On Top of It

Over time, hopefully, most clients will settle into a more mature understanding of their ADHD and how it fits into their life as a whole—it's a part of their life, but not their whole life. The motto for this stage is "Okay, I can do this. It's hard work but there are real rewards for it." They will have gained some acceptance of what their life is about and understand they will have more work to do in some areas than most people, but they also know that that work will pay off in reasonable ways. They have internalized some of the good habits that are especially helpful to them, making those habits a bit more automatic and less consciously driven. They recognize their imperfections and know that sometimes they will fall short. They can accept that it's difficult to live in an information age when one has information-processing deficits (Ramsay & Rostain, 2005a). They may not be happy about this, but they can accept it. See Fully Accepting the Diagnosis, below, for more details on this subject and its relation to self-esteem.

Goal-Setting

It's important to set goals so the therapy doesn't wander or deal exclusively with the day's crises or entertaining events. These are always more exciting subjects to discuss, but part of the dysfunction of ADHD is that planning is perceived as boring and therefore avoided (Weiss et al., 1999). You should help the client to articulate both short-term and long-term goals for change; ideally the short-term goals will lead into or support the long-term goals. Many ADHD folks have difficulty breaking long-term projects into parts and feel overwhelmed as a result, so this can be a good skill to practice with them. Work with your clients to do the following (Brooks, 2002):

1. **Select a few goals to address first.** Whereas some ADHD adults have difficulty articulating goals because they are overwhelmed in too many areas and therefore don't know where to start, others will generate an endless list. Impulsivity and a low tolerance for frustration can cause them to work on all of the issues at once or to jump quickly and haphazardly between too many projects. Work with clients on picking a few goals to start with, preferably those that can be achieved quickly and create positive momentum and investment in the entire process.

2. **Develop realistic, achievable plans to reach those goals.** Given the impulsivity, poor planning skills, and low frustration tolerance of even medicated ADHD adults, it's crucial to work together to create a solid plan that has some hope of succeeding.

3. **Create criteria for evaluating the success of each plan.** It's helpful to know whether a plan is working well. Some goals have concrete measures, such as the frequency of working out, whereas others are more ephemeral, such as "a better relationship with my girlfriend." It may be worth finding concrete measures, such as fewer arguments, but the goal doesn't have to be overly rigid.

4. **Consider possible obstacles to goals and how to handle them.** It's important to normalize failure and discuss it in a problem-solving way to make it less likely that the client will give up prematurely when troubles arise. Having a backup plan, as well as permission to create another plan later, helps people to feel more in control and less at the mercy of fate.

5. **Change the goals if repeated efforts fail.** Some goals seem reasonable but turn out to be too ambitious, overlook obstacles, or don't take into account changes that may occur along the way. Actively choosing to drop a goal is a sign of strength, fundamentally different from being forced to abandon a goal due to circumstances, which too often is the way things work out for untreated ADHD adults. As the old saying

goes, "sometimes wisdom is the greater part of valor"; so it's wiser to remove undone items from the to-do list rather than be forever haunted by them. The lesson to convey to the client is that stubbornly holding onto an unworkable goal is just as problematic as abandoning it prematurely or failing at it due to insufficient planning. Colonel Custer isn't famous for his bravery, after all, but for his stubbornness. Flexibility is a sign of healthy problem solving.

6. **As goals are reached, add new ones to reinforce those successes and the resulting optimism.** When new goals are added, work with the client to continue developing more effective ways to cope that will help to maintain a positive mind-set and strengthen the gains that have been made. After a lifetime of difficulties, it takes hard consistent work to replace a negative mind-set.

Ironically, one of the therapy goals that needs to be continuously worked on is the consistent pursuit of goals. It's almost as if some clients come into therapy saying, "My goal is to stick with a goal." Many ADHD adults have trouble resisting the temptation to force closure prematurely on a project, conflict, conversation, or deal (Hallowell, 1995) simply because they get tired of pursuing it or can't tolerate the ambiguity involved. It can be helpful to point this out to clients because they may not fully appreciate how this fuels later problems or failures.

Maladaptive Coping Strategies

A lifetime of undiagnosed and untreated ADHD will lead to a predictable variety of psychological sequelae that must be addressed in therapy. This section covers the resulting maladaptive core beliefs and habits that many ADHD adults employ.

Maladaptive Core Beliefs

ADHD adults typically display the following maladaptive core beliefs (Rostain & Ramsay, 2006a, p. 15):

- **Self-mistrust.** "I can't rely on myself to do what I need to do. I let myself down."

- **Failure.** "I've always failed and always will fail at what I set out to do."

- **Inadequacy.** "I am basically a bad and defective person."

- **Incompetence.** "I am too inept to handle life's basic demands."

- **Instability.** "My life will always be chaotic and in turmoil."

It's easy to see how a lifetime of undiagnosed and untreated ADHD can lead to these beliefs, as well as how these beliefs can be self-reinforcing by means of the maladaptive habits listed below. The problem is that these beliefs and habits carry too high a price tag compared to some better habits that clients can learn in treatment. Therefore, in working with your clients, you should be alert for comments that suggest these beliefs, then state these beliefs more explicitly so that they can be fully examined for supporting and contradictory evidence.

As much as this is an intellectual exercise, it's also important to help the client change some of the habits that reinforce these beliefs. Because the habits and beliefs are interwoven, you can break the cycle by addressing either one and should therefore use progress in changing one to support progress in changing the other. For example, a client's tendency to procrastinate may be based in beliefs of self-mistrust and instability, which could be addressed in the following way:

Therapist: So how's that big report for work coming along?

Client: Okay, I guess. I'm not really working on it.

Therapist: Are you going to have enough time later?

Client: I'll pull it off. I always do.

Therapist: I'm impressed that you can pull it off like that, but it seems to put you through hell getting it done at the last minute.

Client: I'm used to it [instability].

Therapist: That's how it's usually gone for you, but does that mean you still need to do it that way?

Client: Well, it seems to work out that way anyway, even if I try to do it differently [self-mistrust].

Therapist: I wonder if you could try to start this project at least a little bit earlier. You'll probably never be someone who has a job finished a week ahead of schedule, but maybe you could shoot for not having to stay at work past eight the night before a report is due.

Client: I'm sure my wife would be happier about that.

Therapist: So, to get it done by eight on Thursday night to be ready for Friday morning's meeting, when would you need to start it? Assuming some interruptions, of course.

Client: I guess I could start it on Wednesday, pull the data together before I leave work. Then I just need to do the writing on Thursday.

Therapist: If the data is ready by Thursday morning, you'll have a much easier time getting out of there earlier. Give it a try and let's see how it works out.

Maladaptive Habits

As foreign as these habits may be to some of the people in the ADHD adult's life, they do make sense given the adult's core beliefs and they do work at some level. As with any coping mechanism, the habits that turn out to be maladaptive originally served to protect the person from shame, anxiety, and humiliation. But as time goes by, they don't serve the person as well. We work to help our clients see the price they pay for clinging to these habits and we try to make them understand they would be better served by taking more direct and active approaches. Often, looking at things from a larger perspective, one that includes a solid understanding of ADHD, will help with choosing approaches more likely to be successful, as well as with reframing difficulties.

Due to a lifetime of excessive struggle and failures, many ADHD adults will be more sensitive to the possibility of current failure because they have many bad memories of past failures. Predictably, they may be less willing to get their hopes up again and try new behaviors, for fear of yet another disappointment. If they do take the chance and try new behaviors, they may respond more negatively to the inevitable setbacks along the way, and take them more to heart. You may need to sell your clients on the idea that this time things can indeed work out differently, and that it may be worth trying new strategies and sticking with them. Unlike the past when the promised gains were not achieved, this time can be different because of the solid understanding of ADHD and the integrative treatment model, which provide important aspects to the treatment that were previously lacking.

With resistant or hesitant clients, the goal may be less to convince them to do something they otherwise wouldn't do, but rather to talk about their ambivalence openly. In that way they can make decisions that are well thought-out, rather than emotional and reactive (Ramsay & Rostain, 2005a).

Motivational interviewing techniques can be especially helpful for overcoming ambivalence to trying new strategies, as follows (Young & Bramham, 2007):

1. **Express empathy** by using reflective listening and acknowledging that ambivalence is normal.

2. **Develop discrepancies** by pointing out the difference between the client's current behavior and stated goals.

3. **Roll with resistance** by taking a different tack with the client and suggesting alternate perspectives to how he sees things.

4.   **Support self-efficacy** by encouraging the client to take responsibility for the necessary changes in her life.

Let's now take a look at some of the specific habits that ADHD adults tend to adopt and how to address them.

Avoidance

ADHD adults have difficulty starting and completing tasks, not only because of neurologically based deficits, but also because they make conscious choices not to deal with aversive situations or those they fear will lead to failure. This can also include social withdrawal, which spares them potentially confusing and painful interactions (Weinstein, 1994). Given their rich histories of painful experiences to draw from, it does make sense to avoid previously problematic situations because more of the same usually leads to more of the same. If their skills or circumstances have not changed, then they would be foolish to expect different outcomes.

They may rationalize their avoidance to feel better about it (Ramsay & Rostain, 2005b). For example, they may tell themselves, "I'm too tired now to do that paperwork, so I'll do it first thing tomorrow when I'm more alert." Of course, as they well know, come tomorrow morning, they may forget the paperwork or be distracted by something else, compounding the potential problems.

The avoidance may be based on an accurate self-assessment that the demands exceed their abilities, causing justified feelings of hopelessness. They then cope with those negative feelings by escaping the situation entirely, bringing at least a temporary feeling of relief and thereby negatively reinforcing their avoidance. It may be worth encouraging the client to at least try the avoided task for a brief period, to see how it goes. Frame this as an experiment, so she won't feel that her self-worth is on the line if she doesn't achieve complete success. Rather, the goal is to see if the task is as hopeless as it feels prior to starting it or whether some trial and error refinements can lead to improvement (Ramsay & Rostain, 2005b).

If the client is still resistant, explore why she feels the task is destined for failure and then brainstorm new ways to approach it. This is part of the process of trial and error experimentation and, therefore, failures are not truly failures if they are learned from and the lessons applied forward. Participation in a targeted treatment program may change the client's abilities and therefore alter the odds of succeeding. You're aiming for a guarded optimism from the client, but sometimes grudging optimism is the best you can get.

You may need to cushion the fall in case the client does fail. It may be necessary to educate her about the success-to-failure ratio that other people have, since it's likely that she underestimates the failures that others experience. I will sometimes use the Woody Allen line that 80 percent of success in life is just showing up—that is, just meeting one's obligations without fanfare.

Procrastination

Basically, *procrastination* is temporary avoidance, but often it comes with the added bonus of the adrenaline rush, so to speak, that assists in maintaining focus when the task is finally begun. This habit may also be seen as brinksmanship, discussed next. It is worth discussing the price the client pays in terms of stress and poorer quality work product. Some clients will need help with some of the mechanics of the project if their procrastination is based on the task being too difficult. You may also need to explore the hidden agenda of the convenient face-saving excuse "Sure that report was pretty crummy, but I didn't start it until like an hour before the meeting." It may be helpful to work with the client on ways to make future obligations loom larger in the present; for example, by writing up a list of pros and cons of starting a particular project earlier.

Brinksmanship

Brinksmanship is waiting until the very last minute to complete a project, but not because of lack of earlier opportunities. The pressure of the eleventh hour actually helps those with ADHD to focus better and make more efficient use of their time (Rostain & Ramsay, 2006a). (That's why I facetiously call brinksmanship "nature's Ritalin.") For adults with ADHD, this is in stark contrast to how they work on projects when there is no immediate deadline pressure, when they feel scattered and inefficient and can't fire themselves up to get to work.

Although the adrenaline rush of a looming deadline can be a great motivator, it also leaves no time for unanticipated problems, meaning that too many deadlines will not be met and/or the final product will reflect the haste in which it was completed. There is also the price of the emotional toll on the ADHD adult and/or other people. Therapy involves identifying these risks and stressors, for all concerned, so that the client can make a better informed decision of whether it's worth doing things this way.

For example, I had a client who routinely pushed the limits of his deadlines, despite the fact that it put his teammates in the difficult position of having to rush to not miss their own deadlines. In therapy we discussed this impact on his coworkers and the impact that that had on him. As with many other areas, a proper medication regimen made it easier not only to see the effect of this behavior, but also to self-motivate sooner and reduce the impact.

Pseudoefficiency

Pseudoefficiency consists of working on low priority tasks, such as checking e-mail, rather than on higher priority tasks, thereby creating a false sense of productivity while rationalizing avoidance of the more important tasks (Rostain & Ramsay, 2006a). The person feels busy, but isn't using that time well. The activity makes it easier to rationalize the avoidance. You can address this issue with your client by discussing her priorities and pointing out how they don't match her activities at work or home. You can also point out the tasks that are not priorities are used mostly as time fillers.

Juggling

Juggling involves taking on new and thereby more interesting projects before completing earlier projects that have lost their shine. This also allows the person to feel busy and productive, but it's an empty satisfaction (Rostain & Ramsay, 2006a). Unfortunately, most tasks in life don't get partial credit if they aren't finished. Although it can be helpful to rotate among different tasks if that maintains the client's interest, at some point she needs to finish some of those projects. Juggling can be addressed in therapy in the same way as pseudoefficiency, by reinforcing the fact that they are actively taking care of obligations, but also encouraging them to circle back around and finish some of those tasks before moving on to something new.

You can also reinforce the feeling of satisfaction that comes from completing something, with the understanding that such satisfaction may be less salient for many ADHD folks than the attraction of moving on to the next big, new thing. Medication may also make it easier for the person to not only stay focused on the task at hand, but also tolerate the boredom of finishing something.

Externalizing

Externalizing involves blaming others or external events for unsatisfactory results. It may also involve rationalizing by making excuses for perceived difficulties and failure rather than accepting personal responsibility (Brooks, 2002). Some of this is as much about neurology as it is about psychology; for example, an ADHD adult may genuinely forget that she was told to do something and then swear that the other person never told her. Normalize these kinds of difficulties and frame failures as learning opportunities. If the client is open to it, you may also want to work with her on accepting that some of her processing is imperfect, and to learn to be gracious about accepting responsibility.

For example, the client might say, "I don't remember you asking me to do that, but you might have, so what can we do to fix this now?" For more resistant clients, you can work with them to brainstorm ways that they could have changed the outcome or could do it differently next time, without necessarily accepting full responsibility for what happened, as illustrated in the following conversation:

Client: My boss is a total jerk. He's always giving me a hard time about stuff like this, but he never told me to call that person.

Therapist: It sucks that he's always on your case like that. I wonder if there's anything you can do to keep him from giving you such a hard time?

Client: I doubt it.

Therapist: Well, if your boss isn't good about remembering to tell you stuff, could you check in with him occasionally to make sure there isn't anything hanging out there that's not getting done?

Client: But it should be his job to remember that stuff!

Therapist: Yeah, it should! But if he forgets, then he makes it into your problem, so checking in occasionally can spare you the headache.

This strategy can empower the client to take the control that he does have over a situation, and thereby to take responsibility for at least that part.

Impulsively Rushing

Some clients will impulsively rush through boring, difficult, or burdensome tasks in an effort to get done as quickly as possible to minimize their suffering. Unfortunately and predictably, this makes mistakes much more likely and leads to a worse final product. The negative outcome reinforces the notion that these tasks are to be rushed through because they are hopeless anyway, thus creating a self-fulfilling prophecy (Brooks, 2002). Point out this end result to the client and suggest that he actually try going a bit slower and working a bit harder on some of his projects, perhaps only as an experiment, and see how it works out.

Quitting

Quitting a task before finishing it is somewhat better than not starting it at all (Brooks, 2002). Praise the fact that the client started the task, and then discuss what happened that she quit, as you would work with avoiding. It may be worth discussing the concept of conscious quitting, of making a careful reassessment of the situation and deciding whether the goal is still worth pursuing. If she decides that it isn't, then there shouldn't necessarily be any shame associated with quitting, since "discretion is the better part of valor" sometimes. If, in retrospect, there were things she could have done differently along the way that would have changed the outcome, then use that hindsight as a learning experience.

Controlling

In response to the common feeling of powerlessness that many with ADHD experience, some people go to the other extreme and become dictatorial. If they can't sufficiently control their actions, they may try to control the world around them to put themselves in a better position. These people often have poor empathy and social skills (Brooks, 2002). Discuss with them the idea that letting go of some things allows greater control of others because there are limits to what one person can control. It's best to pick one's battles. In addition, working in various ways to improve these clients' overall functioning may enable them to complete tasks directly and, therefore, not have to rely on controlling as much.

Aggressive Behavior

When avoiding isn't an option, some people use a strong offense as a defense. This is often followed by rationalization of the behavior with claims that the other person deserved it. This can involve physical or verbal bullying (Brooks, 2002). This type of behavior may be more common with hyperactive/impulsive folks. Medication can take the edge off of this aggressiveness and reactivity, as will working with the client to gain a true sense of his competence.

Quasi-Obsessive-Compulsive Behavior

Hypervigilance and frequent checking help ADHD adults to remember everyday things (Weinstein, 1994), which makes them feel they have less to worry about. This is fundamentally different from true obsessive-compulsive disorder where the person pretty much knows that he doesn't need to check, but can't stop himself. In contrast, experience has taught adults with ADHD that they shouldn't trust their memory because it is far too unreliable; so, there's a nugget of truth in their doubts. Some clients may stick rigidly with their routines as a way to ensure that things get done right—for example, their keys always have to go in the same place. Or they may become hyperorganized because anything less than that too quickly degenerates into total chaos. It's important to acknowledge that these clients have good reason for their doubts, and reassure them that they aren't crazy for worrying. However, as their functioning improves, perhaps they can let go of some of their more excessive worries and rigid habits.

Cavalier Lifestyle

Following a lifetime of inability to function by the "normal" rules of society, some ADHD adults may abandon that pursuit and embrace the chaos in their lives. For example, they may rationalize it with "Sure, things are always chaotic for me, but that's just the way I like to live my life. I'm not confined by others' rules." This may evoke a countertransference response of wanting to convince the client that he *should* want to live by those rules, a tack that is likely to evoke strong resistance since he has probably heard this countless times.

A better approach would be to look for any ambivalence he may feel about this way of life. Perhaps he really would like to be more like others but can't pull it off. The cavalier lifestyle is basically a denial of the pain and frustration of not being able to live up to others' expectations. Giving the client some hope and, preferably, some proof that perhaps she can function better may make it easier for her to open up about her frustrated desires and take a chance to invest herself more deeply in the process of change.

Self-Esteem, Self-Perception, and Self-Efficacy

One of a therapist's jobs is to help clients move from feeling victimized to feeling empowered in relation to their ADHD symptoms—they're not just excuses, but rather challenging facts of life that need to be overcome (Nadeau, 1995a). We help our clients to define and understand the assumptions they have about themselves, their ADHD, and other people, as well as how these assumptions prompt certain behaviors and coping strategies that may be self-defeating; we do this with the goal of helping them to employ better strategies and techniques (Brooks, 2002).

Many ADHD adults suffer from the feeling that they don't have enough control over their lives—including their own thoughts and actions. You need to work with them on increasing the amount of control they do have, as well as on accepting the fact that certain areas are beyond their control (Brooks, 2002), or will always be weaknesses. This involves self-acceptance of both positive and negative qualities, because everyone has both. It's just that the ADHD adult's negative qualities might be more visible. The concept of locus of control (LOC) is quite relevant here.

Studies have found that a mixed LOC is best for those with ADHD—they recognize that they have some control over their fate but that there are some forces that are beyond their control (Goldstein, 2006, October). They don't overrely on others to manage their lives, yet neither do they fault themselves for every bad situation. This allows them to actively manage their lives, yet also bounce back from adversity. A significant part of the impairment of ADHD comes from its secondary effects on self-esteem, related to both the outcomes of events as well as to the person's perceptions of how much responsibility he had for them. Whereas medication and coaching work primarily to improve those outcomes, education and therapy work more on altering the person's interpretations of events.

The following table, adapted from Brooks (2002), summarizes how those with low and high self-esteem differ.

SELF-ESTEEM AND PROBLEM SOLVING		
	People with Low Self-Esteem Believe	**People with High Self-Esteem Believe**
Success comes from:	External factors outside of their control, like luck, and can be easily undone by a change in the tides of fortune.	Their own efforts or abilities and therefore can be repeated.
Failure comes from:	Unmodifiable intrinsic factors, such as lack of ability or intelligence.	Modifiable factors, such as inadequate effort, and it is an opportunity to learn from.
In the face of challenges:	They feel helpless and hopeless, retreat from opportunities, don't apply the methods available to them, and don't seek out new knowledge, thus creating a self-fulfilling prophecy.	They increase their efforts and possibly seek compensatory help.

We can probably assume that most adults with ADHD who come in for treatment will tend to have lower rather than higher self-esteem and are looking for ways to feel more effective, as well as to feel better about themselves. Therefore, an important part of the therapy involves convincing them to make an active effort to employ new strategies.

Compounding the difficulties ADHD folks have with success is the fact that they often see the world as unfair and even hostile to them and that too often people are angry, frustrated, or annoyed with them (Brooks, 2002)—which, in truth, they often are. However, those with undiagnosed and untreated ADHD often don't see how their actions contribute to their difficulties or how to change them in realistic ways; for example, telling themselves to "just pay better attention" doesn't work if the person is not actively involved in treatment. Adults with ADHD also may exaggerate the ease with which others achieve success. This sets a standard that they can never hope to live up to, which undermines their motivation even further.

It can be helpful to assess your clients' sense of self-efficacy and LOC. That is, to what extent do they feel willing and able to play an active role in changing their lives for the better? This will have a great impact on their general treatment compliance and on the likelihood of them trying your proposed strategies. If they are too pessimistic, start with something small with good odds of immediate success. If they are too passive or dependent, then push them to come up with their own solutions and to try those solutions on their own. Challenge their negative assumptions by asking for exceptions to typical ways of behaving and thinking or ask for accounts of times when the expected outcome never occurred or occurred less frequently (Brooks, 2002).

Fully Accepting the Diagnosis

Part of fully accepting a diagnosis of ADHD, or any other condition, involves mourning the lost potential for the future and accepting past losses and failures without crumbling into despair or self-hatred. This process goes far beyond mere platitudes. It may involve accepting the need to change his environment or his goals to minimize the inevitable struggles. If at first you don't succeed, then maybe you need different goals. Persistence is admirable, but not to the point of stubbornness. Someone who fully accepts his ADHD can advocate assertively, but appropriately, for himself and not take personally either resistance or misunderstandings because his self-esteem isn't overly dependent on others' opinions or validation.

This is an important point to get across, because there are some people whom he will never be able to fully win over. Unlike Colonel Custer, he recognizes which battles are worth fighting and which are best abandoned. For the battles that can be won, are they worth the price paid? For example, he may be quite successful in his current job, but at what price to his peace of mind? Is the job worth it within the context of his whole life? Accepting ADHD as a part of who he is, but not as all of who he is, allows the client to see his other good and bad qualities more completely.

Touting ADHD's positive qualities, a subject that is addressed below, is a well-meaning attempt to rescue ADHD folks' self-esteem from becoming swamped by the painful feelings stemming from their ADHD deficits, but it gives the ADHD too central a role in their self-definition. It's the difference between "being ADHD" versus "having ADHD." Also, touting ADHD's positive qualities can subtly undermine the need for treatment, because why should we treat something that also has all these good qualities?

People who have ADHD need to learn to control their feelings of shame, embarrassment, defectiveness, unlikeableness, unloveableness, anger, resentment, guilt, and fear, so they can experience these feelings at appropriate times without becoming flooded or having to completely avoid or deny those feelings. Although they aren't pleasant, these are important feelings. At times, they serve a valuable purpose by keeping people honest and striving for self-improvement when present in the right doses. When too powerful, these feelings maintain the status quo at best, and drive self-destructive behavior at worst.

Does ADHD Have Any Positive Qualities?

Some people will seek to bolster ADHD folks' self-esteem by citing the positive qualities that ADHD supposedly brings; for example, that ADHD people have greater energy, intelligence, spontaneity, creativity, fun, and artistic abilities. Although I can certainly appreciate the well-meaning motives behind this sentiment, the unfortunate reality is that no solid studies have found any positive qualities for ADHD nor that it gives any kind of advantage. The studies that have found things like greater intelligence probably suffered from a referral bias with their subjects (Goldstein, 2002). Therefore, it's simply not accurate to say that those with ADHD possess these positive qualities because of their ADHD. Rather, people with ADHD possess many positive qualities, despite their ADHD, and they would have had them anyway, perhaps to an even greater degree, if they did not have ADHD.

Rather than relying on unsubstantiated claims, it's better to emphasize that the client is more than his ADHD, that he has individual strengths and weaknesses. Yes, he has some similarities with others with ADHD, but he is still his own person. Everyone has strengths and weaknesses, so for us all it's a matter of making the most of what we have in order to achieve what we want.

Related to this, some people claim that having ADHD makes a person more successful at certain careers, such as entrepreneurship, sales, military service, computers, or hands-on jobs. Rather, I would say it isn't that they are extra talented in these areas, so much as it is their weaknesses are less problematic or better tolerated in those careers.

Earned Self-Esteem vs. Feel-Good-Now Self-Esteem

Earned self-esteem is based on success in meeting life's challenges. It's hard-won and develops slowly, but it's stable and long-lasting, and provides a secure foundation for future growth. Facing challenges and sometimes falling short is a blow to self-esteem, but it's temporary and necessary for development to occur. By contrast, feel-good-now self-esteem is based on changing standards in the moment to allow the person to succeed, under the premise that the increased self-esteem will make the person more likely to continue pushing forward. Unfortunately, this type of self-esteem is fragile; it doesn't stand the test of time and reality when the person finds himself in less forgiving circumstances (Lerner, 1996).

Earned self-esteem is based on realistic accomplishment. Each success creates a step up the ladder of future success (Brooks, 2002), as the person gains both skills and confidence. Unfortunately, folks with ADHD often lack this history and instead can recount a deep well of failures, shortcomings, and missed opportunities. There is a momentum to both success and failure and to a person's subsequent willingness to take realistic chances. Blowing smoke to make someone feel good in the moment is not helpful, because reality will prove you wrong and you will lose credibility. Instead, work to help your clients learn to value their strengths, work on the weaknesses that they can work on, and accept their remaining weaknesses. This is similar to what the Serenity Prayer tells us.

Some of this work may involve reframing idiosyncratic coping styles, such as staying late at work to get more done when the office is quiet. Counter the client's tendency to feel inferior for being different by fostering acceptance that this is just the way she does things (Weinstein, 1994), and give her credit for being self-aware enough to employ this successful strategy.

A Positive, Resilient Mind-Set

Robert Brooks has done some great work on building resiliency, an especially worthy goal for those who have had more than their fair share of adversity, such as ADHD adults. Brooks (2002, pp. 140–141; adapted with permission) defines the main components of a positive, resilient mind-set as follows:

- *"I will learn to distinguish what I have control over from that which I do not. I will focus my time and energy on those things over which I have control, since I am the author of my life."* Successful people with ADHD don't take on the role of martyr, rather they actively work to improve their lives. They didn't have control over having ADHD, but they do have control over what they can do about it. They don't wait for others to rescue them or look for immediate gratification.

- *"Success can be based on my own strengths and resources."* Although they will credit others for helping, successful people retain a strong sense of being the master of their own destiny.

- *"I have islands of competence."* Many adults with ADHD focus on their negative qualities and ignore their strengths. It can be helpful to explore what strengths the client has and discuss how she uses them effectively in her daily life. You may also want to explore the areas that clients are weakest in and inquire about the times when they actually did reasonably well, to show that even their weakest areas aren't always failures.

- *"I believe that mistakes are opportunities for learning and growth."* No one likes making mistakes or failing, but one of our most important jobs is to help clients become less intimidated by their mistakes, so they are more willing to stretch themselves. Rather than seeing mistakes as awful, work to help them see success as an iterative process in which they learn from trying new things when the first approach doesn't work.

- *"I make a positive difference in the world."* A basic component of emotional well-being is the belief that our actions benefit others. You may want to encourage your clients to find new avenues of generativity, but probably the more reasonable and beneficial tack would be to highlight the value of that which they are already doing.

This mind-set is both a goal of treatment as well as necessary to the entire process. Most clients will not be able to muster this mind-set by themselves, so, initially, you will need to provide it for them, encouraging them to keep working toward their treatment goals.

Social Skills Training

ADHD people sometimes have a poor understanding of social rules, roles, and routines (Young, 2002) that causes predictable difficulties in interacting with others, from casual contacts to friendships to romantic relationships. They mostly know what is appropriate but will act impulsively and regret it afterwards, or they will miss social cues because of their inattentiveness. If asked beforehand or afterward to say what the appropriate response would be in a particular situation, they will have no trouble answering correctly, but nonetheless they do have trouble putting that knowledge into consistent practice, just as they do in many other parts of their lives.

Part of the reason ADHD people have social difficulties may be that they don't adjust quickly enough to changing social situations (Young, 2002), in which case it can be helpful to work with them on remembering to scan the social scene more often, especially when they feel themselves to be out of sync. For example, they could try to remember to step back occasionally to read others' social cues to be sure that everyone is on the same page. ADHD people also may have social difficulties because they have different social agendas than others. For example, they may grow bored when things are going well and will create some drama to spice things up, much to the chagrin of the other people. For that reason you may need to work with them on exploring what their overarching agendas are and whether the disruptions they cause when bored are worth it.

Social skills training programs that focus on teaching more skills can produce only limited benefits for most ADHD adults because, as a rule, the deficit isn't in knowing the skills, but rather in using them at the times that would produce the greatest social benefit (Ellison, 2002). As with so much for adults with ADHD, good intentions and good skills are not always enough—it's doing the right thing at the right time most of the time that's the trick. However, there may be some times when it would prove helpful to give specific pointers to the client (Hallowell, 1995), rather than waiting for him to learn them himself; for example, you might say, "Look people in the eye when talking to them rather than letting your eyes wander around or focusing on something behind them. Many people will take that as a sign of disinterest. When you catch yourself doing that, give the person a quick apology and refocus."

The Value of a Good Apology

Given that ADHD adults tend to make more mistakes and disappoint others more frequently than those without ADHD, it can be helpful to work with your client on how to give a good apology, correct others' misinterpretations of her behaviors, set others' expectations, and show that she brings many other good qualities to a relationship. I tell my clients that if they come across as genuinely concerned and well-intentioned, people will cut them more slack for their social errors. To give a good apology, a person should do the following:

1. Admit what he did wrong.

2. Recognize the impact on the other person.

3. Say what he will do differently in the future, if that is possible.

Under ideal conditions, an apology contains an inherent promise not to make the same mistake again. This is difficult to manage if the person has ADHD, since the odds are good he probably will do the same thing again. Therefore, it's best not to raise the other person's hopes unrealistically, yet to also convey genuine regret. It may be helpful to give the other person permission to address the mistakes directly, such as saying, "If I forget to return this to you, feel free to bug me about it. I tend to forget otherwise."

It may be helpful or even necessary to do some tangible fixing or undoing of a problem and/or make other amends, as well. An apology may be received better if there is some substance behind it. Of course, a good apology requires the ADHD adult to be able to tolerate his legitimate feelings of guilt and frustration without blowing them up into something to be avoided, so it may be that some specific therapy work will be needed to strengthen the client's self-acceptance, as discussed above.

Anger Management

ADHD adults may be more likely to struggle with anger problems than those without ADHD, for two reasons:

1. **Neurology.** Brain-based impulsivity can lead to strong and sudden emotional reactions.

2. **Psychology.** A likely lifelong history of negative social interactions can create the self-fulfilling expectation that whatever can go badly will go badly. Moreover, the stress of feeling constantly behind the eight ball can make ADHD adults more reactive than others.

Impulsively flying off the handle can carry significant social repercussions. In addition, ADHD adults' tempers may flare more suddenly and fade away more rapidly than others would expect, which can be disconcerting. I've had family members tell me, "It's as if once he blows up, he's done with it and then he's surprised that I haven't moved on yet." In addition, many ADHD adults are extremely thin-skinned, especially in emotionally arousing situations, which makes it more difficult for them to respond calmly and thoughtfully.

You can role-play various adaptive and dysfunctional ways to respond to angering situations (Young, 2002), especially for clients who learn better by doing than talking. You can also teach various other ways of dealing with angering situations, such as talking it through with family or friends, walking away from provocation, or cognitively restructuring an event. However, note that many ADHD adults do not have as large or as close a social support network as non-ADHD people do; so care needs to be taken when giving advice to open up to someone whom the ADHD person considers close, if that closeness is not fully reciprocated.

Many ADHD adults need help to learn how to advocate for themselves effectively and appropriately, so that situations don't go bad in the first place (Hallowell, 1995). Some of these adults, however, may be ambivalent about learning to advocate for themselves because they feel undeserving or guilty about asking for anything or feel that they should be able to do it all themselves. Others who have a stronger sense of entitlement may feel too comfortable asking for things or may ask in a way that annoys the other person.

Also, it can be helpful to work on general stress reduction and life management, to help lengthen your client's fuse, since we all do better when less stressed-out. Furthermore, since this is a physiologically based response, ADHD medications should prove helpful.

Sometimes the best thing is to simply walk away from an upsetting or overstimulating situation to calm down (Hallowell, 1995). Therefore, you may want to work with the client to recognize and identify sooner when she is starting to get angry. You can do this by teaching her to pay attention to physiological signals such as feeling hot or having an elevated heart rate and psychological signs such as feeling resentful.

However, since those with ADHD are often weak on self-observation, it also may be worth working with the client to educate others how to not respond to an initial flare-up, because once the dust settles, the flare-up may have subsided and no longer represents how the client feels. At that point, the client can come back, make amends for his overstrong reaction, and then address the situation more productively. This works better if the other person knows that the issue will be addressed again when the person with ADHD has calmed down. People are less likely to pursue a disagreement or misunderstanding if they are confident that the issue will not be left unresolved.

Involving a Romantic Partner in Treatment

One of the goals of therapy is to help the ADHD adult develop skills involving intimacy, diplomacy, and self-regulation; skills that were not developed because of neurological difficulties as well as the secondary effects of a life history too full of negative experiences (Weiss et al., 1999). As with other aspects of their lives, an effective medication regimen will help the ADHD adult to better appreciate their family members and be better able to listen to, learn from, and love them in ways that they could not when unmedicated (Ratey, Hallowell, & Miller, 1995). However, as with most couples who enter therapy, they will have exhausted all the methods of changing the other's behavior and/or attitude that they could think of, without achieving the success they desire. By definition, people come in for help only with issues that they could not solve themselves (Kilcarr, 2002).

Sometimes, bringing a romantic partner or family members into treatment may be more of an adjunct to individual therapy than it is true couples or family therapy. That is, the ADHD adult is the designated patient; the others attend a few sessions primarily to learn what they can do differently to assist in the ADHD adult's progress. Thus, to the extent that you address the partner's behavior, thoughts, and feelings, it's mostly in regard to assisting the primary client. In some couples/families, this intervention is sufficient in that they adapt appropriately and productively to the improvements made by the ADHD adult and no further formal intervention is necessary. In some cases, however, the ADHD is part of a more complex puzzle that does not resolve as easily, and more formal couples/family therapy is required. This may be driven by greater pathology or less effective coping skills in either or both the partner and ADHD adult, as well as by the length of time spent in the unproductive struggle prior to seeking help.

Of course, some partners or family members are more open to therapy and more willing to look at and alter their own contributions to the difficulties and will therefore be more interested in being a greater part of the process. Less productively, some will want to be a part of the therapy as a way of ensuring the ADHD adult "brings up the topics that he's supposed to"; in these cases, the other person's perceived need for control and its possible legitimacy must be addressed.

One of the goals for the therapy is to educate the partner and family members about the neurological underpinnings of the ADHD adult's problematic behavior (Nadeau, 1995a), so that they do not take the behavior personally or see it as willful. A part of that same goal would be to teach the client himself how to educate his family or romantic partner about the neurological bases of his difficulties. This was covered more fully in chapter 4, but it bears repeating. If the partner or family members can see working on the problematic behavior as a common goal and something that they can have some input in, they are less likely to hold onto unrealistic expectations, or to undermine progress by placing the full onus for change on the client.

Initiating Couples Therapy

Especially during the first sessions with a couple, it's crucial to instill hope, often by taking an active role that quickly yields some results and breaks some negative patterns. Insight-oriented therapy can be beneficial but more so once there is some momentum and the couple is invested in the therapy (Kilcarr, 2002). I like to say that "You can't leave the past in the past if it's still happening in the present." The non-ADHD partner will most likely need to see some tangible proof that the therapy will make her life easier if she is to let go of her resentments.

During the initial stages of couples therapy, you will need to do the following (Kilcarr, 2002):

■ Acknowledge the issues that bring the couple to therapy.

- Probe their understanding of ADHD-related issues.

- Define what is working in their relationship.

- Challenge them on what has not been working, such as employing the same tactics that didn't work before, and why they haven't tried alternative behaviors.

- Assist them in mutually defining what they want to have in their relationship.

- Instill in them the fact that for change to occur, it must start with each partner individually.

Many ADHD couples got locked into a downward spiral before seeking help, especially if they weren't previously aware of the diagnosis. Often, the non-ADHD partner internalized, personalized, and attached negative intent to the partner's ADHD behaviors. If the partner with ADHD was aware of the diagnosis, he may have used it as an excuse to avoid responsibility for changing, or minimized the extent of the impact of his ADHD-related deficits because he had been attacked so often, which only made his partner angrier. As a result, both partners may feel unhappy and powerless.

The first step to change this situation is to ask the couple to define what a more satisfying relationship would look like. Basic loyalty to one another is reinforced when there is fairness in the relationship—however that's defined, since "fair" doesn't always mean equal. If we want loyalty, we must assume responsibility for our behavior, so each partner must work to redefine his relational commitments and realign the balance of fairness (Kilcarr, 2002).

Building Empathy

As the expectation for happiness in the relationship dwindles, distressed couples notice selectively and attend disproportionately to their partner's negative behaviors. Positive moments are overlooked in their attempt to justify their dissatisfaction and their own unproductive behaviors. The unhappy couple then tries to change the other's behavior through aversive control tactics, such as strategically presenting punishment and withholding rewards. You can begin to counter this by showing how these negative behaviors can lead to more of the same problematic behaviors from each partner, and to generally negative outcomes overall. It's important to inform the couple that progress will be inconsistent rather than linear. Discussing the inevitability of relapses will diminish feelings of failure when they arise and, ironically, make relapses less frequent (Kilcarr, 2002).

It's important to help the couple communicate individual needs accurately and to maintain realistic perceptions and expectations of the other's behavior. For ADHD folks, it can be hard to really hear everything that the other is saying, so you will need to provide strategies to slow them down and confirm the message sent by their partner. A very helpful tactic to employ is that of mirroring:

1. The couple begins by looking into each other's eyes in a distraction-free environment.

2. One person says what she needs to.

3. The other person paraphrases what was said in a way that conveys full understanding. This does not mean simple parroting, but rather requires some processing and seeking to understand.

4. After the message is confirmed as having been completely heard, the other partner responds, that is, he says what he needs to, which is then mirrored back to him by his partner.

This helps to break the tendency common among distressed couples for neither partner to really hear what the other says. It is especially helpful when one partner has ADHD and thus is prone to missing important details. Mirroring can help each partner to increase understanding for the other partner's position, intentions, and feelings, making it easier for the couple to work together to resolve their differences with less antagonism. In fact, when they really listen to each other, they may be surprised by what they hear. Obviously, not every conversation needs to be this involved, but mirroring is a handy technique to employ when the usual ways haven't been working.

Restoring Balance in the Relationship

Intimate relationships require a complex division of roles, responsibilities, and obligations to function smoothly. This occurs only when there is considerable consensus between the partners regarding which behaviors are appropriate and inappropriate in certain situations. Unfortunately, ADHD behaviors tend to undermine the consistency of these divisions of labor. If a relationship isn't governed by predictable rules, mutually rewarding behaviors tend to decrease in frequency and intensity. The non-ADHD partner is especially likely to feel that her needs aren't being met and to withhold her kind gestures in response to that perception (Kilcarr, 2002).

Relationships where one partner has ADHD are more likely to be imbalanced, where the non-ADHD partner tends to take on a disproportionate share of responsibility for managing the myriad tasks and details of modern life. This imbalance is likely to get worse with the arrival of children since the demands tend to increase exponentially. The stereotype is that of a scattered man with ADHD and a hyperorganized female partner, but the genders can also go the other way.

The good news is that they each balance the other out, at least initially, when things are going well for the couple. The fun-loving ADHD partner brings some levity and spontaneity to the other's life, at least until this behavior is seen as irresponsible. The other partner provides some stability to the ADHD partner, at least until it's seen as boring and controlling. When it works, the ADHD partner is spared the burden of keeping track of all the details of modern life and the non-ADHD partner gets to do things her way, without competition. When it doesn't work, the non-ADHD partner continues to overfunction, taking on more and more of the ADHD partner's responsibilities and growing increasingly resentful. In the meantime, the ADHD partner feels more and more criticized, and thinks he can't do anything right in his partner's eyes, so he does less and less.

As much as the ADHD partner needs to work to improve his overall functioning, the non-ADHD partner, to perhaps an equal extent, needs to learn to feel comfortable backing off and not enabling the other's underfunctioning. Obviously, it's easier for each to change if the other is changing too. To restore balance in the relationship where the non-ADHD spouse is overfunctioning, try these strategies:

- **Assign tasks appropriately** based on each partner's strengths and strongly push for compliance (Weiss et al., 1999). This may involve reshuffling who does what.

- **Get necessary treatment for the underfunctioner** so he can pull his share (Weiss et al., 1999). Untreated ADHD undermines a person's efficiency and effectiveness.

- **Seek out recharging activities for the overfunctioner** (Weiss et al., 1999) in order to maintain balance in her life and minimize resentment for unfair sacrifices.

- **Farm out some activities** like cleaning and babysitting (Weiss et al., 1999) if that will take some of the weight off of the non-ADHD partner. As the saying goes, "A maid is cheaper than a divorce."

- **Notice the things that the ADHD person does do,** rather than just those he doesn't. Also notice his positive attributes and the qualities that he brings to the relationship to dilute the focus on the negative.

- **Allow the ADHD partner to experience his own consequences** without apologizing for him or feeling personally embarrassed, at least in those situations where the non-ADHD partner can step away from it.

- **Change expectations for what will get done and the standards that will be met** rather than be constantly disappointed. As much as the non-ADHD partner may hold to the idea that her expectations are reasonable or "how things should be," the hard reality may be that her partner cannot meet such expectations.

Many couples, regardless of whether one partner has ADHD or not, run into trouble when seeking common ground. With ADHD, finding common ground can be even more difficult. Each person will enter the relationship with strong opinions about how things should be. For example, the ADHD partner may feel that it's acceptable to wait until the last minute to do things, whereas his partner may feel exactly the opposite. It's important to resist the pull of rendering judgment in these debates. Rather, help the couple see what each contributes to the situation, what works and what doesn't, with the idea of making a more conscious choice about whether to continue doing the same things. The ADHD partner will be used to having people tell him that he should change his ways and be "more like everyone else," so he will be sensitized to feeling judged.

Therefore, in the interest of giving both partners a level playing field, it may be helpful to reframe the overfunctioner's standards as being for her own happiness and not necessarily for her partner's, since he may not notice or care as much about the details as she does. For example, it would be disingenuous of me to give my wife the new CD of one of my favorite bands if she's not crazy about them. It doesn't mean that she wouldn't enjoy having the CD, but I need to be honest about who I'm really getting it for, since otherwise it is a rather self-serving gift.

In addition, there are no absolutes for how things have to be done and, therefore, there should be no moral judgments for not meeting absolute standards. For example, if someone doesn't care about paying late fees and sees them as buying the freedom of not having to sweat deadlines, then who am I to judge? Of course, if her partner sees those fees as preventable and therefore wasteful, then that becomes something that they need to negotiate. By framing these as subjective preferences, rather than as absolutes, the couple may become more willing to consider other options rather than holding steadfastly to a standard that is either unachievable or comes with too high a relational price tag.

Once the couple comes to some agreement about what things will be done and how, they will need to work to ensure that those plans actually come to fruition, which is not an ADHD strength. Therefore, the ADHD partner will need occasional reminders to stay on track. This can be formalized in many ways, for example:

- **Use a wall calendar** to record everyone's schedule, events, and tasks to be completed. Hang it in a highly visible place so it will provide automatic reminders.

- **Put up a whiteboard or other reminders** to help keep tasks and events on the ADHD partner's mind.

- **Hold a regularly scheduled family meeting** to discuss schedules and upcoming events, and ensure that the calendar is kept up-to-date. If the couple has children, they may want to include the kids as well, at least for part of the meeting. It helps if the family meeting is held at a regular time, such as Sunday nights after dinner.

For those tasks that are less about meeting obligations and more about doing the little things that make each other happy, it can also be helpful to have each partner write a list of the behaviors from the other that please them and make them feel happy in the relationship. Requests like "Greet me with a kiss when I get home," "Surprise me with a little gift sometimes," and "Rub my back when I'm tired" can be surprisingly effective. Writing out or even posting such lists can be helpful for ADHD people who simply may not think about these acts when they are caught up in their busy days.

Each partner is expected to do his or her best to perform these acts frequently, regardless of what the other does, in order to prevent it from becoming a tit-for-tat arrangement. However, with some couples where there isn't much goodwill left or if there is simply too much inconsistency, it can be helpful to write up a contract of who does what and what the consequences are for noncompliance. This contract needs to have sufficient detail on when, where, and how much of the specified behaviors are necessary (Kilcarr, 2002).

Sexual Functioning

Just as ADHD can have an impact on every other aspect of a romantic relationship, so too can it affect the couple's sex life, in both direct and indirect ways, as follows:

- **Pragmatically** when the inefficiencies resulting from one partner's ADHD means there is simply less time available for sex or romantic intimacy in general, or that one of the partners is not available at the right time; for example, if the person with ADHD is frantically finishing a work project rather than in bed with his wife.

- **Neurologically** when the ADHD interferes with reading or hearing the other's signals, responding patiently, and delaying gratification.

- **Psychologically** when the non-ADHD partner feels resentful about the imbalance in the relationship and this interferes with positive feelings and a desire for closeness, which undermines the restorative effects of sexual activity on the relationship.

These sexual difficulties should be addressed in the same multifaceted way that any other ADHD difficulties are addressed, beginning with framing the sexual difficulties as also deriving from the ADHD in order to reduce blame, guilt, and hurt feelings (Ratey, et al., 1995). It may help to time sexual activity to coincide with medication coverage so that the ADHD partner can perform and connect better. You may also need to work with the couple to learn to communicate effectively about sexual matters, just as they talk about everything else. Note that a more satisfying sex life can be used as a motivator for one or both to change their actions in other ways.

Finally, experimenting with variety as to location, position, and timing can be helpful for the ADHD partner's need for novelty. However, the couple may also need to explicitly delineate mutually agreed upon ground rules in order to make both partners comfortable (Ratey, Hallowell, et al., 1995).

Family Functioning/Parenting

ADHD adults approach parenting in the same way that they approach every other challenge, in that they usually know the right thing to do but don't do it consistently. Books, classes, and unsolicited advice don't usually help the situation because problems aren't based in a lack of knowledge, and pointing out what he isn't doing right only makes the person feel worse. As a result, typical parent training materials will need to be adapted when one parent has ADHD. Moreover, it will likely be impossible for both parents to use the same parenting techniques, so it's better to acknowledge these differences openly, and each parent should strive to be clear about his or her own expectations. Then the couple can work toward at least not contradicting or obstructing each other (Weiss et al., 1999). As much as it's important for parents to be on the same page, the reality is that children are used to there being different rules in different places, and so as long as the two parents don't actively undermine each other, the children should be fine.

For the sake of the relationship as well as the sake of the children, it's important to work on minimizing the very common dynamic of the "fun" ADHD parent and the "strict" non-ADHD parent. It is too easy for the ADHD parent to overidentify with the children against the rules of the other parent, as well as to use a debate over parenting styles to take some potshots in the struggle to define the couple relationship. In the meantime, the non-ADHD parent may feel outnumbered and think that the survival of the entire family rests solely on her shoulders, prompting her to declare martial law over the entire family, including the other parent.

This dynamic is even more likely to occur if one of the children also has ADHD, a fairly likely possibility. Since ADHD children tend to require more parenting resources, the non-ADHD parent may feel even more burdened and overidentify the child with the other parent, taking out her resentment on both parent and child. Therefore, both parents need to work more diligently to ensure that the parent/child hierarchy remains intact and that both parents remain on the same level.

An ADHD parent will have different challenges with an ADHD child, despite and because of their potential similarities. The combination of an easily overwhelmed ADHD adult with a defiant ADHD child can quickly lead to explosive outbursts. You will need to work with that parent on how to avoid being pulled into conflict and how to de-escalate conflicts once they start; the importance of taking time away from the child; and the importance of supportive people in the child's life (Dixon, 1995). It may also help for the ADHD parent to commiserate with the ADHD child about her frustrations and share stories from her own childhood. This empathy-building can help each cut the other some slack when one of them slips up and some wiggle room is needed.

Whether one of the children has ADHD or not, it may become necessary to talk to them, once they are old enough to understand, about the ADHD parent's difficulties so that they do not misinterpret the ADHD behaviors; for example, "If Daddy loved me more he would have remembered to pick me up after soccer." The parents may not have to use the acronym "ADHD," but rather talk more generally about the parent's specific weaknesses. Of course, given ADHD's greater public awareness, the children may come up with that label on their own.

Finally, the topic of family planning may be worth addressing in session, since each additional ADHD child, or even non-ADHD child, can have a seemingly exponential impact on the stress level in the household. Whatever the fantasy of a larger family may be, it is important to frankly discuss the realities before the parents find themselves committed to two decades of obligation. Of course, this suggestion assumes that at least one partner will reliably manage contraception.

Support and Therapy Groups

Although most ADHD adults are treated in individual therapy, there is still something to be said for using a group format. It can be a more efficient use of resources and also allows the group members to learn from each other. Granted, individual therapy, support groups, and therapy groups are neither interchangeable nor mutually exclusive, so it's a matter of matching the client's needs to available interventions.

Support Groups

Don't underestimate the power of a support group. I ran a free monthly adult ADHD support group through Northern Virginia CHADD for five years and found it an excellent experience, as did many of the attendees. The appreciation the members expressed was quite touching. Many ADHD adults haven't met other people whom they know have ADHD, so they may feel they are the only one who struggles with these problems. A support group, whether something formalized through CHADD (Children and Adults with AD/HD, one of the national ADHD advocacy organizations), something online, or just a few people who meet regularly to talk can normalize their experiences. Members of my support group often commented on how great it was to hear other people saying the same things that they had thought and felt.

Attendees also benefit from informal education because members share experiences, tips, and suggestions (Morgan, 2000). However, the leader should be a font of reliable information and may sometimes need to gently override information coming from a group member if it is deemed inaccurate or not helpful to the group. In addition, you will need to keep the group on track, since some ADHD symptoms can interfere with the group process as outlined below:

- Coming in late

- Dominating the conversation

- Impulsively interrupting

- Not listening or communicating clearly

A good leadership style in an adult ADHD group involves clear limit-setting combined with liberal doses of humor. Especially with an ADHD group, humor can really make the structuring more palatable and eliminate power struggles (Kelly, 1995). Note that there are some advantages to having a mental health professional as the leader in terms of better handling the group dynamics and being able to intervene in the unlikely event that a crisis occurs, such as a member expressing excessive anger or emotionality.

You may want to have speakers present on various topics, but it's best to keep the presentations short and leave plenty of time for questions and discussion (Kelly, 1995). However, it depends on the primary goals of the group—is it to be education or discussion? They are both valuable, but they are not interchangeable. From a logistical perspective, discussion groups are much easier to operate.

Often the meetings will attract a core group of members who attend on a semi-regular basis, complemented by people who attend only one or two meetings. The core members provide the group cohesion and consistency from one meeting to the next, but because it is a new group every meeting, there will not be the same cohesion, safety, and group process that develops in a closed group. As a result, you often need to be more active to get each new meeting moving quickly, although a group that has been in existence for a while will require less leader input. To make attendees feel more comfortable about sharing, you should ask for confidentiality but you need to also say that you can't enforce it. When current or former clients attended my group, I told them that I would address them as I addressed any other member of the group, that it was their choice to disclose that they saw me in my professional capacity. Some did, some didn't.

I also found it helpful to have some meetings where family members, romantic partners, and friends were invited to attend, too. I allowed significant others to attend any meeting, but made every third meeting more visitor-focused. This is especially helpful for attendees and their significant others who are new to the diagnosis and have a lot of questions. In addition, hearing other people describe the same difficulties that the ADHD adult has had can help their significant others gain some perspective on what behavior is ADHD-based as opposed to what behavior is more consciously chosen.

Especially with this population, it is really helpful to hold the group at the same time each month, such as every third Thursday, and to send out a reminder e-mail a few days ahead. I collected e-mail addresses when people contacted me about attending and also at the meetings themselves. I promised to not use the list for anything except meeting reminders or notices in cases of inclement weather.

If possible, it's best to run the support group through a sponsoring organization such as a local CHADD chapter, ADDA (Attention Deficit Disorder Association, the national adult ADHD advocacy organization), university, hospital, mental health center, or other institution. This gives the group credibility, especially in the beginning when it can be difficult to recruit members. In addition, the sponsoring organization hopefully will work to promote the group through its website, mailings, and other meeting announcements, in a way that exceeds what an individual can do. Although I send out flyers to professionals and school personnel for the teen ADHD support group I currently run, far more attendees find the group through Chester County CHADD's website and other promotional activities.

I can also say definitively that running these support groups has been the single most effective practice-building activity I've engaged in, both in terms of clients generated and time and money spent. Many of these new clients never even attend the group, but come across my name through the CHADD chapter. Running the group also gave me credibility among the professional community as an expert with this population. Running a support group is very much a win-win for all concerned.

Therapy Groups

Therapy groups allow people to re-create the kinds of challenging social situations that get them into trouble in the real world, but this time with better odds of working them out successfully or of learning from the experience. Specifically for ADHD adults with social skills deficits, therapy groups allow them to practice listening, waiting their turn, sharing, keeping silent for a period of time, staying put, and taking responsibility for what they say and don't say (Hallowell, 1995). It may be easier to make progress in these areas if the client is appropriately medicated, so that he will not only notice these things, but also will retain them better.

Morgan (2000) outlines a detailed ten-session protocol with the following components, most of which are similar to the integrative treatment program advocated in this text (adapted with permission):

- Psychoeducation to impart knowledge and understanding of the impact of ADHD on the person's life

- A discussion of medication and referral to appropriate professionals for pharmacological and other specialized treatment

- Behavioral self-management skills training

- CBT for emotional control and coping with stress

- Relationship and social skills training

- Group interaction to provide mutual support, encouragement, and exchange of ideas and information

Especially in group therapy, you will need to structure the group and keep discussion from wandering too far afield. You will also need to balance everyone's contributions to the group, so one hyperactive or impulsive individual doesn't monopolize everyone's time. It can help to communicate an agenda at the start of the session and to be directive about moving the group forward. Handouts and exercises can keep members on track (Morgan, 2000), as can allowing members to take notes as needed.

Leading an ADHD-focused group will present certain challenges that are not present with a different population. For example, you will need more explicit rules about how lateness, last-minute cancellations, and no-shows will be handled, both financially as well as relationally in terms of how these transgressions will be made up to the other group members. As with any therapy experience, the members bring to the group the weaknesses they are working to improve—ADHD clients will not only bring these into the group therapy room, but also into how and when they make their entrances into the room. Therefore, it is important to handle both the failures and the successes in a consciously thought-out way.

For example, I rarely provide reminders to my clients, partly because I don't have the time, but also partly because it is incumbent on them to learn how to get to my office on time, just as they need to get other places on time. That being said, for a therapy group, however, I might give a reminder call the day before the first session just to ensure that it gets off on the right foot. This whole concept of personal responsibility will be extremely rich ground to discuss in the group, given most ADHD adults' ambivalence toward receiving help or direction. Although, on the one hand, they may expect others to overfunction for them, on the other, they also can react strongly to perceived efforts to control them, based on a lifetime of being the target of nagging.

Conclusion

Doing therapy with ADHD adults requires all the basic therapeutic skills required with any client, but generic therapy will not be sufficiently helpful with this population. I've seen too many clients who were generally dissatisfied with previous therapists who had either never had ADHD on their radar screen or had not fully understood its far-reaching implications. When asked about how these previous therapy experiences had turned out, I get responses ranging from "He really didn't understand me. We just kept talking about the same things but nothing ever changed," to "Well, it was kind of helpful, I guess. She seemed nice."

Of course, ADHD people may have all the same issues that non-ADHD people do and they will therefore respond to traditional therapy to some degree or another, but a more specific focus on their ADHD deficits is needed for maximum benefit. The field of therapy as a whole is becoming increasingly specialized, with specific techniques being developed for use with specific populations. Although a solid foundation of general clinical skills is necessary, it is no longer sufficient.

My hope is that this book has provided you with the tools and knowledge to complement those general skills. I have found ADHD adults to be an extremely interesting and challenging population to work with. It is my hope that this book will increase your interest in this population and reduce some of the challenges.

APPENDIX

Resources for Clinicians and Clients

There is more and more good information available these days on ADHD in adults. Some of this is targeted at clinicians, some at clients. A list of some of the better resources can be found below. This is by no means a definitive list—new items come and old items go—but it's certainly a good place to start looking for resources. An adapted version of this material entitled "ADHD Resources" is also available as a handout for clients on my website, www.TuckmanPsych.com.

Nonprofit Organizations

There are currently two nonprofit ADHD information and advocacy organizations. It's interesting to note that the names of both are still tied to the old term of ADD. I encourage you to join both and to encourage your clients to join as well.

CHADD

CHADD stands for Children and Adults with AD/HD. CHADD has a national headquarters and more than 200 local chapters that hold monthly meetings, offer a local provider directory, and may have other services as well. CHADD National puts on a large annual conference, publishes the bimonthly magazine *Attention!*, and offers other services to clinicians and clients. CHADD also cosponsors the National Resource Center on AD/HD, funded through a cooperative agreement with the Centers for Disease Control and Prevention (www.help4adhd.org). More information can be found at www.chadd.org.

ADDA

ADDA stands for the Attention Deficit Disorder Association. Whereas CHADD covers the full age range of people who have ADHD, ADDA focuses exclusively on adults with ADHD. ADDA puts out a newsletter and offers regional conferences, teleclasses, and a support group directory. More information can be found at www.add.org.

Websites

There are a number of helpful websites that offer information and products for adults with ADHD. These can be useful to both clinicians and clients.

- *www.myadhd.com* This site provides rating scales and history forms that can be electronically transmitted, as well as various treatment tools, available for a fee. They also offer a free monthly teleclass and a biweekly e-mail newsletter.

- *www.addvance.com* This site initially focused solely on the otherwise underrepresented women and girls with ADHD. It has since expanded to address both genders. An online bookstore sells relevant books. They also offer a free monthly e-mail newsletter.

- *www.addwarehouse.com* This site provides an extensive list of books on ADHD and related disorders, plus a few other items. If it's relevant to ADHD, you'll find it here.

- *www.addconsults.com* This one offers a wide range of resources, including articles, online chats, a monthly e-mail newsletter, and books and other ADHD-related items for purchase.

Professional Directories

A number of websites offer searchable directories where potential clients can find providers who specialize in ADHD. I have found these sorts of online directories to be surprisingly fruitful and to justify the expense involved.

- www.chadd.org

- www.add.org

- www.addconsults.com

- www.psychologytoday.com

- www.adhdcoaches.org

Reading List

In addition to the growing number of books on adult ADHD, there are other publications that you and/or your clients may find useful. In the following list, *ADDitude* is most appropriate for clients, *Attention Research Update* is appropriate for both clients and therapists, and the remainder are generally more targeted at a professional audience.

- *ADDitude:* A bimonthly magazine devoted to living with ADHD. More information is available at www.additudemag.com.

- *Attention Research Update:* A free monthly e-mail newsletter summarizing current journal articles on ADHD. More information is available at www.helpforadd.com.

- *The ADHD Report:* A bimonthly newsletter edited by Russell Barkley that provides new information about ADHD. More information is available at www.guilford.com.

- *Journal of Attention Disorders:* The only journal devoted exclusively to research and clinical issues related to attention. Quarterly. Edited by Sam Goldstein. More information is available at www.sagepub.com.

- *The NYU School of Medicine Adult ADHD Newsletter:* A free bimonthly electronic newsletter that provides up-to-date information. More information is available at www.med.nyu.edu/psych/psychiatrist/adultadhd newsletter.html.

Value-Added Materials

A large collection of additional materials related to this text is available at no charge on my website. You will find handouts to give to clients, as well as forms available for your own use. You can find these materials at www.TuckmanPsych.com.

References

American Psychiatric Association. (2000). *Diagnostic and statistical manual of mental disorders, 4th ed., text revision.* Washington, DC: American Psychiatric Association.

Arnstein, A. F. T. (2006). Fundamentals of attention-deficit hyperactivity disorder: Circuits and pathways. *Journal of Clinical Psychiatry, 67*(suppl. 8), 7-12.

Barkley, R. A. (2006a). History. In R. A. Barkley (Ed.), *Attention-deficit hyperactivity disorder, 3rd ed.* (pp. 3-75). New York: Guilford Press.

Barkley, R. A. (2006b). Primary symptoms, diagnostic criteria, prevalence, and gender differences. In R. A. Barkley (Ed.), *Attention-deficit hyperactivity disorder, 3rd ed.* (pp. 76-121). New York: Guilford Press.

Barkley, R. A. (2006c). Associated cognitive, developmental, and health problems. In R. A. Barkley (Ed.), *Attention-deficit hyperactivity disorder, 3rd ed.* (pp. 122-183). New York: Guilford Press.

Barkley, R. A. (2006d). Comorbid disorders, social and family adjustment, and subtyping. In R. A. Barkley (Ed.), *Attention-deficit hyperactivity disorder, 3rd ed.* (pp. 184-218). New York: Guilford Press.

Barkley, R. A. (2006e). Etiologies. In R. A. Barkley (Ed.), *Attention-deficit hyperactivity disorder, 3rd ed.* (pp. 219-247). New York: Guilford Press.

Barkley, R. A. (2006f). ADHD in adults: Developmental course and outcome of children with ADHD, and ADHD in clinic-referred adults. In R. A. Barkley (Ed.), *Attention-deficit hyperactivity disorder, 3rd ed.* (pp. 248-296). New York: Guilford Press.

Barkley, R. A. (2006g). A theory of ADHD. In R. A. Barkley (Ed.), *Attention-deficit hyperactivity disorder, 3rd ed.* (pp. 297-334). New York: Guilford Press.

Barkley, R. A. (2006, October). Research symposium I: A decade of research. Seminar at 18th annual CHADD International Conference, Chicago, IL.

Barkley, R. A., Cunningham, C. E., Gordon, M., Faraone, S. V., Lewandoski, L., & Murphy, K. R. (2006). ADHD symptoms vs. impairment: Revisited. *The ADHD Report, 14*(2), 1-9.

Barkley, R. A., & Murphy, K. R. (2006). Identifying new symptoms for diagnosing ADHD in adulthood. *The ADHD Report, 14*(4), 1-7.

Barkley, R. A., Fischer, M., Smallish, L., & Fletcher, K. (2003). Does the treatment of attention-deficit/hyperactivity disorder with stimulants contribute to drug use/abuse? A 13-year prospective study. *Pediatrics, 111*, 97-109.

Barkley, R. A., & Gordon, M. (2002). Research on comorbidity, adaptive functioning, and cognitive impairments in adults with ADHD: Implications for a clinical practice. In S. Goldstein & A. T. Ellison (Eds.), *Clinician's guide to adult ADHD: Assessment and intervention* (pp. 43-69). San Diego, CA: Academic Press.

Barkley, R. A. (1997). *ADHD and the nature of self-control*. New York: Guilford Press.

Biederman, J., Faraone, S., Monuteaux, M. C., Bober, M., & Cadogen, E. (2004). Gender effects on attention-deficit/hyperactivity disorder in adults, revisited. *Biological Psychiatry, 55*, 692-700.

Biederman, J. (2006, October). Advances in the neurobiology of AD/HD. Seminar at 18th annual CHADD International Conference, Chicago, IL.

Biederman, J., Spencer, T. J., Wilens, T. E., Prince, J. B., & Faraone, S. V. (2006). Treatment of ADHD with stimulant medications: Response to Nissen perspective in The New England Journal of Medicine. *Journal of the American Academy of Child & Adolescent Psychiatry, 45*(10), 1-4.

Brooks, R. B. (2002). Changing the mind-set of adults with ADHD: Strategies for fostering hope, optimism, and resilience. In S. Goldstein & A. T. Ellison (Eds.), *Clinician's guide to adult ADHD: Assessment and intervention* (pp. 127-146). San Diego, CA: Academic Press.

Brown, T. E. (1995). Differential diagnosis of ADD versus ADHD in adults. In K. Nadeau (Ed.), *A comprehensive guide to attention deficit disorder in adults* (pp. 93-108). New York: Bruner Mazel, Inc.

Brown, T. E. (1999, October). AD/HD inattentive type. Seminar at 11th annual CHADD International Conference, Washington, DC.

Brown, T. E. (2005). *Attention deficit disorder: The unfocused mind in children and adults*. New Haven, CT: Yale University Press.

Conners, C. K. (2002). Foreword. In S. Goldstein & A. T. Ellison (Eds.), *Clinician's guide to adult ADHD: Assessment and intervention* (pp. xvii-xviii). San Diego, CA: Academic Press.

Connor, D. F. (2006a). Stimulants. In R. A. Barkley (Ed.), *Attention-deficit hyperactivity disorder, 3rd ed.* (pp. 608-647). New York: Guilford Press.

Connor, D. F. (2006b). Other medications. In R. A. Barkley (Ed.), *Attention-deficit hyperactivity disorder, 3rd ed.* (pp. 658-677). New York: Guilford Press.

Crawford, R., & Crawford, V. (2002). Career impact: Finding the key issues facing adults with ADHD. In S. Goldstein & A. T. Ellison (Eds.), *Clinician's guide to adult ADHD: Assessment and intervention* (pp. 187-204). San Diego, CA: Academic Press.

Dixon, E. B. (1995). Impact of adult ADD on the family. In K. Nadeau (Ed.), *A comprehensive guide to attention deficit disorder in adults* (pp. 236-259). New York: Bruner Mazel, Inc.

Editors. (2005, December/January). In the news. *ADDitude*, 11.

Editors. (2006, June/July). Methylphenidate skin patch approved. *ADDitude*, 12.

Ellison, A. T. (2002). An overview of childhood and adolescent ADHD: Understanding the complexities of development into the adult years. In S. Goldstein & A. T. Ellison (Eds.), *Clinician's guide to adult ADHD: Assessment and intervention* (pp. 1-23). San Diego, CA: Academic Press.

Epstein, J. N., Conners, C. K., Sitarenios, G., & Erhardt, D. (1998). Continuous performance test results of adults with attention deficit hyperactivity disorder. *The Clinical Neuropsychologist, 12,* 155-168.

Faraone, S. V., Biederman, J., Spencer, T., Wilens, T., Seidman, L. J., Mick, E., et al. (2000). Attention-deficit/hyperactivity disorder in adults: An overview. *Biological Psychiatry, 48,* 9-20.

Faraone, S. V., & Khan, S. A. (2006). Candidate gene studies of attention-deficit/hyperactivity disorder. *Journal of Clinical Psychiatry, 67*(Suppl. 8), 13-20.

Friedman, S. R., Rapport, L. J., Lumley, M., Tzelepis, A., VanVoorhis, A., Stettner, L., et al. (2003). Aspects of social and emotional competence in adult attention-deficit/hyperactivity disorder. *Neuropsychology, 17,* 50-58.

Goldstein, S. (2002). Continuity of ADHD in adulthood: Hypothesis and theory meet reality. In S. Goldstein & A. T. Ellison (Eds.), *Clinician's guide to adult ADHD: Assessment and intervention* (pp. 25-42). San Diego, CA: Academic Press.

Goldstein, S. (2006, October). Advanced interventions for AD/HD. Seminar at 18th annual CHADD International Conference, Chicago, IL.

Goldstein, S., & Ingersoll, B. (2005). Controversial treatments for children with attention-deficit hyperactivity disorder. www.ADDWarehouse.com, 4/7/2005.

Goldstein, S., & Kennemer, K. (in press). Neuropsychological aspects of attention-deficit hyperactivity disorder. In C. R. Reynolds & E. Fletcher-Janzen (Eds.), *Handbook of clinical child neuropsychology, 3rd ed.* New York: Springer Publishing Company.

Gordon, M., Barkley, R. A., & Lovett, B. J. (2006). Tests and observational measures. In R. A. Barkley (Ed.), *Attention-deficit hyperactivity disorder, 3rd ed.* (pp. 369-388). New York: Guilford Press.

Hallowell, E. M. (1995). Psychotherapy of adult attention deficit disorder. In K. Nadeau (Ed.), *A comprehensive guide to attention deficit disorder in adults* (pp. 146-167). New York: Bruner Mazel, Inc.

Hallowell, E. M. (2006). *CrazyBusy: Overstretched, overbooked, and about to snap! Strategies for coping in a world gone ADD.* New York: Ballantine Books.

Harman, P. L. (2004, August). Addressing fears and prejudices about AD/HD: An interview with Thomas Brown, Ph.D. *Attention!,* 28-31.

Ingersoll, B. (2006, October). Complementary treatments. Seminar at 18th annual CHADD International Conference, Chicago, IL.

Jaffe, P. (1995). History and overview of adulthood ADD. In K. Nadeau (Ed.), *A comprehensive guide to attention deficit disorder in adults* (pp. 3-17). New York: Bruner Mazel, Inc.

Johnson, D. E., & Conners, C. K. (2002). The assessment process: Conditions and comorbidities. In S. Goldstein & A. T. Ellison (Eds.), *Clinician's guide to adult ADHD: Assessment and intervention* (pp. 71-83). San Diego, CA: Academic Press.

Katz, L. J. (2004, August). College success: Accommodations and strategies that work. *Attention!,* 32-37, 46.

Kelly, K. M. (1995). Adult ADD support groups. In K. Nadeau (Ed.), *A comprehensive guide to attention deficit disorder in adults* (pp. 352-374). New York: Bruner Mazel, Inc.

Kelly, K. M., & Ramundo, P. (2006). *You mean I'm not lazy, stupid, or crazy?!* New York: Simon & Schuster.

Kilcarr, P. J. (2002). Making marriages work for individuals with ADHD. In S. Goldstein & A. T. Ellison (Eds.), *Clinician's guide to adult ADHD: Assessment and intervention* (pp. 219-240). San Diego, CA: Academic Press.

Klingberg, T., Fernell, E., Olesen, P. J., Johnson, M., Gustafsson, P., Dahlstrom, K., et al. (2005). Computerized training of working memory in children with ADHD—A randomized, controlled trial. *Journal of the Academy of Adolescent Psychiatry, 44,* 177-186.

Lavenstein, B. (1995). Neurological comorbidity patterns/differential diagnosis in adult attention deficit disorder. In K. Nadeau (Ed.), *A comprehensive guide to attention deficit disorder in adults* (pp. 74-92). New York: Bruner Mazel, Inc.

Lerner, B. (1996, Summer). Self-esteem and excellence: The choice and the paradox. *American Educator*, 9-13, 41-42.

Morgan, W. D. (2000). Adult attention deficit disorder. In J. R. White and A. S. Freeman (Eds.), *Cognitive-behavioral group therapy for specific problems and populations*. Washington, DC: American Psychological Association.

Murphy, K. (2002). Clinical case studies. In S. Goldstein & A. T. Ellison (Eds.), *Clinician's guide to adult ADHD: Assessment and intervention* (pp. 85-106). San Diego, CA: Academic Press.

Murphy, K. R. (2006). Psychological counseling of adults with ADHD. In R. A. Barkley (Ed.), *Attention-deficit hyperactivity disorder, 3rd ed.* (pp. 692-703). New York: Guilford Press.

Murphy, K., & Gordon, M. (2006). Assessment of adults with ADHD. In R. A. Barkley (Ed.), *Attention-deficit hyperactivity disorder, 3rd ed.* (pp. 425-450). New York: Guilford Press.

Murphy, P., & Schachar, R. (2000). Use of self-rating in the assessment of symptoms of attention deficit hyperactivity disorder in adults. *American Journal of Psychiatry, 157*, 1156-1159.

Nadeau, K. G. (1995a). Life management skills for the adult with ADD. In K. Nadeau (Ed.), *A comprehensive guide to attention deficit disorder in adults* (pp. 191-217). New York: Bruner Mazel, Inc.

Nadeau, K. G. (1995b). ADD in the workplace: Career consultation and counseling for the adult with ADD. In K. Nadeau (Ed.), *A comprehensive guide to attention deficit disorder in adults* (pp. 308-334). New York: Bruner Mazel, Inc.

Nadeau, K. G. (2002). The clinician's role in the treatment of ADHD. In S. Goldstein & A. T. Ellison (Eds.), *Clinician's guide to adult ADHD: Assessment and intervention* (pp. 107-127). San Diego, CA: Academic Press.

Phelan, T. W. (2002). Families and ADHD. In S. Goldstein & A. T. Ellison (Eds.), *Clinician's guide to adult ADHD: Assessment and intervention* (pp. 241-260). San Diego, CA: Academic Press.

Prince, J. B., & Wilens, T. E. (2002). Pharmacotherapy of adult ADHD. In S. Goldstein & A. T. Ellison (Eds.), *Clinician's guide to adult ADHD: Assessment and intervention* (pp. 165-186). San Diego, CA: Academic Press.

Prince, J. B., Wilens, T. E., Spencer, T. J., & Biederman, J. (2006). Pharmacotherapy of ADHD in adults. In R. A. Barkley (Ed.), *Attention-deficit hyperactivity disorder, 3rd ed.* (pp. 3-75). New York: Guilford Press.

Quinn, C. A. (2002). Detection of malingering in assessment of adult ADHD. *Archives of Clinical Neuropsychology, 18,* 379-395.

Ramsay, J. R., & Rostain, A. L. (in press). Psychosocial treatments for ADHD in adults: Current evidence and future directions. *Professional Psychology: Research and Practice.*

Ramsay, J. R., & Rostain, A. L. (2005a). Adapting psychotherapy to meet the needs of adults with attention-deficit/hyperactivity disorder. *Psychotherapy: Theory, Research, Practice, Training, 42,* 72-84.

Ramsay, J. R., & Rostain, A. L. (2005b). Cognitive therapy for adult ADHD. In L. VandeCreek (Ed.), *Innovations in clinical practice: Focus on adults.* Sarasota, FL: Professional Resource Press.

Ramsay, J. R., & Rostain, A. L. (2005c). Girl, repeatedly interrupted: The case of a young adult woman with ADHD. *Clinical Case Studies, 4,* 329-346.

Rapport, L. J., VanVoorhis, A., Tzelepis, A., & Friedman, S. R. (2001). Executive functioning in adult attention-deficit hyperactivity disorder. *The Clinical Neuropsychologist, 15,* 479-491.

Ratey, J. J., Hallowell, E. M., & Miller, A. C. (1995). Relationship dilemmas for adults with ADD: The biology of intimacy. In K. Nadeau (Ed.), *A comprehensive guide to attention deficit disorder in adults* (pp. 218-235). New York: Bruner Mazel, Inc.

Ratey, J. J., Miller, A. C., & Nadeau, K. G. (1995). Special diagnostic and treatment considerations in women with attention deficit disorder. In K. Nadeau (Ed.), *A comprehensive guide to attention deficit disorder in adults* (pp. 260-283). New York: Bruner Mazel, Inc.

Ratey, N. A. (2002). Life coaching for adult ADHD. In S. Goldstein & A. T. Ellison (Eds.), *Clinician's guide to adult ADHD: Assessment and intervention* (pp. 261-277). San Diego, CA: Academic Press.

Riccio, C. A., & French, C. L. (2004). The status of empirical support for treatments of attention deficits. *The Clinical Neuropsychologist, 18,* 528-558.

Richard, M. M. (1995). Students with attention deficit disorders in postsecondary education: Issues in identification and accommodation. In K. Nadeau (Ed.), *A comprehensive guide to attention deficit disorder in adults* (pp. 284-307). New York: Bruner Mazel, Inc.

Robin, A. L. (2002). Lifestyle issues. In S. Goldstein & A. T. Ellison (Eds.), *Clinician's guide to adult ADHD: Assessment and intervention* (pp. 279-291). San Diego, CA: Academic Press.

Rostain, A. L., & Ramsay, J. R. (2006a). Adult with ADHD? Try medication + psychotherapy. *Current Psychiatry, 5*(2), 13-16, 21-24, 27.

Rostain, A. L., & Ramsay, J. R. (2006b). A combined treatment approach for adults with ADHD—Results of an open study of 43 patients. *Journal of Attention Disorders, 10*(2), 1-10.

Safren, S. A. (2006). Cognitive-behavioral approaches to ADHD treatment in adulthood. *Journal of Clinical Psychiatry, 67*(Suppl. 8), 46-50.

Schab, D. W., & Trinh, N. T. (2004). Do artificial food colors promote hyperactivity in children with hyperactive syndromes? A meta-analysis of double-blind placebo controlled trials. *Journal of Developmental and Behavioral Pediatrics, 25,* 423-434.

Skibbins, D. (2007). *Becoming a Life Coach.* Oakland, CA: New Harbinger Publications.

Spencer, T. J. (2006a). ADHD and comorbidity in childhood. *Journal of Clinical Psychiatry, 67*(Suppl. 8), 27-31.

Spencer, T. J. (2006b). Antidepressant and specific norepinephrine reuptake inhibitor treatments. In R. A. Barkley (Ed.), *Attention-deficit hyperactivity disorder, 3rd ed.* (pp. 648-657). New York: Guilford Press.

Tudisco, R. (2005, February). Living with ADHD. Chester County CHADD conference, West Chester, PA.

Tzelepis, A., Schubiner, H., & Warbasse, L. H., III. (1995). Differential diagnosis and psychiatric comorbidity in adult attention deficit disorder. In K. Nadeau (Ed.), *A comprehensive guide to attention deficit disorder in adults* (pp. 35-57). New York: Bruner Mazel, Inc.

U.S. Census Bureau; Census 2000, Summary File 1; generated by Ari Tuckman; using American FactFinder; http://factfinder.census.gov; (26 February 2007).

Weinstein, C. S. (1994). Cognitive remediation strategies: An adjunct to the psychotherapy of adults with attention-deficit hyperactivity disorder. *Journal of Psychotherapy Practice and Research, 3,* 44-57.

Weiss, M., Hechtman, L. T., & Weiss, G. (1999). *ADHD in adulthood: A guide to current theory, diagnosis, and treatment.* Baltimore: The Johns Hopkins University Press.

Wells, R. D., Dahl, B. B., & Snyder, D. (2000, May/June). Coping and compensatory strategies used by adults with attentional problems. *Attention!, 22-24.*

Wilens, T. (2004). Impact of ADHD and its treatment on substance abuse in adults. *Journal of Clinical Psychiatry, 65,* 38-45.

Wilens, T. (2006). Mechanism of action of agents used in attention-deficit hyperactivity disorder. *Journal of Clinical Psychiatry, 67*(Suppl. 8), 32-37.

Wilens, T. E., Faraone, S. V., Biederman, J., & Gunawardene, S. (2003). Does stimulant therapy of attention-deficit/hyperactivity disorder beget later substance abuse? A meta-analytic review of the literature. *Pediatrics, 111,* 179-185.

Wilens, T. E., Zusman, R. M., Hammerness, P. G., Podolski, A., Whitley, J., Spencer, T. J., et al. (2006). An open-label study of the tolerability of mixed amphetamine salts in adults with attention-deficit/hyperactivity disorder and treated primary essential hypertension. *Journal of Clinical Psychiatry, 67,* 696-702.

Young, S. (2000). ADHD children grown up: An empirical review. *Counselling Psychology Quarterly, 13,* 191-200.

Young, S. (2002). A model of psychotherapy for adults with ADHD. In S. Goldstein & A. T. Ellison (Eds.), *Clinician's guide to adult ADHD: Assessment and intervention* (pp. 147-163). San Diego, CA: Academic Press.

Young, S., & Bramham, J. (2007). *ADHD in adults: A psychological guide to practice.* Chichester, England: John Wiley & Sons, Ltd.

Index

anger management, 219-220

antidepressants, 128, 130

antisocial personality disorder, 53

anxiety, 51-52

Anxiety & Phobia Workbook, The (Bourne), 182

apologies, 218-219

appetite suppression, 124, 126

Areas of Impairment Form, 34-35

arousal: coaching and, 148; self-regulation of, 61

assessment: impairment, 23; instruments used for, 42-48; substance abuse, 122

assessment instruments, 42-48; continuous performance tests, 46-47; intelligence and achievement tests, 44; memory tests, 44-45; neuropsychological, 43-44; problems with using, 42-43; projective tests, 47; rating scales, 45-46

attention: coaching and, 149; regulation of, 12-13; subfunctions of, 13-14. *See also* inattention

Attention Deficit Disorder Association (ADDA), 229, 234

Attention Deficit Disorder in Adults: Practical Help for Sufferers and Their Spouses (Weiss), 10

attention regulation, 12

Attention Research Update newsletter, 235

attributions, 94

avoidance, 170-171, 208

B

Barkley, Russell, 60

Barkley's ADHD Rating Scale, 45

Barkley's response inhibition theory, 60-62

Becoming a Life Coach (Skibbins), 145

behavioral inhibition, 60-62

biofeedback, 137

biological fallacy, 94

biological treatments, 109-140; medications, 109-135; nontraditional, 135-140

bipolar disorder, 50-51, 125

black-box warnings, 119, 129

blood pressure issues, 124, 126

borderline personality disorder (BPD), 54

Bourne, Edmund, 182

Brain Gym program, 139

brain injuries, 55

brain scans, 48-49

brinksmanship, 209

Brooks, Robert, 217

Brown, Thomas, 19, 31

Brown Attention-Deficit Disorder Scales, 45

Brown's six clusters of executive functioning, 62

C

caffeine, 29, 110, 128

calendars, 156-157, 225

career counselors, 187-189

careers: counseling related to, 187-189; finding better jobs and, 105-106. *See also* work problems

Catapres, 133

causes of ADHD, 57-58

cavalier lifestyle, 212-213

CHADD (Children and Adults with AD/HD), 228, 233

chaos/messiness, 176-178

checking behaviors, 212

cigarette smoking, 75

classroom performance. *See* academic functioning

cleaning up problems, 149

client handouts, 93, 164, 235

Clinical Assessment of Attention Deficit-Adult scale, 46

clocks, 161-162

coaching, 89, 141-189; career counselors and, 187-189; clinical benefits of, 147-149; core deficits and, 151-152; definition of, 142; on eliciting support from others, 182-185; explanatory overview of, 141-143; four-part model of, 164-182; general theory of, 149-151; goal management and, 178-182; insurance reimbursement for, 145; long-term goal of, 154; memory management and, 164-167; organizations related to, 146; process of, 149-151; professional organizers and, 186-187; psychotherapy compared to, 143-144; referring out, 144-145; setting goals in, 153-155; short-term goal of, 153-154; structure provided through, 154-155; stuff management and, 175-178; technology/systems used with, 155-163; time management and, 167-174; training and certification for, 145-147; work accommodations and, 187-189

Cogmed system, 138-139

cognitive behavioral therapy, 201

collateral information sources, 40-41

college students, 70, 103-105

Common ADHD Medications form, 131

comorbid conditions, 49-55; antisocial personality disorder, 53; anxiety, 51-52; bipolar disorder, 50-51; borderline personality disorder, 54; depression, 49-50; head injuries, 55; learning disabilities, 53; medical conditions, 55; post-traumatic stress disorder, 52; psychotherapy

expectation management, 150, 224
explanations vs. excuses, 192
extended-release medications, 118
externalizing, 210-211

F

failure: as core belief, 205; reframing of past,
195-197
family issues: causation theories and, 57-58;
coaching process and, 184-185; education
process and, 97-99; parenting behavior and,
83-84; psychotherapy and, 220-221, 227-228;
scheduled meetings for, 225. *See also* romantic
relationships
feel-good-now self-esteem, 216
Feingold diet, 136
fidgetiness, 24, 26, 198
financial management, 74
Focalin, 116, 131
focus cluster, 62
forms: Adult ADHD Interview Form, 32-33; Areas
of Impairment Form, 34-35; Common ADHD
Medications, 131; Medication Monitoring
Sheet, 132
four-part coaching model, 164-182; goal
management, 178-182; memory management,
164-167; stuff management, 175-178; time
management, 167-174
free recall, 166
frustration tolerance, 181-182

G

gender differences, 30-31
*Gender Issues and ADHD: Research, Diagnosis, and
Treatment* (Quinn & Nadeau), 31
genetic factors, 58-59
goals: coaching, 153-155; management of, 178-182;
psychotherapy, 204-205; treatment, 89, 90
Gordon Diagnostic System (GDS), 46
groups: support, 228-230; therapy, 230-231

H

habits: acquisition of, 159; maladaptive, 207-208
Hallowell, Ned, 52
handouts for clients, 93
head injuries, 55
headaches, 124, 126
homework assignments, 39-40, 199
hyperactivity: adult ADHD and, 26-27; coaching
process and, 152; diagnosis of ADHD and,
10-11, 21, 26-27; goal management and, 181;
soft signs of, 28; symptom evolution and, 24

hyperfocus, 12, 28, 169, 171-172
hypertension, 124, 126
hypervigilance, 212
hypomania, 125, 127

I

impact of ADHD, 63-87; academic functioning
and, 68-71; daily life functioning and, 72-75;
executive functioning and, 66-68; occupational
functioning and, 71-72; parenting behavior
and, 83-84; personality evolution and, 64-65;
prognostic indicators and, 84-86; psychological
functioning and, 75-79; romantic relationships
and, 81-83; situational effects and, 65-66;
social functioning and, 79-84
impairment: Areas of Impairment form, 34-35;
diagnosing, 22-23, 34-35
impulsivity: adult ADHD and, 27; coaching
process and, 152; decision making and,
197; diagnostic criteria for, 21; lack of, 85;
psychotherapy and, 201; rushing and, 211; soft
signs of, 28-29; time management and, 174
inadequacy, 205
inattention: adult ADHD and, 25-26, 52; anxiety
and, 52; coaching process and, 151; soft signs
of, 28
incompetence, 205
inconsistent performance, 13
inefficient use of time, 167-168
information: collateral sources of, 40-41. *See also*
resources
insomnia, 123-124, 126
instability, 206
Institute for the Advancement of AD/HD
Coaching, 146
insurance coverage, 145
integrative treatment model, 89-91; coaching and,
141-189; education and, 93-107; medications
and, 109-135; nontraditional treatments and,
135-140; psychotherapy and, 191-232
intelligence: academic functioning and, 69;
compensating for ADHD with, 85
intelligence tests, 44
Intermediate Visual and Auditory (IVA) CPT, 46
International Classification of Diseases-10, 11
International Coach Federation, 146
interpersonal relationships. *See* relationships
interviews: diagnostic, 31-41; motivational,
207-208
intimate relationships. *See* romantic relationships
irritability, 124, 126

organizational systems: professional organizers and, 186-187; stuff management and, 176-178
outcome indicators, 84-86
overdiagnosis of ADHD, 17-18
overwhelm, 203

P

paper planners, 160
parenting behavior: causation theories and, 57-58; couples therapy and, 227-228; social functioning and, 83-84
PDAs (personal digital assistants), 160-161
persistence of effort, 68
Phelan, Thomas, 64
physiology of ADHD, 57-62; environmental factors and, 59; etiology and, 57-58; genetic factors and, 58-59; neurology and, 59-60; unifying theories and, 60-62
planners, 157-160
Play Attention program, 139
polypharmacy, 133
positive outcomes, 85-86
post-traumatic stress disorder (PTSD), 52
preventing problems, 149-150
problem solving, 214
procrastination, 170-171, 209
professional advocacy, 185
professional directories, 234
professional organizers, 186-187
prognostic indicators, 84-86
projective tests, 47
prospective memory, 67-68, 166-167
provider directories, 234
Provigil, 133
pseudoefficiency, 72, 209-210
pseudohoarding, 176
psychodynamic therapy, 200-201
psychological functioning, 75-79; anger problems and, 219; defense mechanisms and, 77-79; self-image and, 76-77; sexual problems and, 226
psychosis, 125, 127
psychotherapy, 89, 191-232; adapting for ADHD adults, 200-201; adjusting to ADHD diagnosis in, 201-203; anger management and, 219-220; coaching compared to, 143-144; cognitive behavioral therapy and, 201; comorbid diagnoses and, 193-194; family issues and, 220-221, 227-228; goal-setting process in, 204-205; group process for, 228-231; maladaptive coping strategies and, 205-213; past treatment failures and, 195-197; psychodynamic therapy and, 200-201;

reframing used in, 192-193, 195-197; research on ADHD and, 194-195; resilient mind-set and, 217; romantic partner involvement in, 220-228; self-esteem issues and, 213-217; social skills training and, 218-219; substance abuse management and, 194; traits that interfere with, 197-199; transference/countertransference in, 199-200
pulse irregularity, 124, 126

Q

quasi-obsessive-compulsive behavior, 212
Quinn, Patricia, 31
quitting, 211

R

rambling, 198
Ratey, Nancy, 148, 154
rating scales, 45-46
reactive decision making, 197
reading list, 235
rebound effect, 118, 124, 126
reconstitution, 61
recording devices, 163
reframing: four part process of, 193; limited benefits from past treatments, 195-197; past struggles, 192-193
relationships, 79-84; empathy in, 222-223; parenting, 83-84, 227-228; restoring balance in, 223-226; romantic, 81-83, 220-228; social skills and, 80-81, 218-219
reminder alarms, 159, 162
repetitive tasks, 180-181
resilient mind-set, 217
resources, 233-235; adult ADHD websites, 234; author's website, 235; nonprofit organizations, 233-234; professional directories, 234; reading list, 235
response inhibition theory, 60-62
restlessness, 24, 27, 181
Ritalin, 115, 131
role playing, 219
romantic relationships: ADHD-friendly lifestyle and, 102; building empathy in, 222-223; coaching process and, 184-185; couples therapy and, 220-228; education process and, 97-99; impact of ADHD on, 81-83; parenting issues in, 227-228; restoring balance in, 223-226; sexual functioning in, 82-83, 226-227. See also family issues
rule interpretation, 198
running late, 172-173

treatment: coaching as, 141-189; education as, 93-107; goals of, 89, 90; integrative model of, 89-91; medications as, 109-135; nontraditional, 135-140; psychotherapy as, 191-232
TuckmanPsych.com website, 235
Tudisco, Rob, 188

U
underdiagnosis of ADHD, 18-20
unifying theories, 60-62; Barkley's response inhibition theory, 60-62; Brown's six clusters of executive functioning, 62

V
verbal working memory, 61
video games, 66
Visual Mind program, 163
vitamin supplements, 137
voice recorders, 163
Vyvanse, 115, 122, 131

W
watches, 162
websites: adult ADHD information, 234; alarm technology, 162; author's resources, 235; coaching information, 146; computer programs, 163; professional organizers, 187; provider directories, 234
Wechsler Memory Scales-III (WMS-III), 45
Weiss, Lynn, 10
Wellbutrin, 130, 131
Wender, Paul, 10
whiteboards, 225
withdrawal symptoms, 127, 128
work problems: adult ADHD and, 71-72; disclosure of ADHD and, 183-184; finding a better career/job, 105-106; missed deadlines and, 173-174; seeking accommodations for, 187-189
working memory, 67, 138
working memory training, 138-139

Y
You Mean I'm Not Lazy, Stupid, or Crazy?! (Kelly & Ramundo), 78, 94, 192

Z
zombie-like state, 125, 127

Ari Tuckman, PsyD, MBA, is a clinical psychologist who specializes in diagnosing and treating children, teens, and adults with ADHD. He is a dynamic presenter and has given more than one hundred presentations on ADHD and other topics. He is on the board of the Attention Deficit Disorder Association, is a contributor for *Additude* Magazine's section Ask Additude, and writes a monthly column for myADHD.com's e-mail newsletter. He facilitated a monthly adult ADHD support group for the Northern Virginia chapter of CHADD for five years and was named Professional of the Year. He has appeared on national television and radio and been quoted in magazines and newspapers. He is in private practice in West Chester, PA and is currently at work on a book for adults with ADHD.